Breaking the Cycle

Civil Wars in Lebanon

Edited by

YOUSSEF M CHOUEIRI

BREAKING THE CYCLE
Civil Wars in Lebanon

Edited by Youssef M Choueiri

Copyright © Stacey International
First printed 2007

Stacey International
128 Kensington Church Street
London W8 4BH
Tel: 020 7221 7166 Fax: 020 7792 9288

www.stacey-international.co.uk

ISBN: 9781905299539

CIP Data: A catalogue record for this book is available from the British Library

Design: M.G. Daniels

Printing & Binding: Oriental Press, Dubai.

Contents

Contributors

Alexandra Asseily

As witness of the pain of the civil war in Lebanon, Alexandra Asseily decided to explore her own responsibility for war and peace and became a psychotherapist. She is a governor and founder of the Centre for Lebanese Studies, Oxford, on the Board of the Guerrand Hermes Peace Foundation and Balamand University and a former member of the Advisory Board of the Centre for the Study of World Religions at Harvard University. She has travelled widely to help various ethnic and social groups to nurture understanding and co-operation. She initiated The Garden of Forgiveness in central Beirut. Alexandra is married to George Asseily and lives between Beirut and London.

Ahmad Beydoun

Ahmad Beydoun is a writer and sociologist. He is the author, most recently, of *Le Liban, Itineraires dans une guerre incivile*, Paris-Beirut, 1999, and *Identité confessionnelle et temps social chez les Historiens libanais contemporains*, Publications de l'Université Libanaise, Beirut 1984.

Beydoun is professor of Sociology in the Institute of Social Sciences at the Lebanese University. He received his PhD from Université de Paris-Sorbonne (Paris IV) in 1982.

Youssef Choueiri

Youssef Choueiri is Reader in Islamic Studies, School of Arts, Histories and Cultures, University of Manchester. He previously taught Middle Eastern History at the University of Exeter and was appointed in 2005-06 to a research fellowship by the Centre for Lebanese Studies in association with St. Antony's College, Oxford. His publications include *Modern Arab Historiography*, *Arab Nationalism* and *A Companion to the History of the Middle East*.

Pamela Chrabieh

Dr Chrabieh holds a PhD in Sciences of Religions (University of Montreal). She is currently conducting a post-doctoral research (Canada Chair of Islam, Pluralism and Globalisation, University of Montreal/Institute of Islamic-Christian Studies, St Joseph University, Lebanon), financed for two years by the Social Sciences and Humanities Research Council of Canada. Author of: *Icônes du Liban, au carrefour du dialogue des cultures* (Carte Blanche, Montréal, 2003); *A la rencontre de l'islam, itinéraire d'une spiritualité composite et engagée*, (Médiaspaul, Montréal, 2006).

Mark Farha

Mark Farha was born and raised in Zurich, Switzerland. Upon graduating from Georgetown's School of Foreign Service, he obtained a Master's degree in World Religions at Harvard.

He has recently completed his PhD Thesis in History and Middle Eastern Studies entitled, 'Secularism under Siege in Lebanon's Second Republic'. He served as Head Teaching Fellow for Harvard Core Class 'Thought and Change in the Contemporary Middle East' and 'Religion and Modernisation: Cultural Revolutions and Secularism 1998-2005'. Recipient of two Teaching Awards, he lectures on secularism in the Arab world and Turkey at Harvard, Columbia and Singapore's Foreign Ministry, as well as the IDSS at Nanyang University.

Sune Haugbolle

Sune Haugbolle obtained his doctorate in Middle East Studies at St Antony's College, Oxford. He has published several articles on memory in relation to the Lebanese civil war, one of which is 'Public and Private Memory of the Lebanese Civil War,' pp. 191-203 in *Contemporary Studies of South Asia, Africa and the Middle East*, vol. 25 no. 1, 2005.

Rudy Jaafar

Rudy Jaafar is founding member and General Coordinator of Nahwa al-Muwatiniya (Na-aM), a political NGO engaged in enhancing good governance, transparency, and accountability in Lebanon and the wider Arab world. Rudy obtained his MA from the Fletcher School of Law and Diplomacy, and is presently a visiting Adjunct Professor at the PSPA Department at the American University of Beirut.

Michael Johnson

Michael Johnson is Senior Lecturer in Politics and Dean of the School of Social Sciences and Cultural Studies, University of Sussex. His research interests include politics and political economy of the Middle East, with particular reference to ethnic and confessional conflict. Publications include *Class and Client in Beirut: The Sunni Muslim Community and the Lebanese State, 1840-1985* and *All Honourable Men: The Social Origins of War in Lebanon.*

Michael Kerr

Michael Kerr is Leverhulme Research Fellow in the Department of International History at the London School of Economics and Political Science. In 2001-02 Dr Kerr completed research for his PhD in Lebanon and his recent publications include *Imposing Power-Sharing: Conflict and Coexistence in Northern Ireland and*

Lebanon (Irish Academic Press, 2005), 'Approaches to Power-Sharing in Northern Ireland and Lebanon' in Rory Miller (Ed.) *Ireland in the Middle East: Trade, Society and Peace* (Dublin: Irish Academic Press, 2007).

Mohammad F Mattar

Mohammad Mattar is the managing partner of Mattar Mouawad Majdalany el Khazen law firm in Lebanon. He has thirty years of experience as a litigation lawyer. Mr. Mattar pursued his studies in law at the Lebanese University and his studies in philosophy at the American University of Beirut. He did his postgraduate studies at the School of Oriental and African Studies (SOAS) and St Anthony's College. He is a lecturer at the University of St Joseph in Lebanon and is presently the Chairman of the Lebanese Transparency Association (LTA).

Nawaf Salam

Nawaf Salam is an Associate Professor of Political Science and the Chairperson of the Political Studies and Public Administration department at the American University of Beirut. He holds a Master of Laws (Harvard), a Doctorate in History (Sorbonne) and a *Doctorat d'Etat* in Political Studies (Sciences-Po/Paris). Author of several books and numerous articles on Lebanon and the Arab world, he recently edited *Options for Lebanon* (London, 2004) and co-edited (with Theodor Hanf) *Lebanon in Limbo: Postwar Society and State in an Uncertain Regional Environment* (Baden-Baden, 2003).

Halim Shebaya

Halim Shebaya is a postgraduate student in Middle Eastern Studies at the School of Oriental and African Studies in London. He holds a Bachelor in Business Administration (2002) from the American University of Beirut and a Master of Divinity (2005) from the Near East School of Theology. He is interested in Lebanese politics and inter-religious dialogue. He has been active in different forms of work with Palestinian refugees and Lebanese youth for the past seven years. He also served as a NEST student representative on the Joint Committee for Islamic and Christian Religious Institutions.

Maha Shuayb

Maha Shuayb graduated from the Lebanese University with a BSc in Sociology in 2000. She has an MEd in Guidance and Counselling in Education from Newcastle University. She went on to study for a doctorate in Educational Research at the University of Cambridge and graduated in 2002. Maha graduated with a PhD in Education from the University of Cambridge in 2005. She has researched citizenship education in Lebanon and the aims of the new curriculum and their social and political impacts. She has also conducted research on a variety of topics such as students' psychological, personal, and vocational needs at universities in Lebanon post the civil war. Maha is currently working at the National Foundation for Educational Research in Britain where she is researching citizenship and curriculum design and goals in Europe.

Foreword

In September 2005 the Board of the Centre for Lebanese Studies, in co-operation with the Middle East Centre at St Antony's College, Oxford, appointed Dr Youssef Choueiri as Visiting Fellow for a full academic year. His mission was to do extensive research on past civil wars in Lebanon from the 1840s to 1990. The culmination of this work was to be a conference in June 2006 organised by the Centre in Lebanon to bring together academics, historians, politicians and lay people from Lebanon, the US, Europe and the Arab states.

Lebanon was experiencing quite an economic revival in early summer 2006, and indeed our aim at the Conference was to discuss and put forward ideas and proposals that could translate into laws to be adopted by the political establishment in order to help prevent civil war in the future. This publication is coming out after the July-August Israeli war on Hezbollah and Lebanon, and after the subsequent political and social divisions that were exacerbated by the war and its consequences.

I hope that by the time it is printed, the present unsettled conditions will have been resolved, and that the proposals put forward by our contributors will be taken seriously by Lebanon's leaders and lawmakers in order to go some way towards avoiding future conflict within.

My thanks go to all those who contributed towards the success of the conference. The importance of the subject, the quality of the speakers and their contributions were widely recognised and reported.

Finally, I take this opportunity to thank the Patrons of the Centre for Lebanese Studies and the sponsors of the Conference, without whom an event such as this could not have taken place.

George Asseily
Chairman of the Centre for Lebanese Studies

The Centre for Lebanese Studies is an independent academic research institution. It was founded in 1984 in association with the Middle East Centre at St Antony's College, Oxford. Its aims are to promote international understanding of Lebanon and the issues facing it.

The Centre initiates and publishes research papers and books on relevant historical, economic, political, sociological and cultural issues affecting Lebanon. It also organises conferences and seminars in order that ideas and views on the country's state of affairs may be exchanged.

Introduction

Youssef M Choueiri

This book is the product of a conference organised by the Centre for Lebanese Studies, England, from 6 to 8 June, 2006, held at al-Bustan Hotel, Lebanon, under the title: Breaking the Cycle: Civil Wars in Lebanon.

The conference programme was divided into four sessions. Each session dealt with a particular topic designed to stand on its own and form at the same time an integral part of our overall theme.

Thus, the first session dealt with the various models and analytical studies advanced to understand civil war in general, and the Lebanese civil war in particular. The second session carried our analysis forward by concentrating on the last civil war 1975-1990. The reason for singling out this particular civil war stemmed from its direct impact on present-day Lebanon and its implications for the future development of its society. The third session revisited the post-war settlement and its ramifications in the political, cultural, religious, economic and legal fields. The conference culminated in the fourth session with its focus on the most appropriate means and methods that could be deployed to avoid the outbreak of a new civil war.

Our last general session, designated as a roundtable discussion, was meant to bring together as many of our contributors and participants as possible, in order to conduct a wide-ranging discussion on the best way forward and how to enable Lebanon to turn its back on civil strife and build a prosperous and just society for all its citizens.

Seventeen contributors, drawn from all over the world, offered presentations on the above-mentioned topics. The conference was also addressed by its guest of honour HE Fouad Siniora, the Lebanese Prime Minister. Other distinguished guests included HE Ghassan Tueni who delivered a keynote speech on cultural change and political reconciliation, and HE Tarek Mitri, Minister of Culture ,who gave a dinner speech on the perils of civil wars and the idea of building a new Lebanon. This book includes a selection of a number of the presentations as revised by the contributors and transformed into chapters. Youssef Choueiri, the organiser of the conference, has also added a chapter of his own on the general theme of Lebanon's civil wars.

The idea of the conference was based on the assumption that Lebanon seems to have had its fair share of civil wars, both in the nineteenth and twentieth centuries. Yet, the threat of a new civil war is ever-present as both an expectation by some analysts, and an ambition by others. Such a situation necessarily makes us realise that there must be a reason for the persistence of this culture of civil strife and violence. Hence, one has to revisit each civil war in its particular historical context, while trying at the same time to detect a certain pattern that could be seen to be running through most, if not all, of these civil wars.

Furthermore, by a process of elimination, one cannot simply fall back on obvious or banal explanations. In other words, these civil wars are not to be seen as the result of the personal whims of a few individuals, no matter how powerful or significant they may appear to be. Nor can one take for granted theories of a recurring conspiracy, double-dealing and the external interference of various parties. Although these explanations should not be discounted completely, the contribution of these factors to the outbreak of civil strife should always be bracketed and assigned a secondary role.

Needless to say, civil wars have been a prominent feature in a number of countries, both old and new: the English civil war in the seventeenth century, the American civil war in the nineteenth and the Spanish civil war in the twentieth century, to mention only a few well-known cases. However, what one immediately notices is that these civil wars ended with a clear winner and a clear loser. More importantly, the winning party invariably took care to consecrate its victory by devising a new political formula and corresponding institutions designed to underline the emergence of a different order. Unfortunately or fortunately, such an outcome was never fully arrived at in our Lebanese case.

A recent study estimates that 'more than 140 civil wars around the word since 1945 have killed approximately 20 million people and displaced 67 million. Despite this massive human misery, the academic community had not paid much attention to the scale of civil war until very recently.'[1] In this sense, Lebanon's last civil war is not a unique case, nor does it signify the persistence of an aberrant political system. Nevertheless, the recurrent problem of having to live through yet another civil war, ever since the 1840s is in many ways a worrying state of affairs.

As to the causes of these civil wars, a major survey commissioned by the World Bank under the guidance of Paul Collier, now at Oxford University, argues that contemporary civil wars are not caused by political or socioeconomic grievances, but as a result of the financial rewards warlords stand to reap from their perpetuation. In other words, civil wars are rooted in greed, not grievance. However, Samir Makdisi and Richard Sadaka, of the American University of Beirut, found the so-called Collier-Hoeffler (CH) model is not particularly helpful in trying to understand the underlying factors behind the last civil war in Lebanon. They single out 'religious, rather than ethnic, fractionalisation' as a crucial factor. They also point to 'external interventions... as another significant factor in accounting for the causes of the war.'[2] If we substitute 'sectarian' and 'social' for the term 'religious', as their more detailed analysis seems to imply, then we begin to grasp the perennial problems of the Lebanese polity and its pluralist multi-confessional society. However, further research is still needed to arrive at a more rounded picture. Our conference represented such a preliminary endeavour. This is not to say that there was agreement on a general approach to these civil wars. Be that as it may, towards the end of the conference there seemed to be a common diagnosis that called for drastic measures if Lebanon was to avoid the outbreak of a new civil war.

Hence, the present book is divided into three parts: 1. The Historical Context; 2. Memories of War and Forgiveness; and 3. The Politics of Reform: An Agenda for the Future.

Part I offers a general description and analysis of the various civil wars in the context of the modern and contemporary history of Lebanon. Ahmad Beydoun in Chapter One contends that despite the fact that Lebanon has witnessed in the last 150 years or so three major civil wars, each war should be seen in its historical context, rather than a prelude to a new cycle of violence.

Hence, causes of violence and civil strife in Lebanon are to be sought in the peace formulae or settlements arrived at by internal and external parties. In other words, these forms of settlement were meant to regulate new social relations that were blocked by the old historical structures and their rigidity. By attempting to renew their internal structures, various Lebanese groups saw civil war as the only option that would allow them to amend their relationship with other groups or communities. Unfortunately, no formula has so far resolved this historical paradox as its authors endeavoured in their turn to freeze it in time, perpetuating thereby the possibility of new conflicts.

In order for Lebanon to overcome such a deadlock and avert the possibility of a new civil war, it has to conclude a new contract or pact between its citizens. Such a pact has to be based on the new developments and changes which Lebanon has undergone in its contemporary history, particularly in the period since the end of the last civil war.

Youssef Choueiri in Chapter Two discusses, interprets and compares the three major civil wars of 1860, 1958 and 1975-90, with particular emphasis on the last two. The purpose of this historical analysis is geared towards uncovering the major underlying causes of these civil wars, their duration and conclusion. By so doing, the study aims to arrive at a rigorous evaluation of both domestic factors and external intervention. However, the function of a number of interlocking factors and their interplay, the factor of institution-building and modes of political governance, figure more prominently in guiding the general thrust of the chapter.

Choueiri goes on to explore the contemporary configuration of domestic forces and external pressures. This particular aspect is singled out in view of a number of reasons related either to the previous civil wars or the uncertain trajectory of future development.

In Part II, three chapters deal with the traumas, manipulations and festering wounds of past conflicts and individual recollections. Pamela Chrabieh alludes to an 'invisible war', gripping an entire society with its fantasies and state of denial, whereby 'the other' is either ignored or dehumanised. However, she cites many examples of individual and collective efforts undertaken across Lebanon to heal the wounds and achieve reconciliation. Sune Haugbolle turns his attention to the various narratives articulated by Lebanese intellectuals in art, literature, the media and public debates, and how they ended up forming in a culture of war memories. Sectarian violence and civilian resistance to its perpetrators, the militias, are often remembered in different ways by different social and political groups. He concludes his analysis by calling on the Lebanese to invent new ways of reaching out to each other in order to lay to rest the ghosts of the past. Alexandra Asseily takes up the same theme from a different angle. Her approach is to show how past conflicts affect the psychology of individuals and consequently that of a particular community as a whole. In order to defuse such 'emotional charges', creating at the same time a new mode of thinking and behaving whereby the propensity to pass on these beliefs to the next generation is invalidated, she discusses the implications of forgiveness as a central mechanism.

Part III includes seven chapters recommending a wide range of reforms so as to bolster the Lebanese political system against civil war or to arrest the fragmentation of Lebanese society into self-enclosed sectarian cantons. This is the main theme of Michael Johnson's chapter. He thus considers confessionalism to be an outmoded form of allocating political posts or an unviable system incapable of delivering genuine political participation. He, moreover, sees civil marriage, which is still banned in Lebanon, as an essential step towards tackling a number of chronic problems, such as gender equality, inheritance, divorce and marital rights in general. He also highlights corruption in public life as a major obstacle to the emergence of a fully accountable system of government. Finally, Johnson pins his hopes on a revitalised civil society organised to work for a united and secular society. The education system is also severely criticised by Maha Shuayb for its repeated failures to instil a proper and enduring sense of citizenship. Her study revealed a significant gap between public and private religious schools. Religious schools seemed to achieve the highest level of student satisfaction. Private schools catered for students' diverse needs and involved them in various activities in the same religious institution. This resulted in a strong sense of belonging to the institution. In contrast, the majority of students in public schools suffered neglect and consequently developed negative feelings towards officialdom. Her findings reveal that the young generation trust religious institutions to fulfil their needs rather than the public secular system. She concludes by showing how the supremacy of religious schools over public ones will lead to a more fractured society comprising different ghettos.

Mark Farha went even further, offering a panoramic view of all the deficits of the Lebanese polity. These range from the failure to embrace secularism and apply its tenets in all spheres of public life to a dismal record of economic performance. His chapter gauges the exuberant optimism which followed the 14 March demonstration, and assesses to what degree a word of caution is in order. The current political polarisation in Lebanon is compared (and contrasted) to that prevailing prior to the last Civil War of 1975, with a focus on three commonly cited causes for hostilities: Lebanon's unresolved identity, skewed economic development and continued exposure to the Israeli-Arab conflict and its ramifications.

Michael Kerr offers a nuanced depiction of the way external support and linkages, both regional and international, could be harnessed by the local elite to bolster its consociational democracy. However, such an outcome, as Kerr argues, has to be underpinned by a political culture of elite cooperation and conflict management. In other words, power-sharing in Lebanon depends on a positive regional context and an internal culture of national allegiance. Halim Shebaya highlights the alienation of Lebanon's Christians in the wake of the meagre results of 'the Cedar Revolution' following the departure of Syria's troops in April 2005. He views the emergence of General Aoun as a victorious leader of the Christian community as a golden opportunity that his political opponents in the Sunni and Druze camps failed to garner to regain the trust of a substantial component of the Lebanese landscape. His short-term solution is to reconfigure political alliances by having Aoun as the linchpin and president of the republic. Rudy Jaafar tackles the necessity of reforming the electoral system as the most efficient way of building a lasting democracy. He offers a compelling argument revealing the flawed structures of the state and its inherent weaknesses. Thus, the Lebanese confessional system created a balance of sectarian power rather than a national unity and a common sense of loyalty to state or society. His solution consists of recommending a flexible electoral system known as the Single Transferable Vote (STV). Such a mechanism, as Jaafar demonstrates, would ensure fairer representation and allow the consolidation of non-sectarian parties.

Shortly before the conference got under way, a report by International Crisis Group published in June 2006 (*Crisis Watch* No.34, 1 June 2006), listed Lebanon alongside Afghanistan, Brazil, DR Congo, Israel/Occupied Territories, Mali, Somalia, Sri Lanka, Timor-Leste, Turkey, as 'a deteriorated situation.'[3] Furthermore, in early June, riots erupted in south and east Beirut in protest against a Lebanese satire show that seemed to parody the leader of Hezbollah in an undignified way. Both the report and the event were in retrospect a disturbing backdrop, and constituted at the same time a timely reminder of Lebanon's fragile peace and its history of violence and civil wars, coupled with persistent efforts to chart a different course.

Finally, during the conference, the Lebanese political system was analysed, dissected and found to be wanting. Although some scholars and statesmen have hailed this system as a good example of consociational democracy[4], almost all of the conference participants came to a different conclusion. This system was thus seen as an outmoded collection of confessional institutions, blighted by notions of obsolete loyalties, crippled by bygone patriarchal networks of family ties and rotten to the core by age-old indubitable practices of corruption. We hope that this book will have served its purpose by demonstrating to all Lebanese and their friends throughout the world the absolute necessity of immediate action and comprehensive reform.

Notes

1 Nicholas Sambanis, 'Expanding Economic Models of Civil War Using Case Studies', p.1. Website: www.nyu.edu/gsas/dept/politics/seminars/ns1110.pdf,p.1.

2 Samir Makdisi and Richard Sadaka, 'The Lebanese Civil War,1975-1990', in P Collier and N Sambanis (eds.) *Understanding Civil War: Evidence and Analysis*, Vol. II , The World Bank, 2005, p.59. See also, Paul Collier and Nicholas Sambanis, 'Understanding Civil War: A New Agenda' (2002).

   Journal of Conflict Resolution. 46(1): 3-12; Paul Collier and Anke Hoeffler, 'Greed and Grievance in Civil Wars,' Working Paper Series 2002. Centre for the Study of African Economies, Oxford.

3 The report was based on the following incidents and events: 'Worst cross-border fighting in six years erupted 28 May after rockets fired into Israel in apparent response to killing of Islamic Jihad group leader in south. Israeli air strikes targeted Popular Front for the Liberation of Palestine camps, leading to exchange of artillery fire, and border skirmishes with Hezbollah: three guerrillas reportedly killed before truce brokered by UN.

Political leaders held seventh round of 'national dialogue' talks 16 May but failed to find consensus on future of pro-Syrian President Lahoud or disarmament of Hezbollah: talks to continue 8 June. Rival leaders' March pledge to peacefully disarm guerrillas outside camps within 6 months yet to be implemented. Lebanese soldier killed in skirmish with pro-Syrian Palestinian guerrillas 17 May. UN Security Council called for disbandment of all militias inside Lebanon.'

4 For an example, see Richard Hrair Dekmejian, 'Consociational Democracy in Crisis: the Case of Lebanon', *Comparative Politics*, Vol. 10, No 2, (1978), pp. 251-265.

Part I

The Historical Context

Chapter One

Movements of the Past and Deadlocks of the Present: Did the violence of the nineteenth century generate a society prone to civil war?

Ahmad Beydoun

It is no wonder that in a society, whose recent history saw each of its major political crises turn into violent civil strife, some observers – be they specialists or not – anticipate the outbreak of another war whenever a difficult crisis with no foreseeable solution emerges. Such is the case of the Lebanese today facing, as they do, the current crisis that cripples their political system and that was revealed (rather than emerged) more than a year ago. Naturally, they recall the latest war that swept through their country between 1975 and 1990 as well as older crises that led to civil strife, such as in 1958 and in the nineteenth century, or the so-called 'movements'[1] crisis that raged for about two decades in the mid-1800s and attained its peak and its end in 1860.

However, the Lebanese who know their country's history well, might also recall other situations where serious omens of civil strife spread or where violence erupted before it was brought under control by external influential forces which had a dissuading presence in the country or had no interest, under the given circumstances, in fomenting war. Such was the case in 1918-20 and again in 1936.[2]

By recalling previous crises, one tends to let wars of the past pervade the way the present crisis is perceived and dissected. Such an attitude is reinforced by a hasty tendency claiming that all wars are the same regardless of any change of circumstances or facts, no matter how important.

The question that has to be asked: will previous wars necessarily generate new ones or will they be a source of contrition and learnt lessons, enhancing thereby the desire to reach peaceful solutions for political and/or socio-political crises?

This chapter can only include a general diagnosis of the first war of the three that were waged in Lebanon in the nineteenth and twentieth centuries. This diagnosis aims at unveiling constant denominators that were passed on to existing conflicts, if such denominators do exist. It also aims at deducing the unique features of the present crisis in comparison to the previous ones, attempting at the same time to verify the existence of links between these past wars and the potential violent tensions currently prevailing in Lebanon.

Different evolutions

The events of 1840-60 were inaugurated by a general rebellion against unbearable policies adopted by the Egyptian occupation forces and their ally Prince Bashir Shihab II. The rebellion was general in the sense that it unified the ranks of the various religious denominations of the coast and the mountain, notably the Maronites and the Druze. This unity was mainly expressed in memorable popular uprisings such as that of Entelias and Dayr al-Qamar. We tend to forget, though, the other events that preceded or followed these two popular movements by months or even years.

In fact, prior to the general insurrection, the Maronites had adopted for a certain period of time, the project of Bashir Shihab, and accepted thus to fight the Druze who stood against him and the Egyptian ruler, Ibrahim Pasha. The Druze believed, then, that such a war, waged against them by the Maronites, aimed at breaking their back, so as to cripple forever those who had been for a long time the powerful lords of the southern mountain.

At the end of the insurrection, the Druze became more attached to their leaders who returned from exile and attempted to regain the feudal privileges they had lost, and which had been a heavy burden on the Maronites. Prince Bashir had in fact released the Maronites from a great part of that burden before the arrival of Ibrahim Pasha, only to indulge later on, with the Egyptians, in more unjust measures against Christians and Druze alike. These measures were worse than any previous feudal privileges the two communities had known.[3]

The situation in the mountain after 1841 was not the same for the two camps, however. In fact, the Druze held on to the customary guarantees of their status in the mountain as a substitute for their small number and to make up for their lagging behind the new trends introduced by the Europeans. These trends should have led them to change existing patterns of investment in agriculture, education, industry and commerce alike. This was what the Christians did in the second quarter of the nineteenth century, and even earlier.[4]

The Christians had already started to appreciate the advantages of independent work and its association, in many cases, with what amounted to private landownership rights. It would be true to say that private ownership was not fully applied in the 1840s from a purely legal point of view. However, the decline of feudalism during the rule of Bashir had made it a *fait accompli* in practice.[5] As a result, the first glimmers of patriotic aspirations and dreams of national independence started to appear among the Christians, as mirrored in the works of their scholars. Christians were, thus, calling for either autonomy in an expanded mountain with an integrated economic system or for a Syrian kingdom open to Christian activity. In fact, Boulous Nujaym had no hesitation in describing such activity as '*isti'mar*', an Arabic word that meant '*umran* .i.e., cultivation or construction[6] at that time. However, Syrian nationalism had not by the middle of the nineteenth century gained acceptance at the level of Christian leadership, i.e., the Church. It was rather advocated by 'heretics', such as Boutros al-Bustani[7], converted by Anglo-Saxon missionaries and whose horizons were broadened by an Arabism movement founded in the Syrian provinces by Ibrahim Pasha as a means of countering the legitimacy of Ottoman rule[8].

While espousing modernisation, this Maronite leadership found itself trapped in a paradoxical situation. On the one hand, it was weakening feudalism by empowering elements that were opposed to it, and by promoting the status of peasants' sons who aspired to be priests and monks. On the other hand, this leadership was still feudal in its origins in the 1840s and the church had become by then, despite the fact that it followed a different way of accumulating capital and managing labour, the leading feudal lord in its own right. Patriarch Youssef Hubaysh had combined utter allegiance to Prince Bashir II and Druze allegiance to his person, since he was seen as the guardian of a system of values akin to theirs[9].

A Mixed partition

Following 1841, the Maronites, headed by the patriarch, failed to promote a stable national rule except through the reinstatement of Bashir II at Beit Eddeen. Such a solution constituted a catastrophe for the Druze[10]. When the Ottoman statesman Omar Pasha had failed to reinstate stability, the mountain was divided into two Qa'imaqamates (provinces) each having a sectarian council with judicial capacity[11]. The two Qa'imaqamates fared no better[12]. This led to the system of Shakib Effendi in the aftermath of the '1845 movement'. Feudal lords worked hard on sabotaging this new formula since it delegated some of their prerogatives to the councils and to the local governors and they persisted in their efforts to violate[13] and paralyze the new system.

Nevertheless, the new system failed to solve other issues such as that of the mixed districts (*cazas*), notably in the southern province. There, power was given to the large minority of Druze while the Christians were left to wonder whether, according to religious affiliations, they were expected to follow the Christian governor in the North or his Druze counterpart in the South, where he headed a bunch of dignitaries to whose authority the Christians were reluctant to submit again.[14]

Under the regulations of this partition, which lasted 15 years, the rising fury of the new enlightened Christian forces was directed against both the Druze and the northern Maronite feudal lords. This mounting anger was eventually to culminate in the Peasants' Revolt led by Tanious Shahin, who proceeded to establish his own rule in Kisrwan in 1858, dubbing the new order a 'republic'. The new republic expelled landlords in a part of the Northern Mountain, not only out of their own farms but out of their own homes as well[15]. Some historians found a correlation between the above-mentioned movement and the ascendance, within the church, of new forces which resulted in the election of Boulous Mas'ad, a son of a peasant, to the headship of the Maronite church upon the death of Patriarch Youssef Al Khazen in 1854[16]. Such views are corroborated by the unconditional support on behalf of the church of the rising movement at its early beginnings and the aspirations of religious dignitaries to set up their own direct rule of the mountain[17]. However, due to the institutional vocation of the church and its overall interests, the church could not relinquish its unifying and reconciliatory role and persist in its support of a movement that became violent and chaotic. It opted, thus, for an ambivalent position dictated by interrelated clerical interests and sectarian considerations. This allowed the new patriarch to turn a blind eye when Youssef Karam led a campaign to put an end to the republic of Tanious Shahin[18].

Friction

The result of this internal situation was persistent friction between two denominations: on the one hand, the Druze, who did not manage to find any other solution to maintain their inherited status except to rally, as a somewhat unified bloc, around feudal leaders who rose from the ashes of the Bashir-Egyptian era, and on the other hand, the Maronites who were witnessing the emergence of new forces which linked agriculture to international trade and were embracing new professions and lifestyles. This resulted in further social differentiation within the ranks of the Maronites. Moreover, Maronite individuals were able to consolidate their positions, since they were being defined by their professional achievements rather than by their inherited social standing. They also started, under the leadership of the church, to strengthen sectarian ties, lending less importance to family and town identities. Thus, new power paradigms emerged embracing voting rights and the right to choose. There were confrontations because of the social intermixing of the two communities and because the question of the administrative authority in the southern province remained unsolved for the Christians as was the case for the Druze in relation to socio-economic authority[19].

The underlying factor, fuelling such extended friction in the southern province in particular, was the fate of feudalism. Feudalism often served to mask sectarianism as a system promoting both solidarity and conflict. It had often minimized its manifestations and prevented it from assuming an autonomous form, and from being controlled by a majority whose ultimate aim would have been to remove feudal allegiances at least in one community. The first omen of civil war was, in fact, the loss by the feudal lords of absolute allegiance to their authority, which was guaranteed by the Ottomans and the traditional system they had installed, but was now opposed by one community while the other still considered it to be a safe haven for which there was no substitute[20].

This feudal crisis took place in an Ottoman and international environment that exacerbated the crisis and embraced its sectarian dimensions. The Ottoman Tanzimat or 'organisational measures', inaugurated mainly under European pressure, by the Noble Rescript (Khatti Sharif) in 1839, were largely controversial. While some voiced their disapproval of certain notions, others welcomed them, while still others were totally opposed. These measures were thus partially implemented and a subject of controversy and reluctance depending on the advantages or disadvantages the central administration found in their implementation[21].

In Mount Lebanon, the new Christian forces welcomed the new measures regarding feudalism, and the consecration, by the Decree of 1856 (Khatti Hamayoon), of equality among the Sultan's subjects regardless of religion. However, the same forces opposed the consequences of such measures, reinforcing as they did central administration, and weakening at the same time the prerogatives of local governors, which were equated in their eyes with autonomous rule[22].

By contrast, the Sunnite majority rejected this equality in rights which was caused, in its opinion, by a growing European influence in the sultanate, coupled with an enfeebled Ottoman rule. The supporters of the new measures were considered, therefore, to be agents working for the Europeans[23]. Moreover, the Ottoman administration was not always honest in its will to implement reforms that deprived it of its privileges and prerogatives[24]. The Druze, on the other hand, felt this Sunnite resentment in the coastal cities vis-à-vis the new reforms and thought of proving their devotion to Islam through their attendance of prayers at mosques and the flaunting of their newly-found devotion. Soon, however, they resented the tendency to centralise the administration and deny them autonomy over their region. They also grew weary of the Sunnite preachers sent to spread Sunnite faith amongst them[25].

Europe: a double-edged sword

On the European side, British influence had by then attained its peak in the Ottoman Empire, notably in the Syrian provinces. This was particularly the case after Britain led the Syrian fight against Mohammed Ali and helped solve the Egyptian problem. France, on the other hand, was quite embarrassed by its support of the Egyptian invasion and soon decided to play the unconvincing role of mediator[26]. The British attempted, thus, to seduce the Maronites in the hope of replacing the French. However, the Church perceived the British as heretics and fought British and American Missions as best as it could[27]. Hence, the British turned to courting the Druze who were favourable to their initiative. Being a Catholic empire,

9

Austria had better luck with the Maronites. However, its success was limited and short-lived due to the adherence of the Church to its French protector. The Orthodox, on the other hand, sought the protection of the Russian Tsar[28].

This distribution of protection (which was entrenched during the Mutasarrifiyya era 1860-1914) provided the respective denominations with a feeling of relative security vis-à-vis the state, and bestowed legitimacy on any interference by these protective states in Ottoman policies. However, it also exacerbated Muslim resentment of protected communities. This is how massacres spread to Damascus in 1860, where more than 5,000 people were killed in one day on July 9 in what was the peak of violence in that wretched year[29].

Strangely, the majority of Damascus victims were Orthodox though the Lebanese Orthodox took the side of Druze not that of the Maronites in the events of 1860 and in other confrontations.[30]

The 'Movements': made in the mountains

One cannot deny the role of European powers in the 'movements' of the nineteenth century in Lebanon. However, one cannot accuse the European consuls and their superiors or assistants of having direct responsibility for the waves of civil violence in Lebanon. In other words, these Europeans did not create this violence. In fact, the French tried to pacify the uprising of 1840 but to no avail[31]. The British, on the other hand, attempted to protect Bashir III from the Druze, only to abandon him later on[32]. Moreover, there is no proof to the direct involvement of foreign consulates either in the conflict of 1845 or in the massacres of 1860. They simply tried to protect those who sought refuge from Ottoman rule, after each wave of civil violence. European countries also intervened to force the Ottoman emperor to take measures to counter the spread of violence. They even took these measures themselves when the need arose. This is how the British sent their fleet in 1840 and the French both in 1841 and 1860. In addition, both coordinated their political action in 1845[33].

The Ottoman officials, in the mountain, knew that civil violence caused them embarrassment vis-à-vis European countries and increased their intervention in the affairs of the empire. At the same time, they opposed the rapprochement between Lebanese communities and any of the foreign countries the Ottomans suspected. Therefore, they crushed any step they considered as a move away from the empire. They spread discord among the straying party and its opponent, relying on an existing predisposition for war and replicating a known tactic used to deal with insurrection within the empire. In fact, the Ottomans did not invent this tactic in the mid-1800s, since it had been the way feudalism had dealt with similar matters[34].

Nevertheless, one has to admit that not all Ottoman rulers had the same attitude towards preventing bloodshed or dealing with insurrection. Mustapha Pasha, Omar Pasha, Wajihi Pasha and Khorshid Pasha were no match for As'ad Pasha, Khalil Pasha, Shakib Effendi and Fouad Pasha in this regard[35]. In any case, the behaviour of Ottoman officials – in all its different forms – was not far off what was expected from them. In fact, one may accuse the likes of Wajihi Pasha and Khorshid Pasha of either turning a blind eye to planned atrocities or being accomplices to the planning. However, neither Ottoman nor European attitudes can explain the wave of civil violence that spread in these times.

What does this all mean? It means that the civil violence that swept the country was genuinely civil or locally-based, sparked by socio-economic transformations that heralded similar ones at the socio-political levels. These transformations were imposed by some and opposed by others. The capacity of outside forces to split a given community and mobilise the other respectively stems from the mountain's history itself. Depending on the angle one chooses, this history may include the years of Egyptian occupation or may extend to the past three centuries. Whether in the former or the latter eras, Mount Lebanon was always affected by the changes stirring in its immediate Ottoman environment and the fluctuations of relations between this environment and the rest of the world and its most influential powers. It would, however, be ludicrous for Lebanon to blame the rest of the world for its major transformations and for how these transformations paved the way for the violence that gripped Lebanon. Such blame would suggest that the Lebanese should have isolated themselves from the rest of the world or that the world should have given the Lebanese the prerogative of engineering its whole history so that it could exclude all that might generate violence amongst them. Instead, the Lebanese should consider whether they did their best to use other means, besides civil wars, to cope with the inevitable obligations of history. Once such questions are answered, one can ask how others are to be blamed and what can be attributed to simple misfortune.

A classification of legacies

What legacy did the movements of the nineteenth century leave us with that might justify the likelihood of a civil war every time we face a difficult crisis? The answer includes three elements: First, constant structures created and rooted in a certain period and passed on to future eras. Second, past scenarios that are supposed to be recreated in the present and the future; and third, events or series of events, that are unique by nature and cannot be passed on from era to era but could be repeated occasionally due to an intrinsic relation with constant structures.

Regarding the 'structures' we have inherited from the movements of the nineteenth century, we can mention what was dubbed 'sectarianism' or the designation of religious denominations as units of conflict and substitutes to feudalism. However, the movements were simply – in the words of Marx – the violent midwife of sectarianism. They did not create denominations or their disposition to play this role. In fact, the denominations that met in 1920 were not, in their social composition and power, the same as when they first formed in 1861. Moreover, they were not equal in their formation as sects or institutionalisation as such, rather than mere conveyers of other forms of group solidarity. However, the model passed on by the Mutasarrifiyya imposed itself, though in a modified form, on the new partners, forcing them to embrace it and reproduce it through various paces and patterns. The erstwhile confrontation between the Maronites and the Druze was now a confrontation between Christians and Muslims. The state and the city – Beirut in this case – became the main stage of this confrontation, a factor that did not figure in the structures of the nineteenth century[36].

Today, we might be standing at the threshold of a new transformation where distinctions between Muslims and Christians have become politically insignificant, and have been replaced by new dividing lines between the various sects i.e. the Sunnites, the Maronites, the Shi'ites, the Druze, the Orthodox, etc. These lines of division need to be redefined and might prove ever-shifting. The situation is not new. It was clearly seen as such when the Lebanese political society was looked at from Beirut, rather than Paris or Cairo, for instance. However, the divide amongst sects rather than religions seems to be more exacerbated in the current crisis. 'Gender' experts assert, nowadays, that the distribution of humanity to females and males has become, due to change of roles, obsolete. Such is the case of the division of Lebanese into Muslims and Christians today.

As for the inherited scenarios, one cannot acquit old wars of either their facts or myths, exploited by existing wars to justify their cause and continuation or by efforts aiming at sparking a new war with the purpose of attaining certain objectives. Old scenarios are, in fact, used to emphasize existing divisions among the various communities. However, they may, according to the circumstances and the will of decision-makers, fuel another war or become a source of collective indignation or mockery. The truth is that old scenarios are not passed on to us without being altered and we all have our version of any given war or event. There are, therefore, various conflicting versions of the same war and its motives. The questions we ask about wars are reflections of our own questions coupled with questions about the era during which this or that war took place. In fact, the spiritual fuel of any war is not past images, despite their importance, but rather current violence itself through its realities and stories. This violence is founded on what we once called 'the exacerbation of differences' where every divergence in views between two communities is turned into a 'contradiction' that shuns peaceful solutions[37].

As for inherited circumstances, the movements of the nineteenth century revealed the incapacity of the Lebanese to deal with the accumulation of changes through peaceful means. The Lebanese failed to recognise the different balance of forces within their society and did not act accordingly. This incapacity was not due to constraints imposed by third parties, as their leaders always communicated with each other and exchanged demands during those days without any major obstacle. When they reached agreement over a given problem, they always managed to implement it without anyone preventing them from doing so.

What is being repeated?

It was, in fact, agreed upon that the pact of 1943 would serve as the guideline of public policy. The pact was, however, seriously violated, on the eve of 1958[38], and during the 1960s when supporters of reform and economic growth turned a deaf ear to those calling to preserve the role of the state and national security and vice versa. We arrived, thus, at the war of 1975 after which the Ta'if Agreement was signed to put an end to the cycle of violence in the country. That agreement was, unfortunately, not fully implemented. It was also violated in many ways. The Syrians rejected the question of their withdrawal from Lebanon and the Arab identity of Lebanon was understood to mean steering Lebanon's affairs away from Damascus. The only articles within the Ta'if agreement that were implemented were transitional or distributive political reform articles such as those pertaining to the distribution of parliamentary seats, and the handing of the executive power to the cabinet, whose posts were also distributed according to sectarian considerations. All other articles, pertaining to the dynamic chapter of the agreement, i.e. to the elimination of political sectarianism, were dismissed. All those who received a share in the deal seemed quite content with what they had received and only demanded –when there was any demand– to be given their full share, no more and no less. Such content drained the country and prevented any reform or proper governance.

These realities remained hidden under the rule of the neighbouring master. They were only unveiled when the main Lebanese political actors were left to communicate directly with each other. Contrary to what some might think, the new situation was revealed not because the old ruler still had some followers to obey him in Lebanon – even if that were true. Neither was it revealed because the other Lebanese actors followed other foreign countries – even if that were also true.

It was rather revealed because Lebanese leaders, and hence Lebanese communities, became compelled to put behind them a political system that had long become dysfunctional and posed a hurdle to national independence, security and development, confining the country's choice to either collapse or explosion.

Freezing peace, generating violence

We believe that the reasons behind violence in Lebanon do not lie within the previous wars but rather within the peace settlements that were adopted in theory and in practice in Lebanon. In fact, these settlements established a system of relations among various communities whose socio-historical structures underwent major transformations. Unfortunately, the failure to take into account these transformations strengthened the chances of war. We believe that it was not war that led to the formation of communities, though it might have consecrated them and altered their orientation and development. It was rather that these groups waged wars as the only available means of renewing their internal structures and their relationship with other stakeholders. War imposed itself because the afore-mentioned system and settlements were thought to have a sustainability that was neither deserved nor acknowledged by history. Therefore, it is the various 'pacts' or 'agreements', rather than previous wars which are thought to be everlasting, that are more worthy of being considered the real cause of future violence.

We thus believe that in the interests of averting war the Lebanese should adopt a pact among themselves to alter the existing system of governance if need be. The desire to maintain old systems despite changing circumstances, and consequently to deny history itself, becomes sooner or later a will to kill and die.

A new pact involves, however, the holding of negotiations amongst stakeholders who believe that new changes should be incorporated into the self image each one retains of themselves, of other parties, of the country and of the whole world. Such is the effort that is required. The various Lebanese parties may not have the capacity to deliver, since each still clings to a self image that existed years ago and since each believes that the country's fate has been settled once and for all a thousand years ago, if not more. There is no doubt that there are certain constants in every political system. However, political systems should always live up to the tests imposed upon them by the various social, historical and political changes because war becomes probable when constancy is valued more than survival and when the former is made the enemy of the latter.

Notes

1 Many books were written regarding the 'Movements' of the nineteenth century and the war of 1975-1990, which is not the case of the events of 1958. Regarding the Movements see: Adel Ismail, *Histoire du Liban du XVIIe Siècle à nos Jours, Vol.* IV, *Redressement et Déclin du Féodalisme libanais (1840-1861),* Beirut 1958. An analysis of this book and other books dedicated to the movements of the nineteenth century can be found in the following: Ahmad Beydoun, *Identité confessionnelle et Temps social chez les Historiens libanais contemporains,* Beirut 1984, third part, chap. II.

Ismail has also published an Arabic synopsis of his book entitled 'The Era of Chaos and Unrest 1840-60' in *Lebanon: History and Legacy,* (in Arabic), Beirut 1993. Volume II, pp. 329-382. Regarding the war of 1975-1990 see:

Ghassan Tueni, *Une Guerre pour les Autres,* Paris 1985 ; Samir Kassir, *La Guerre du Liban, de la Dissension nationale au Conflit régional, 1975-1982,* Paris-Beirut 1994. For the events of 1958, see: Caroline Attie, *Struggle in the Levant, Lebanon in the 1950s,* Oxford 2004.

2 For the events of 1918-20: Meir Zamir, *The Formation of Modern*

Lebanon, Cornell 1988, Chapter II.

For the events of 1936, see: Meir Zamir, *Lebanon's Quest, The Road to Statehood, 1926-1939,* London-New York 1997, pp.199-213

3 For an account of the 1840 Rebellion, see Ismail, *Histoire...*, *Vol.* IV, pp. 39-103.

4 Regarding the socio economic transformations that led to these 'movements', see: Dominique Chevallier, *La Société du Mont-Liban à l'Époque de la Révolution industrielle en Europe,* Paris 1971.

5 Chevallier, *La Société...*, pp. 80-81.

6 Jouplain, *La Question du Liban,* Paris 1908, p. 529

7 A reading of the political texts of Boutros al-Bustani in Nassif Nassar, Towards a New Society, Fundamentals to the Critique of Sectarian Societies, (in Arabic), Beirut 1970, pp.16-32

8 With reference to the Arabism of Ibrahim Pasha, see: Zein Noureddine Zein, *the Emergence of Arab Nationalism',* Beirut 1968, pp.45-46 and 187-188 (of the Arabic version).

9 Regarding transformations within the church, see: Chevallier, *La Société...*, pp. 245-256. Waddah Sharara , *On the Origins of Sectarian Lebanon,* (in Arabic), Beirut 1975 pp.63-39. Regarding the role of Patriarch Hobeish in the beginning of that period, see: Ismail, *Histoire...*, Vol IV, pp. 71, 113-117 et 133.

10 Idem, pp 113-115. Regarding the relation between Bashir II and Druze dignitaries refer to: Hussein Ghadban Abu Shaqra (narrator) and Khattar Yussef Abu Shaqra (editor), *Movements in Lebanon during the Times of the Mutasarrifiyya,* (in Arabic) p.1-24.

11 Ismail, *Histoire...*, Vol.IV, pp.284-289. Unanimity was prerequisite in both councils. Otherwise the decision is referred to the Wali (governor of Sidon). The two Qa'imaqamates could also be removed by that governor. If we consider that this system was the first institutional form of sectarianism in Lebanon, we must admit that the unanimity of vote required and the foreign arbitration imposed in case no unanimity was reached, were elements that accompanied the birth of that system. The truth is that it accompanied it throughout its history. During the Mutasarrifiyya times, there was an administrative council. However, power was given to the Mutasarrif (ruler) who was not Lebanese. The various dignitaries from various denominations still relied on European councils to gain leverage vis-à-vis the foreign ruler as well as vis-à-vis each other. During the French Mandate, power was given to the high commissioner who had the right to suspend the constitution, remove the president, dismiss the cabinet and dissolve the national assembly. Lebanon did not achieve the removal of foreign arbitration and a unanimous vote as a prerequisite for keeping the decision making process as an internal one except during the three decades

following the independence of 1943, in other words for 30 years out of 160 years which constitute the real age of sectarianism. We believe that the 30 years were an exception, and the re-establishment of the former conditions (which failed to prevent conflicts, anyway) is impossible. To overcome the unanimity (which is impossible and will cripple the authorities) and foreign arbitration conditions (which might be implicit or explicit) depends on overcoming political sectarianism altogether which is something the Ta'if Agreement seems to have recognised. However, what happened to that agreement clearly demonstrates that overcoming sectarianism is not an easy task to say the least.

12 Ismail, *Histoire...*, Vol IV, pp. 175-201

13 idem, p. 301

14 Ibid, pp. 216-219

15 Id, p. 321-327

16 Chevallier, *La Société...* p. 271

17 Ismail, *Histoire....*, Vol. IV, pp. 324-325

18 Chevallier, *La Société...*, pp. 277-278 and 289

19 Sharara, *Origins,,p p.52-60*

20 Ismail, *Histoire..., Vol* IV, Conclusion

21 Regarding the impact of the movements on sectarian relationships in Damascus refer to: Iskandar Bin Ya'coub Abacarius, *Narratives of Mount Lebanon events,* (in Arabic) edited by Abdel Kareem al-Sammak, London 1987, p253-254. Regarding the same topic in Mount Lebanon refer to: Abu Shakra, *movements...*, id, p32-34

22 Regarding the fight of both Druze and Maronites against the Austrian Omar Pacha and the will of the Maronites to reinstate Bashir II refer to: Ismail, ' the Era of Chaos and Unrest...' , in *Lebanon: history and legacy, Vol 2, p 352-354*

   Also: Ismail, *Histoire..., Vol* IV, pp. 257-261

23 Chevallier, *La Société...*, pp. 267-269

24 Ibid, p 269

25 Ismail, *Histoire...*, Vol IV, pp. 139-140 and 188

26 Riad Ghannam, *Lebanese provinces during Egyptian Rule 1832- 1840,* (in Arabic), Chapters 4, 5, 6, Beirut 1988, and Ismail, *Histoire...*, Vol. IV, pp. 16-17

27 Chevallier, *La Société....*, pp. 256-260, and Ismail, *Histoire....*, Vol. IV, pp. 156-160

28 Ismail, *ibid.,* pp. 106 et 146-148

29 Abacarius, *Narratives,* chapter 8

30 Ismail, *Histoire...*, p. 137 and Ismail, *the Era of Chaos,* p356

31 Ismail, *Histoire...*, pp. 78-88. On the other hand, Ismail (pp 73-77) asserts that the British and the Ottomans encouraged the rebels and provided

them with promises and arms. However, the movement of 1840 was a collective rebellion and was not a civil war.

32 Ibid, pp. 110-111 and 121.

33 Ibid, pp. 73, 89-99, 154-156, 277-280, 333-334, 346-351.

34 In 1840, disarming the population and arming the formal authority became the objective of the Ottomans when dealing with the Lebanese crisis. It aimed at disempowering the feudal lords and replacing them with civil servants. However, this tendency truly materialised during the times of the Mutasarrifiyya. Regardless, the Lebanese tend until today to arm their respective communities.

35 In the references we cited, there is a depiction of the Ottoman rulers. All these references commend the second group while accusing the first of partiality, conspiracy, neglect and corruption.

36 Ahmad Beydoun, *The Discontinuous Republic, Sources of the Lebanese System after the Ta'if Agreement*, (in Arabic), Beirut 1999, p461-463.

37 id, p 295-296.

38 Chamoun, accepted, unlike other Arab leaders, the 'Eisenhower Doctrine' and engineered the defeat of the leaders of the opposition in the parliamentary elections of 1957.

Chapter Two

Explaining Civil Wars in Lebanon

Youssef M Choueiri

A perennial problem of Lebanese society is the weakness of the state and its inability to acquire legitimacy from all or most of its citizens. The weakness of the state is mirrored in the continuing and growing role of local and sectarian communities in the fields of education, health, social welfare and political mobilisation. Moreover, since the nineteenth century Lebanon has been plunged into at least three civil wars.

From 1861 to 1989, each civil war was launched and settled under similar conditions. These included:

1. The absence of an adequate political formula.
2. The emergence of new sectarian configurations demanding political recognition.
3. The imposition of a new settlement by outside forces, or through their mediation.
4. No Lebanese civil war has so far come to an end as a result of direct and unmediated negotiations by the parties concerned.

Patterns and configurations

There is clearly a pattern running through the previous three civil wars, despite the fact that it tended to assume different forms under different historical circumstances. The recurrence of such a pattern has to be read against the background of a weak Lebanese state and its failure to win legitimacy or tacit approval. Furthermore, both sides of each civil war actively sought external support or became convinced of a favourable outcome on the basis of a certain reading of the regional and international balance of forces.

In the nineteenth century various experiments were made to devise a viable formula. Bashir II (1788-1840) was the first ruler of Mount Lebanon who tried to centralise political authority. He did so by a combination of policies and measures designed to deprive his opponents or rivals of their power base and properties. These policies, often violently executed, served to reduce the number of feudal families. The only powerful rival he had to contend with was Bashir Junbulat (or Jumblatt) who was the wealthiest and most influential chieftain in the Shuf and beyond. After his return from exile in Egypt, having concluded an alliance with the Viceroy Muhammad Ali, Amir Bashir finally succeeded in disposing of his rival by defeating him in a military battle in 1825. This opened the way for further confiscations of land and properties throughout Mount Lebanon.

However, Bashir's policy of centralisation, which paved the way for the emergence of strong local institutions, was cut short by the Egyptian invasion of Syria and Lebanon, under the command of Muhammad Ali's son, Ibrahim, in 1831. Bashir, despite his initial reluctance, threw his weight behind the Egyptian campaign in its confrontation with the Ottomans and, subsequently, various local forces. The European powers, particularly Britain and Austria, were alarmed at the rapid advances made by Ibrahim and decided to reverse his seemingly relentless drive to topple the sultan himself. Finally in 1840, local Lebanese rebels joined forces with a European expedition led by Britain and Austria and put an end to the

Egyptian adventure. Consequently, Bashir II's experiment based on centralisation and institution-building came to an end as he was sent into exile immediately after the defeat of his Egyptian ally.

For the next twenty years Mount Lebanon became the scene of constant civil strife and intense external interventions. A new political vacuum was clear for all to see. The Ottomans[1] were constantly striving to reassert their authority, but never quite succeeding in achieving their aims. On the other hand, the former Druze feudal lords sought to reclaim their former privileges and often managed to do so. Nevertheless, in the new age of reform or Tanzimat, inaugurated by the Ottoman authorities, such privileges were felt to be flagrantly outmoded and blatantly oppressive. The Maronite church, in its turn, was becoming more involved in the political destiny of its community in the absence of the former lord of Mount Lebanon. Mounting clashes between Druze and Maronites led the Ottoman state to propose the division of the Mountain into two districts: northern and southern, or the double Qa'imaqamate composed of a northern Maronite district and a southern Druze district. But owing to the fact that both communities were not geographically separated as neatly as the proposal had assumed, the formula turned out to be highly impractical and was turned down by both Druze and Maronites. In 1845 another civil war erupted. Appeals by the European powers forced the Ottomans to intervene to put an end to the war and devise a new political solution. This was done under the supervision of the Ottoman Foreign Minister, Shakib Effendi. His solution amounted to a final recognition of the complexity of Lebanese society by granting representation to all sects on the two councils of the double Qa'imaqamate. Thus, in addition to Druze and Maronite representatives, there were Sunni, Greek Orthodox, Greek Catholic and Shi'ite representatives, assisted by *wakils* or deputies in both districts.

However, this new arrangement turned out to be highly flawed. The outbreak of the Kisrwan peasant rebellion of 1858 dealt it a mortal blow. The 1860 civil war erupted in a political space largely dominated by local forces and in the absence of an effective political power.

Once again, external intervention played a decisive role in bringing an end to the new civil war. By that time, each Lebanese sect was protected by or linked in one way or another to a particular European power. Thus, whereas the Maronites were backed by France, Austria and France as Catholic sponsors, the Greek Orthodox were supposed to shelter under the protection of Russia, and the Druze had the tacit support of Great Britain. These European powers, together with the Ottoman establishment, came to a new agreement on the future government of Mount Lebanon. It was now decided that the Mountain would become a single political unit, Mutasarrifiyya, under the authority of a non-Lebanese Christian governor, to be appointed by the Ottoman Sultan in consultation with the major European powers. The governor was to be supported in his tasks by an administrative council composed of twelve elected Lebanese members on the basis of sectarian representation. By 1864 the Council included four Maronites, three Druze, two Greek Orthodox, and one each from the Greek Catholic, the Sunni and the Shi'ite communities. It is important to bear in mind, that these quotas did not reflect actual sectarian proportions, as the Druze, for example, did not form more than ten per cent of the total population. By 1913 the breakdown of the population was as follows:

Table 1. Source: KH Karpat, *Ottoman Population 1830-1914*, Madison, 1985

Maronites	242,308 (58.4%)
Druze	47,290 (11.4%)
Greek Orthodox	52,356 (12.6%)
Greek Catholic	31,936 (7.7%)
Shi'ite	23,413 (5.7%)
Sunni	14,529 (3.5%)
Others	2,968 (0.7%)
Total	414,800

The Administrative Council, as its name implied, had a consultative role. In this sense, it could offer advice on matters referred to it by the appointed governor. But it was also charged with allotting taxation, overseeing the management of revenue and the distribution of expenditure. Each councillor represented one district or qada'. Councillors gained their seats by an indirect system of election whereby village *Shaykhs* or elders were elected by the local population who in turn elected their particular representative in the Council. Moreover, the Mutasarrifiyya enjoyed fiscal autonomy and recruited its own local gendarmerie or police. Social and economic life was dominated by two features, silk production by French-owned and local factories and the rise of the Maronite church, particularly its monasteries, as the owner of one-third of agricultural land in Mount Lebanon.

Another feature, which was to persist down to the present time, was the mounting emigration of Lebanese to North and South America, as well as Egypt and the Sudan, in search of better opportunities or mere employment. Between 1860 and 1908 it is estimated that up to 100,000 emigrated from Mount Lebanon to the Americas and adjacent Arab countries. Thus this steady emigration acted as an index of poor economic conditions and the inability of the local economy to absorb the country's surplus labour. Consequently, members of the nascent Maronite middle class began to voice demands for incorporating Beirut and other areas to the south and east into Mount Lebanon. This trend was eloquently exemplified by Paul Jouplain's publication (pseudonym Boulous Nujaym) in French of a history book entitled: *La question du Liban* (1908).

This historian, who was a civil servant working within the institutions of the Mutasarrifiyya set up between 1861 and 1864, captured the mood of a new social group which came into being as the result of Ottoman reforms and European intervention. He argues the case for a Lebanese fatherland that could play the role of a Syrian Piedmont, thus re-enacting the movement of Italian unification. More importantly, he delves into the history of Lebanon as a connected development, evolving over time in its manifold levels. However, his main assumption envisages direct European intervention, calling on France to assume its role as a liberator of the oppressed Christians of the East. He also charges the Lebanese Christians, particularly the Maronites, with the task of transforming a new Greater Lebanon, incorporating Beirut and the other coastal cities, into a modern European state.

By 1914 and the outbreak of the First World War, the Ottoman state which had entered the war on the side of Germany, abolished the special privileges of the Mutasarrifiyya and appointed its own Muslim governor. Such a state of affairs persisted until 1918, when Anglo-French and Arab forces succeeded in pushing the Ottoman military occupation out of Syria and Lebanon completely. It was under these circumstances that Greater Lebanon was born as a result of French imperial policies and the tacit support of the British government. Hence, in 1920 when the French Mandate was officially declared, Greater Lebanon was not a predominantly Christian country, but one in which its Muslims formed at least half of the population.

In 1926 a new constitution was introduced for the Republic of Lebanon, with its own president, cabinet of ministers and chamber of deputies. However, the French High Commissioner retained the ultimate authority in the republic and remained so until Lebanon achieved its independence in 1943. However, the formal niceties of the constitution did not do away with the former Ottoman system with its clear confessional nature of representation. It was thus assumed that the president would always be a Christian and exclusively Maronite after 1933, whereas the premiership was assigned to the Sunnis on a permanent basis in 1937. After independence this confessional distribution of state and civil service posts was fixed as a concrete expression of a new National Pact concluded in 1943 between the leading representatives of the Maronite and Sunni communities. In 1947 it was agreed that the Speaker of Parliament would always be a Shi'ite.

The main political rift that emerged under the French Mandate was between those who advocated allegiance to the new republic as a final and permanent fatherland or nation and those who stressed the importance of its identity and consequently the possibility of merging the republic into a wider Arab federation. But this broad categorisation, adopted by some Lebanese and Western historians, often hides more subtle nuances which did not conform to a simplified classification of political allegiance. To be sure, the newly incorporated Sunni coastal cities, or the Shi'ite of south Lebanon and the Biqa' Valley were not initially disposed to accept the new French order for political, economic and cultural reasons. Nevertheless, by the early 1930s there gradually began to emerge a more positive Muslim attitude towards the new republic, provided certain conditions were met. In other words, a majority of Muslims were inclined to settle for a Lebanese identity in exchange for a clear official policy based on the idea of full independence and political equality. This meant that Lebanon had to free itself of French or Western direct influence and align itself with other Arab movements or states struggling for the same aims. In the Christian camp, a similar stance, albeit less keen on relinquishing earned privileges, such as the presidency of the republic, made its appearance after the outbreak of the Second World War. However, in both camps there were those who insisted on continued full protection, and others who thought that the establishment of Greater Lebanon came about at the expense of Greater Syria and its territorial integrity. The mainstream position eventually won the day in the battle for independence throughout 1943.

Had equality and inequitable economic system of production and distribution been achieved, the Lebanese state might have weathered the storms of the 1950s and 1970s. But this was not to be.

In a sense, the future of Lebanon has never been conclusively settled ever since its independence in 1943. The political formula devised at the time to ensure Lebanon's survival as an independent country was an unwritten national pact between the representatives of its Christian and Muslim communities, or to be more precise, the Maronite president of the republic, Bisharah al-Khoury and the Sunni Prime Minister Riyadh al-Sulh. The formula simply required the Maronites to recognise the Arab character of Lebanon and the Sunnis to accept the country as an independent state not to be absorbed at a future date by one of its Arab neighbours, namely Syria.

This formula broke down in 1958 when civil war broke out over issues of foreign policy, mainly the Eisenhower Doctrine, and the domestic distribution of wealth and power. This was largely a war between the main Maronite political establishment represented by President Camille Chamoun and his Sunni opponents in Beirut, Tripoli and Sidon, in addition to the veteran Druze leader, Kamal Jumblatt. The civil war was brought to a swift end after the fighting had reached a stalemate, and both Egypt and the United States decided to strike a deal whereby Camille Chamoun would not seek a new term of office and General Fouad Shihab, the Commander of the Lebanese army since 1945, would be elected as the new president.

Although the national Pact remained intact, the foreign policy of Lebanon under its new president became more neutral, and more often than not closely associated with the general thrust of Nasser's Arab alignments. More importantly, the Lebanese state became for the first time in its modern history an engine of social change and economic transformation. Hence, networks of roads, schools and hospitals were extended over the entire country, thus benefiting the marginal and deprived areas, in addition to a host of social and welfare programmes designed to lessen social and sectarian tensions. Nevertheless, Shihab's Pro-Arab Policy and his domestic reforms created a backlash within the Maronite Community, particularly the Phalanges, led by Pierre Jumayyil, and his two allies, Camille Chamoun and Raymond Eddeh. With the death of Nasser, the relocation of the PLO's headquarters and centre of operation to Lebanon, in addition to new vocal demands calling for reforming the system of government as a whole, the stage was set for another round of violent confrontations. The old formula was severely tested and turned out to be woefully lacking in meeting the emergent set of challenges. Thus, between 1975 and 1990 Lebanon became the theatre of a plethora of overlapping wars, pitting Christians against Muslims and Palestinians, with the Israelis going out of their way to prop up the Maronite camp against all the others, while the Syrians supported different factions, be they Christian, Muslim or Palestinian, and succeeding by the end of the war in gaining the upper hand as the sole arbiters of Lebanese domestic and foreign policies.

Ascendant Sects and State Structures

The working assumption is that each civil war exposed the inadequate mechanisms of Lebanese institutions to channel political and socio-economic changes. Consequently, effecting change had to fall back on, or was associated with, the ascendancy of a particular sect, either politically, culturally or economically, and the defensive responses such ascendancy elicited from the other sects. Nevertheless, civil strife would not have occurred without the absence of a legitimate and efficient state.

In 1860 the Maronites were such an ascendant sect, while the Druze desperately tried to stem the tide of their political and economic decline. The civil war took place in the virtual absence of a viable political system. Paradoxically, the Maronite assertiveness and subsequent control of the levers of power, underpinned by French sponsorship, turned sectarian strife in Lebanon into a struggle for power and the ultimate control of political authority.

In 1958 the state was still a minimalist set of weak institutions in an era of rapid economic changes and increasing demands for social justice. It was largely the Sunnis who thought the time had come to challenge the hegemony of the Maronites. The resultant civil war announced a Sunni endeavour, led by urban political bosses, to tip the balance of power in their favour, relying in the process on the backing of Egypt and Syria under the leadership of Gamal Abd al-Nasir (Nasser). Although there was no clear-cut victory for either side, the Sunnis had become by the end of the war almost equal partners of the Maronites, having as much stake in the new state as the Maronites. However, it must be borne in mind that it was often the political elites of these sects who claimed victory and reaped its benefits in the name of their communities.

General Fouad Shihab's endeavours to strengthen the presence of the Lebanese state were eventually thwarted by a combination of local entrenched interests and regional developments. Both the Maronite and Sunni leaderships, each for their own reasons, became alienated or deeply alarmed as they saw their function being whittled away and taken over by state institutions.

By 1975, it seems that the Shi'ites had finally reached a similar conclusion, while at the same time Maronite political organisations sensed the imminent threat to their status and partnership with the Sunnis. The outbreak of the third civil war was largely played out against a highly charged atmosphere punctuated by the grievances of various Shi'ite groups affiliated to different political parties and factions, as well as Maronite pre-emptive attacks. The initial Shi'ite-Palestinian alliance signalled the persistence of a familiar pattern of internal and external factors coalescing to achieve particular goals, albeit for different reasons. As we know, this alliance did not endure as other external forces entered the field, such as the Syrians, the Iranians and the Americans. The Israelis also entered the scene to promote their own strategic interests.

Population: Table 2

	1932	1984
Shi'ite	154,208 (19.6%)	1,100,000 (30.8%)
Sunni	175,000 (22.4%)	750,000 (21.0%)
Druze	53,047 (6.8%)	200,000 (5.6%)
Maronite	226,378 (28.8)	900,000 (25.2%),
Other Christians	21.1%	17.5%
Muslims	48.8%	57.3%
Christians	50.0%	42.7%

Source: *Lebanon: A Conflict of Minorities* (Minority Rights Group, London (1983).

As can be seen from this sketch, these civil wars were largely politically motivated and ultimately linked to the ambitions or fears of particular sects. In other words, these were sectarian rather than religious wars. Their outbreak, duration and mode of conclusion reveal the failure of Lebanese institutions to respond to rapid change with the appropriate mechanisms to direct social transformation through peaceful channels.

Hence, it becomes important to identify the essential elements of the present political system and its ability to respond to societal changes. Furthermore, the existence of a new ascendant sect and the possibility that a number of other sects are likely to feel threatened by such an ascendancy, bring to the fore the significance of discussing the inadequate characteristics of the Lebanese political institutions. In this sense, a civil war may break out as a result of the aggressive drive of a particular sect or the pre-emptive riposte launched by other sects. At this stage the Shi'ite ascendancy has so far failed to translate itself into enduring and dominant political forms at the legislative and executive levels. Ironically, it seems that Syria by its sheer presence in Lebanon, and as a trusted ally of various Shi'ite groups, obviated the need for such an ascendancy to capture the highest levers of power. However, such a need has now reasserted itself in the wake of Syria's withdrawal from Lebanon. It is in this context that one should read the real significance of various incidents and political realignments, as actions and counter-actions are being formulated and carried out to meet the challenges of this entirely new situation.

As the Lebanese state is still incapable of managing social and political transformations through properly transparent, legitimate and accountable institutions, Lebanon is once again faced with a new civil war or descent into sheer chaos. However, there are indications that the present or forthcoming crisis is unlikely to be a repeat performance of previous civil wars. This was amply demonstrated by the emergence of new social movements cutting across almost all sects. Nevertheless, these movements represent in the main a coalition of Christian, Sunni and Druze forces pitted against the inexorable ascendancy of political Shi'ism.

It is this complex encounter between various internal elements that has to be highlighted as the main engine of change without, however, neglecting to take into account regional and international pressures capable of either restraining the outbreak of widespread violence or unleashing the destructive energies of various Lebanese and non-Lebanese social forces. Moreover, it is ultimately the responsibility of the Lebanese themselves to devise new institutions and practices designed to put an end to yet another cycle of violence.

With the end of these various wars, and the emergence of Syria as the dominant power in Lebanese affairs, Lebanon entered a new phase in its modern history. This was characterised by the signing of the Ta'if Accord at the end of 1989 and the subsequent implementation of some of its terms and stipulations. The Ta'if Accord was supposed to settle the future of Lebanon as no formula has done before, enshrining as it did the acceptance of almost all the Lebanese deputies, political forces and community leaders of Lebanon as 'a sovereign, free, and independent country and a final homeland for all its citizens.'[2] Moreover, it called for parity of parliamentary representation between Christians and Muslims, and highlighted at the same time the Arab Identity of Lebanon and its active role as a founding member of the Arab League. It also stated that 'efforts [will be made] to achieve comprehensive social justice through fiscal, economic, and social reform.' More importantly, it stipulated disbanding 'of all Lebanese and non-Lebanese militias.' As to sectarianism, the accord called for its abolition in all appointments to the institutions of state save parliament, the three top political posts, and 'the top-level jobs and equivalent jobs which shall be shared equally by Christians and Muslims without allocating any particular job to any sect.'

Nevertheless, the Accord's call for the abolition of political sectarianism, and the redeployment and eventual withdrawal of Syria's armed forces was never fully implemented. Although all militias were disbanded, Hezbollah, which emerged after the 1982 Israeli invasion as a resistance guerrilla movement, was exempted from this general requirement given the continuing Israeli occupation of a security belt in the south of the country.

Owing to a configuration of local, regional and international factors, particularly in the wake of the assassination of former Prime Minister and foremost Sunni leader, Rafiq al-Hariri, on 14 February 2005, a coalition of Maronite, Druze and Sunni forces that enjoyed open French and American support, compelled Syria to withdraw its troops from Lebanon by the end of April of the same year. In the meantime, Syria had managed in 2004 to convince a majority of Lebanese members of parliament to amend the Lebanese constitution in order to allow President Emile Lahoud to extend his term of office for an additional three years. Syria had also before its withdrawal succeeded in nurturing a special political relationship with Hezbollah, which often matched that party's other special relationship with Iran. By weaving close ties with a number of other Lebanese parties, personalities and factions, Syria remained as a force to be reckoned with even after its military withdrawal. Hence, the end of Syria's military presence did not lead to the emergence of a broad Lebanese consensus, or betoken the advent of national unity. Rather, it left the Lebanese political scene a polarized arena whereby demands for radical reforms resurfaced as the platform of a new coalition centered on Hezbollah, Amal, the other Shi'ite movement led by the Speaker of Parliament, Nabih Berri, and the former General Michel Aoun, who does not hide his ambition to become the next president of the republic in 2007. In other words, whereas the Syrian military presence had served to freeze the Shi'ite drive for change, its removal has reactivated such an agenda and widened its appeal to embrace different political forces and confessional groups.

The Future of Lebanon

At a time when the future of our entire planet is being intensely debated, the future of Lebanon may not seem to be an urgent matter to discuss. However, the future of this tiny country is paradoxically interconnected with the unfolding Arab-Israeli conflict, the war in Iraq and the ambitions of Iran to develop its own nuclear programme. Given these considerations, the future of Lebanon takes on a global dimension and is of direct interest to the United

States with its present imperial policies, the European Union, not to mention Russia and China.

The future of Lebanon will to a large extent depend on the looming outcome of the confrontation, be it peaceful or violent, between political Shi'ism and the so-called 14 March forces grouped around al-Hariri's son and heir, Saad, his Prime Minister Fuad al-Siniora, Walid Jumblatt and his Druze faction, and Samir Ja'ja'(Geagea), the leader of the Maronite Lebanese forces. In this sense, the last Israeli bombardment and invasion of Lebanon only served to galvanise the underlying dynamics of change and political reckoning. Bearing this in mind, in trying to depict a number of alternative scenarios, it would useful to highlight the following points:

1. The Shi'ite community is the only Lebanese sect that speaks with one voice on all major issues affecting the future of Lebanon. This state of affairs was the result of the changes witnessed by the Shi'ites since the 1970s. Its traditional leadership, represented by, among others, the al-As'ad and Hamadeh families, has been swept aside and replaced by members of a new Shi'ite middle and lower middle class who have risen to prominence by their professional and individual efforts. This political transformation was, moreover, accompanied by a social mobility and demographic growth, with the result that the Shi'ite community has become the largest Lebanese sect, despite the disputed figures of its real numerical strength. Social mobility and demographic growth were helped in no small measure by the burgeoning of a new economic development spurred by investments from migrant businessmen and entrepreneurs in North America and West Africa, in addition to subsidies provided by various Iranian agencies.

Furthermore, the Shi'ites are the only Lebanese community that has undergone such radical changes, straddling the political, social and economic dimensions.

2. Compared with the different voices emanating from the leaders of the Sunnis, the Druze and the Maronites, the Shi'ites of Lebanon are thus able to formulate a single political programme, gain non-Shi'ite allies for its implementation, and sustain a long campaign to turn it into a permanent feature of the Lebanese landscape.

3. In order to achieve its aims and appeal to the widest constituency outside its own community, Hezbollah, as the main Shi'ite force, has made a number of amendments to its original political programme. It has first accepted and recognised Lebanon as a sovereign state and a fatherland for all its inhabitants. Secondly, it has dropped its demand for the establishment of an Islamic state, opting instead for a pluralist polity based on the rule of law, democratic accountability and the consensus of its religious communities. Thirdly, its leader, Hassan Nasrallah, has recently spoken of the Shi'ite belief in the government of the Imam as no more than the establishment of a strong and just state capable of protecting its citizens and defending the territorial integrity of the country.

   The immediate demands of Hezbollah and of its coalition partner, the Free Patriotic Movement, led by Michel Aoun are the formation of a government of National Unity and the introduction of a new electoral law more expressive of the diversity and new political forces in the country.

4. The 14 March Coalition Forces, which dominate parliament and government, contend that their agenda encompasses the following points: A. Preserving the status quo as long as possible, while endeavouring at the same time, to introduce minor economic reforms; B. Resolving any outstanding issues with Israel or Syria by appealing to the international community, particularly the United States and France, and enlisting their goodwill to launch new diplomatic and political initiatives; C. Seeking to convince Hezbollah to disarm once the issue of Sheba' Farms and the release of Lebanese prisoners has been formerly adopted by the United Nations.

   After the failure of Hezbollah and its allies to renegotiate the formation of a cabinet of national unity in early November

2006, Hezbollah and Amal cabinet ministers resigned from the Lebanese government, thereby exacerbating a deepening political crisis that gripped the country at all levels.

Three Scenarios:

The immediate causes of the present crisis can be traced back to 2004. This year could be seen as a watershed that set off a chain of events culminating in the Israeli invasion of July 2006.

On 11 May 2004 President George Bush signed an executive order implementing the Syria Accountability and Lebanese Sovereignty Restoration Act.[3] The act was meant to introduce a number of sanctions against the Syrian state. Such sanctions were justified by referring to Syria's support of 'terrorist groups', its development of various categories of weapons of mass destruction, its continued violation of 'the spirit of the 1989 Ta'if Accord" by maintaining a military presence in Lebanon, thereby preventing the local government from extending its rule over the entire national territory, and for Syria's failure to police its borders with Iraq against foreign fighters.[4] On 2 September 2004 the Security Council passed Resolution 1559. The Resolution was adopted by a vote of nine in favour, to none against, but with six abstentions. Those voting in favour included The United States, Germany, France and Spain. China, the Russian Federation, Algeria, Brazil, Pakistan and the Philippines abstained.

Sponsored by the US and France, the Resolution was mainly confined to reaffirming the necessity of respecting Lebanon's sovereignty, territorial integrity and political independence. It also stressed the need for Lebanon to have a government that enjoyed the right to exercise 'the sole and exclusive authority throughout its country.' More importantly, the Resolution stipulated the urgent task of disbanding and disarming 'all Lebanese and non-Lebanese militias.'[5]

It also referred to the 'upcoming presidential Lebanese election' by highlighting the need to exclude 'foreign interference or influence.' Leaving no doubt as to its target, it went on to call on 'all remaining foreign forces to withdraw from Lebanon.' In other words the Resolution had set out to achieve two interrelated objectives: to disarm Hezbollah as a non-official Lebanese armed group and to place direct pressure on Syria to withdraw all of its military forces from Lebanon.

In 2003, as Syrian-American relations rapidly deteriorated amid allegations of Syrian meddling in Iraq, the US government began openly criticising Syria's occupation of Lebanon, a policy reversal that inspired the opposition movement in Lebanon to reassert itself. By early 2004, France had also ended its official silence on the occupation, and both Western powers were openly calling for a Syrian withdrawal, leading most other European governments to follow suit. Defying these calls, Damascus moved to consolidate its control by pressing the Lebanese parliament to approve a constitutional amendment extending the tenure of President Emile Lahoud, a staunch Syrian ally and rival of Prime Minister Rafiq al-Hariri, beyond his six-year term. In September 2004, on the eve of the parliamentary vote, the UN Security Council passed Resolution 1559, calling for a constitutional presidential election, the withdrawal of all foreign forces, and the disarmament of militias. Syria's decision to push ahead with the amendment provoked an unprecedented international outcry and veiled threats by Western governments to take 'further measures.'

On 1 October 2004, one of Jumblatt's close aides, Marwan Hamadeh, who had resigned his cabinet post as an act of protest against the extension of president Lahoud's mandate for a further three years, suffered severe injuries as a result of a car bomb. In December 2004 various political factions opposed to Syria formed a united front against interference in Lebanon's internal affairs, but did not demand an outright military withdrawal. However, two months later, the anti-Syrian forces did demand full military withdrawal in compliance with resolution 1559. It was thought that Hariri favoured such a move. On 14 February 2005, Rafiq al-Hariri[6] was assassinated as his motorcade went past the St George Hotel located in one of Beirut's fashionable seafront districts. Various factions were blamed for his murder, but the finger of accusation was firmly pointed at Syria by Hariri's allies, both locally and internationally.[7] Hariri's assassination led to intensification of international pressure on Syria to withdraw its troops from Lebanon. Such pressure, accompanied by anti-Syrian mass demonstrations in Beirut, robbed Damascus of its legitimacy and cast it as a foreign occupying power. Thus, within seven weeks, beginning on 5 March 2005 the withdrawal of 14,000 Syrian troops was complete. Moreover, Omar Karami's pro-Syrian government was forced to resign. A transition government, headed by moderate statesman and entrepreneur Najib Mikati, was appointed to prepare the ground for new parliamentary elections.

In June 2005 parliamentary elections were held in three stages. The anti-Syrian camp comprising Saad al-Hariri, Jumblatt, Ja'ja' (or Geagea) and their allies won 72 seats, whereas the other camp comprising Amal, Hezbollah and Aoun's Free Patriotic Movement won 56. The total number of parliamentary members is 128. Hence, Saad al-Hariri and his allies failed to secure their two-thirds majority in order to be able to force President Lahoud, largely perceived as pro-Syrian, to resign. Initially, Hezbollah and Amal, together with representatives of Jumblatt , Ja'ja' and President Lahoud, joined the new cabinet under the premiership of Fuad Siniora, a staunch member of Hariri's camp. On the other hand, General Aoun's movement, calling for sweeping reforms, was the only block that declined to become part of the new government.

However, this relatively broad-based government was soon to show signs of fragmentation. This was the result of a number of disagreements relating to the implementation of Resolution 1559 and the future of Hezbollah as an armed group. In December 2005 Hezbollah's two ministers, along with their three Amal colleagues, suspended their participation in the government. This came after Prime Minister Siniora asked the cabinet to endorse a proposal outlining the establishment of an international court to try those accused of Hariri's assassination. Hezbollah and Amal objected to the decision because it was taken on the basis of a majority vote rather than consensus. In other words, officials of both parties considered the manner in which the principle of voting was conducted a clear violation of the conditions upon which they had agreed to join the government. After the withdrawal of the Shi'ite ministers, Hassan Nasrallah, the Secretary General of Hezbollah, stipulated a second pre-condition to be agreed upon before he would authorise his ministers to resume their duties. He now asked for an unequivocal statement from the cabinet declaring Hezbollah to be a national resistance movement, not a militia, and therefore not to be disarmed as predetermined by the terms of Resolution 1559.

At first Siniora tried to play down the claims and fears of Nasrallah and his allies. He argued that the international community had already endorsed his government's position in considering Hezbollah's weaponry a mere domestic affair. But he went on to envisage the possibility of disarmament as the outcome of an internal dialogue among the Lebanese.[8] Siniora also revealed that his government policy statement was discussed with Nabih Berri, Amal's leader and Speaker of Parliament, and that both had agreed to amend some of its clauses to address Hezbollah's concerns. However, he went on to disclose that his allies, namely Jumblatt and Ja'ja', rejected the amendment.[9]

The political crisis was played out against the background of increased diplomatic pressure by the United States and France. On 14 January 2006, US Assistant Secretary of State for Near Eastern Affairs, C David Welch visited Lebanon for meetings with Siniora and his cabinet. In a press release coinciding with his visit, Welch reiterated US support for a free and democratic Lebanon and the determination of his administration to uphold the rule of law and ensure that Hariri's murderers were brought to justice.[10] Despite these and other international assurances, political assassinations continued to plague the Lebanese landscape and daily lives of ordinary citizens. Between June and December car bombs claimed the lives of a number of prominent Lebanese personalities: George Hawi, a former Communist party Secretary-General; Jebran Tueni, a parliamentarian, publisher, Chairman of the Board and General Manager of the influential daily *An-Nahar*; and Samir Kassir, a columnist on *An-Nahar* and one of the leaders of the Cedar

Revolution. Various parties were accused of their murder, but their supporters blamed Syrian intelligence personnel.

By the end of 2005 the Druze leader, Walid Jumblatt had become one of the most vociferous and outspoken critics of Hezbollah, as a pro-Iranian organisation, and of the pro-Syrian Popular Front for the liberation of Palestine General Command, led by Ahmad Jibril. These two groups were accused of blind defence of the Syrian regime and subservience to its hidden agenda in Lebanon. But in early February 2006 Fuad Siniora succeeded in defusing the crisis by stating publicly that Hezbollah was indeed a resistance movement. He, moreover, affirmed his belief in conducting the affairs of his government by consensus. As a result, Amal and Hezbollah ended their boycott of the government.

In order to resolve the wider political crisis, ranging from relations with Syria to President Lahoud's legitimate re-election, a series of sessions dubbed the National Dialogue were held at the Lebanese Parliament building from early March to the second half of June 2006. These talks were attended by all political leaders of the Lebanese communities. The fact that exclusive sectarian representation was the only criterion for being included in the dialogue denoted the true state of fragmentation in Lebanese society. Saad al-Hariri, Hassan Nasrallah, Walid Jumblatt, Michel Aoun, Samir Ja'ja', Amin Jumayyil, Fouad Siniora and Ghassan Tueni were all invited as spokesmen of their respective confessional factions. Some progress was made. They all agreed on supporting the UN investigation of the Hariri assassination, and the need to collect by August 2007 all Palestinian weapons deployed outside the refugee camps. The participants further agreed to normalise bilateral relations with Syria and open Syrian and Lebanese embassies in Beirut and Damascus respectively. However, the two thorniest issues turned out to be finding a candidate to replace President Lahoud and disarming Hezbollah. Thus the talks stalled and then ground to a halt before the Israeli bombardment of Lebanon in early July.

It is important to recall that, at one of these National Dialogue sessions, Hassan Nasrallah, the leader of Hezbollah, gave a lengthy presentation on his views on disarming his organisation and the threat Israel still poses to Lebanon.[11] Nasrallah called for a comprehensive 'defence strategy' in the military, security, political and economic fields in order to counter Israeli schemes against Lebanon. He went on to describe at length 'the flexibility, dynamism, discipline, complete secrecy and exceptional ability" of his party. He contended that such qualities enabled Hezbollah to make quick and decisive decisions. While praising 'the sacrifices, heroism and courage' of the Lebanese armed forces, he offered a frank assessment of its weaknesses and inability to confront the Israeli enemy on its own. In other words, the Lebanese state had to accept and endorse the continuing presence of Hezbollah as the only armed force capable of protecting the country's national interests.

In the meantime, Israeli military and intelligence experts were, according to Seymour Hersh of the New Yorker[12], discussing with US administration officials 'the profound threat' of Hezbollah's military arsenal to the security of Israel and American interests in the region. This took place in April and May 2006. As a result, an initial plan was outlined by the Israelis calling 'for a major bombing campaign in response to the next Hezbollah provocation...Israel believed that, by targeting Lebanon's infrastructure, including highways, fuel depots, and even the civilian runways at the main Beirut airport, it could persuade Lebanon's large Christian and Sunni populations to turn against Hezbollah." The plan was put into effect immediately after Hezbollah fighters launched a surprise attack on an Israeli military post across the border from southern Lebanon. The operation ended with the capture of two Israeli soldiers and the death of at least six. For the next 34 days more than 1,300 Lebanese civilians were killed and over 900,000 were displaced and at least 4,000 were wounded. However, Hezbollah fought a highly coordinated guerrilla campaign from well-defended positions and launched thousands of rockets into northern Israel. One of its notable military feats was the destruction of an Israeli warship stationed along the Lebanese coast. By the end of the war, Israel had failed to achieve its two main aims: the freeing of its kidnapped soldiers and the liquidation of Hezbollah as a military force. Nevertheless, it did inflict severe damage on the Lebanese economy and infrastructure which wiped out fifteen years of economic recovery and reconstruction.

The adoption by the Security Council of Resolution 1701 on 11 August paved the way for a ceasefire and led to the withdrawal of Israeli troops and the deployment of the Lebanese army throughout south Lebanon. It also called for increasing the size of UNIFIL to 15,000 in order to monitor the cessation of hostilities and assist the Lebanese army in keeping law and order in the south. The resolution also called for the implementation of all United Nations resolutions demanding the disarmament of all militias, including Hezbollah. However, this last demand was left to the discretion of the Lebanese government.

As far as our initial analytical assumption is concerned, the last war exposed the fragility and brittleness of the Lebanese state and the persistence of parallel agencies capable of sidestepping its authority as the sole representative of the country. Moreover, the vibrancy and vitality of the Lebanese civil society during and after the war dwarfed all efforts by state institutions to respond to the relentless Israeli onslaught on its territory. The unity of almost all Lebanese during the last war contrasts sharply with the mounting enmity between the leaders of the government and the opposition since the cessation of hostilities and the withdrawal of the Israeli army. More importantly, Hassan Nasrallah has gained as a result of the war a stature far beyond his Lebanese constituency and has become an acclaimed symbol of resistance and patriotism to Arabs and Muslims across the world. It was only a matter of time before he would seek to translate his popularity, and consequently that of his party, into clear political gains. Leading a broad coalition of political forces cutting across the familiar sectarian lines, he issued a series of declarations and made a number of speeches calling for a new government and the introduction of a more equitable electoral law so as to allow his party, and that of his partners, to attain a fairer representation in parliament and other institutions of the state. His emphasis on the necessity of building 'a strong and just state' reflected a general Lebanese mood and a demand put forward by almost all Lebanese political factions and forces.

On 1 December 2006 Hezbollah and the Free Patriotic Movement, together with an array of other political factions and parties[13], called for open protests and demonstrations, and staged sit-ins in two squares in the centre of Beirut. The immediate demands of the opposition were the formation of a government of national unity giving them the legal right to veto any cabinet decision. The Prime Minister and his coalition insisted that the opposition and consequently the Lebanese parliament should approve the creation of an International Tribunal to reach a judgement on the assassination of Rafiq al-Hariri and other politicians.[14] Despite the mediation of several Arab and foreign envoys and the intense efforts of the Secretary-General of the Arab League, 'Amr Musa, no proposal seemed to be acceptable to both parties as 2006 drew to its end.

Although it would be difficult to speculate about the future course of events, the most likely scenarios could be summarised as follows:

1. Civil disobedience by Hezbollah and General Aoun's Free Patriotic Movement. Such a drastic step would virtually paralyse the state and erode the vestiges of its meagre authority.
2. New parliamentary elections, leading to the election of a new president. Such an outcome would definitely be the most desirable, as it implies a peaceful transition of power and the possible emergence of more stable procedures of governance.
3. Civil War. This last scenario, although the least desirable and certainly the most tragic, should not be ruled out, given the history of Lebanon and the repeated failures of its political institutions and culture to accommodate or meet the demands of new social forces. Political Shi'ism and the grievances of other social groups represent at the moment a challenge that can no longer be ignored.

Conclusion

Lebanon is a state, which generates civil wars as a result of its confessional structures and their contradictory interests. In this sense, one could explain the various civil wars in Lebanon in terms of the uneven development of the social, economic and cultural structures of the various sects in their co-existence within a certain political arrangement. This friction is an inbuilt mechanism that is triggered into violent confrontations whenever a certain sect feels itself capable of tipping the balance of power in its favour.

In the nineteenth century Druze were pitted against Maronites. The latter as the ascending sect faced and attempted to replace the former, a rapidly declining sect, both economically and politically. Moreover, a sect that is in the ascendant often resorts to foreign or non-Lebanese regional powers in order to win control and secure its dominance. It is well-known that the Maronites combined their newly-established ascendancy in the economic and cultural fields with French interests and prestige in order to win political control. In the twentieth century both the Sunnites and the Shi'ites tried to enact a similar scenario by allying themselves with regional forces and power blocs. The Sunnites sought the support of Nasser's Egypt in 1958, while the Shi'ite between 1975 and 1980 relied on their Palestinian allies and after 1982 attempted to involve either Syria or Iran on their behalf. However, in these three instances, it is worth mentioning the following:

1. No sect managed to achieve total victory or impose its authority without offering concessions to or reaching compromise with the other parties.
2. The degree of triumph by each sect has largely been determined by the internal organisation of the parties concerned as well as the extent to which outside forces were prepared to become involved in Lebanese affairs. The eagerness of the French to acquire Syria and Lebanon as part of their empire made it possible for the Maronites to draw on an almost inexhaustible military and political commitment. On the other hand, the

reluctance of Nasser's Egypt to be drawn into the Lebanese quagmire accounts for the partial victory achieved by the Sunnites in 1958. The complicated and uneasy alliance between the Shi'ites and the PLO explains to a large extent the deterioration of relations between the two camps by 1980, while Iran's inability to intervene directly on behalf of some Shi'ite groups and Syria's reluctance to engage the Lebanese on their own terms made a Shi'ite complete ascendancy highly improbable.

By 2005 the confrontation between the sects had reached a stalemate, or these sects had fought each other to a standstill. The stalemate was broken by two new developments: the withdrawal of Syrian troops in the same year and the Israeli bombing campaign and invasion the following year. The first event forced political Shi'ism, as it was propelled by the sheer logic of its dynamism, to fall back on its own resources, while the second afforded it an opportune leverage to stake a claim to power-sharing in a restructured state.

Notes

1 Mount Lebanon and Syria became part of the Ottoman Empire in 1516 after the battle of Marj Dabiq when Sultan Selim the Grim defeated a Mamluk army.
2 The Ta'if Accord was achieved through the efforts of Saudi Arabia, Morocco and Algeria, in addition to the tacit approval of the United States and Syria.
3 The President of the United States signed into law the Act in December 2003, but did not put it into effect until May the following year. According to the White House factsheet the Act included the following sanctions:

'Prohibition on the export to Syria of any items that appear on the United States Munitions List (arms and defense weapons, ammunition, etc.) or Commerce Control List (dual-use items such as chemicals, nuclear technology, propulsion equipment, lasers, etc.); Prohibition on the export to Syria of products of the United States, other than food and medicine; and Prohibition on

aircraft of any air carrier owned or controlled by the Syrian government to take off from or land in the United States.'

Moreover, the President decided to impose the following additional sanctions:

'Under Section 311 of the USA Patriot Act, the Secretary of the
Treasury is to issue a notice of proposed rulemaking with respect
to a measure to require US financial institutions to sever corre-
spondent accounts with the Commercial Bank of Syria based on
money laundering concerns.'

4 Other violations relating to Iraq included Syria's failure to send back to
Iraq approximately $200 million in frozen assets in Syrian banks.

5 For the text of the Resolution see Security Council Press Release 8181.

6 Hariri served as Prime Minister for relatively long terms: from 1992 to
1998 and from 2000 until October 2004. It was estimated that at least 16
others were blown up with him as explosives detonated his motorcade.

7 In an article in the *Guardian*, 23 February 2005, Patrick Seale, the British
writer and biographer of Hafiz al-Assad, Bashar's father, enumerated a
long list of suspects. However, he believes that Syria's enemies, namely
Israel, Lebanese Christian extremists and an array of Islamist groups, had
most to benefit from Hariri's murder.

8 See *As-Safir*, Beirut, 16 January 2006.

9 See the policy statement of Siniora's government as reported as reported
by the *Daily Star*, 29 July, 2005

10 An-Nahar Tuesday, 17 January 2006.

11 As reported by al-Manar Television Archives: www.moqawama.org,
accessed on 1 November 2006.

12 Seymour Hersh, 'Watching Lebanon: Washington's interests in Israel's
war', the *New Yorker*, 21 August 2006.

13 These included Amal, the Syrian Social Nationalist Party, al-Marada of the
Maronite leader Suleiman Frangieh, the Druze notable Talal Irslan, the
Tripolitan veteran politician and former Prime Minister Omar Karami.

14 Including the assassination of the Industry and Trade Minister on 21
November 2006.

Chapter Three

Is Lebanese Confessionalism to Blame?

Mohammad F Mattar

The question, 'Is Lebanese Confessionalism to Blame for the Civil War of 1975-90?' presumes the need to pass judgement. To pass judgment requires stating the case for and against the indictment of the confessional system of Lebanon. This has been one of the main preoccupations of concerned laymen and specialists alike.

This essay, therefore, will attempt to avoid passing judgment. It will try to establish whether there is a cause-effect relationship, or a causal connection, between confessionalism and the civil war that devoured Lebanon during the bloody years of conflict between 1975 and 1990. If and when this is established, remedies will be suggested. An account of the background story is necessary, albeit that the narrative is essentially reflective and impressionistic.

Civil war is a highly charged and divisive phrase in Lebanon. The Lebanese do not see eye to eye on whether the 1975-90 events were exceptional in their nature, or simply one episode in a string of conflicts that had plagued their country since the second half of the nineteenth century, and which are traditionally recognised as civil wars. Opinions also differ on the nature and causes of this particular episode, on the apportionment of responsibility amongst its actors, and whether it constituted a 'civil war' or a 'war of others'.

Archbishop Grégoire Haddad captured the spirit of this multifaceted and, more often than not, heated debate, saying in an interview:

> The battle is between the Palestinians and Lebanese. No! It is between the Palestinians and the Christians. No! It is between the Christians and Muslims. No! It is between leftists and rightists. No! It is between Israel and the Palestinians on Lebanese soil. No! It is between International Imperialism and Zionism on the one hand, and Lebanon and neighbouring states on the other.

Each interpretation or facet of this conflict has its ardent followers among the Lebanese. However, there is general agreement that, since the nineteenth century, three bouts of fighting qualify, more or less, as instances of civil war or conflict, these being: the 1860-64, the 1958 and the 1975-1990 conflicts.

Underlying this tacit agreement is the belief that from the different interpretations of these instances one can discern or extract some common features, a pattern of sorts. But what are those common features, or this pattern that subsumes these three episodes; and do they really share in some common characteristics and how do they differ, if at all?

In brief, these episodes occurred in, or were accompanied by, a climate that demonstrated the following similarities:

1. Intense international and/or regional rivalry, pressures and sabre-rattling;
2. Breakdown or collapse, partial or total, of the state apparatus;
3. Standoff between and among domestic groupings;
4. Internal political, social, or economic changes or redressment;
5. Realignment of domestic forces with foreign powers;
6. Changes in the power structure or balance of power within and between communities;

7. The direct cause or causes that triggered the conflict.

The 1975-90 conflict unfolded in a climate of turmoil; its dramatic events played out in a framework of an interplay of domestic, regional and international elements and dynamics. The facts of this episode are universally acknowledged and amply documented; its lessons, however, are not.

For the purpose of convenience and to avoid semantics or being drawn into pedantic exchanges, I suggest defining 'civil war' as a conflict that unravels on a national soil involving factions or segments of the same people and sometimes others, irrespective of its root causes, whether internal or external.

As to 'confessionalism', I suggest defining it as the sectarian power-sharing formulae, the confessional practices and institutions (customary, legal and constitutional) and the ensuing political system that have obtained in Lebanon from 1860, and especially after 1920, up to now. In general, it is: the 'communal culture' that serves as the engine of Lebanese politics; the instinctive and visceral determinants of the individual and collective conduct of the Lebanese; and the justifying pretexts they usually deploy, consciously and unconsciously, in good faith or in bad faith, to either dissociate confessionalism from, or water down its relationship with, the bleak state of affairs they presently live under.

It is the contention of this essay that, for reasons intrinsic to their confessional make up and composition, and for related ancillary and interlaced historical reasons, the Lebanese have developed and become inherently divisive, and as such they have failed to evolve into a unitary cohesive polity. External pressures and meddling of outside forces only help to perpetuate and, in cases of heightened regional or international crises, to exacerbate this divisive proclivity.

Greater Lebanon was conceived in the wake of the collapse of the Ottoman Empire and the restructuring of the Middle East by the British and the French after the First World War. Both powers invented the Sykes-Picot Agreement that refashioned the post-Ottoman Middle East. However, in the Balfour Declaration, Great Britain alone promised the Jews a National Homeland in Palestine;

it simultaneously encouraged Sharif Hussein to revolt against the Ottomans promising him independence and an Arab Kingdom.

The British, it seems, were more abreast of regional politics than the French when they encouraged the Administrative Council of Mount Lebanon (*Majlis Al-Idarat*) in 1920 to declare Greater Lebanon a neutral entity. With increasing Jewish settlement in Palestine, the British could probably foresee what was to come. Was it that they wanted to cushion Greater Lebanon from impending future vicissitudes, or, as is more likely, did they want to contain French colonial power? The French opted for a French mandated Christian Lebanon; it is probable that colonial hubris clouded their better judgment of forestalling future dangers.

Lebanon, originally and foremost, is a Christian idea. Building on the mainly Druze and Christian political and social traditions, and the customs of nineteenth century Mount Lebanon, the French concocted Greater Lebanon in 1920. To ensure the economic viability and the better survival of the new born entity, they annexed to it the four *cazas* (provinces or districts) of Beirut, the North, the Biqa' and the South. Along with these new acquisitions came fresh communities (mainly Sunni, Shia, Greek Orthodox and Greek Catholic) with their traditions and customs.

The 'newcomers' also brought with them their own predilections, affinities and world views. Predominantly urban (city dwellers in Beirut, Tripoli and Sidon), the Sunnis were especially receptive to the calling of pan-Arabism. In comparison, the Shias, predominantly provincial (from the South and the Biqa'), were not less receptive than their coreligionists to the pull of pan-Arabism, but proved more ready to come to terms with the idea of Lebanon, having been formally recognised as a community for the first time. The Greek Orthodox were especially attracted to the calling of the Syrian Social National Party (SSNP) of Antoun Saadé, while the Greek Catholics, in general, positioned themselves with the Maronites.

The French ruled Greater Lebanon from 1920 to 1943, through the introduction of the 'Confessional System' in which public posts and benefits were allocated on the basis of religious affiliation, privileging the Christians in general and the Maronites in particular. Intellectually and schematically described, it was a period of accommodation between a mainly inward-looking, Lebanese-centered and western (especially French) orientated ideology, and a predominantly outward-looking, Arab-centered and Muslim orientated one. The ideology of the Syrian Social National Party stood in the middle by advocating Greater Syria. This divide was not rigid; it was in fact fluid and symbiotic. For not long before, Lebanese (or more accurately Syrian) Christians were in the forefront of Arabism, when it represented a useful tool to ascertain national identity vis-à-vis the Turks, or a potent weapon to ward off the 'Turkification' policies of the Union and Progress Party (*Al-ithad wa Al-Taraki Party*).

In fact, those three outlooks vied for dominance. An ambitious pan-Arab outlook intent on restoring lost Arab glory pursued the vision of a strong Arab state rooted in a long historical heritage. A more modest outlook of a Christian Lebanon – tinged by Druze, Sunni and Shia constituencies – built on the new and short tradition since 1861 of having a Christian rule over Mount Lebanon, an anomaly in the Arab World. And a conciliatory Syrian Social Nationalist outlook advocated a staunchly secular Syrian Nation based on a social consciousness it presumably had developed through history, even when it was a part of a bigger unit or entity.

It was only after the Second World War, and with the acceleration of Jewish settlement in Palestine and the creation of the State of Israel in 1948, that a fourth ideology came forward. Entrenched in the historical claim of the Jews to a 'National Homeland' in Palestine, the gist of their calling was that minorities cannot escape persecution except by having an exclusive Jewish state of their own.

Lebanon gained its independence in 1943, thanks to a favourable international climate in which the British outmanoeuvred and coerced the French into its acceptance, a rare instance of the Lebanese overcoming their sectarian differences in the face of French colonial hegemony and heavy-handedness, and an historic deal known as 'the National Pact' (*al-Mithaq al-Watni*).

The Confessional System continued. The Christians maintained a majority in parliament, despite the gradual demographic shift in favour of the Muslims. The Maronites were ensured the presidency, control over the army and a majority in the civil service – practically over all political control. The Muslim elite was slowly being co-opted into the system, with a Sunni in the prime ministry and a Shia in the speakership of the parliament. Intellectually, however, both Christians and Muslims were to, supposedly, relinquish their attachment to outside callings.

Within Lebanon, therefore, there were three contending nationalisms: Arab, Syrian and Lebanese. The 'National Pact', in that sense, was paradoxical. It expressed the difference as well as the unity of sects. By negative definition, it was not meant to express unity but to reconcile differences. The three holders of the presidency, the prime ministry and the speakership of the house considered, and reflected, more the interest of their own respective community than a national one.

The 'National Pact' would have been less likely to take place, had King Faysal the First succeeded in installing his Hashemite Kingdom in Damascus. Nevertheless, independent Lebanon was not contracted on an anti-Arab tone. On the contrary, the deal, in essence, provided that, in return for the acceptance by the Muslims of the entity (*Kiyan*) of Lebanon, the Christians will not embrace anti-Arab policies. The power sharing and apportionment of posts were a detail, albeit an increasingly important one. Independent Lebanon was neither a venue nor an avenue for colonial, anti-Arab machinations (*La Makar wala mamar*). As such, Lebanon presented itself as an especially accommodating Arab model. This did not necessarily go down well with neighbouring Syria, nor did it conform to the Israeli model of an exclusive minority state, a predicament that will haunt this small country for a long time to come, and that will foment crises, again and again.

Post Independence Lebanon, during the presidency of Bishara Khoury (1943-52), witnessed the gradual decline and eventual replacement, of the French influence by the British. This was consecrated domestically by the loss of the pro-French president Emile Eddé to president Khoury. Within the pro-French camp, however, lingered a nostalgic longing for the smaller Christian Lebanon; a longing that continues to surface in times of crises. Khoury's term of office, that also witnessed the first wave of Palestinian refugees to settle in Lebanon after the State of Israel was declared in 1948, hinged and thrived on Arab solidarity, especially within the Saudi-Egyptian camp. It was, however, tarnished by his re-election and eventual demise before finishing his second tenure, and by the execution of SSNP leader Antoun Saadé, a black and shameful chapter in the annals of Lebanese judiciary and politics and a serious blow to secular politics.

In the vein of being a unique Arab model, Lebanon, during this period, was quite active and instrumental in the formation of the Arab League in 1945 and the drafting of the Universal Declaration of Human Rights in 1948 – a role that reflected Lebanese openness and keenness for a role bigger than their capabilities, an urge to engage in regional and international affairs and an awareness of the importance of international legitimacy.

A window of opportunity offered itself for the Lebanese to build a national identity and an all-inclusive state. They, however, missed the opportunity by failing to foster a national identity that would ultimately have put in check communal identities, mitigated parochial interests and reined in outside appeal. This was in great part due to two main reasons. The first, the early departure of the French which left the Lebanese with the confessional system but not sufficiently initiated in the craft of French liberalism and its practices or in the tradition of French nationalism and republicanism. The second, the extreme strain the first Arab-Israeli confrontation, and its reverberations, exercised on Lebanon. The outcry over their defeat in Palestine galvanised the Arab masses and divided the Lebanese between those who wanted to join in the fight against Israel and those who wanted to remain on the sideline. Needless to say here, that this divide was more or less sectarian in nature.

This state of affairs inspired to deflect Lebanon's internal political development from a domestic process unfolding in a, more or less, normal climate, into an abnormal, sometimes convulsive, one overwhelmed by turbulent regional and international complexities. Over and above, the geopolitical posture of Lebanon was drastically compromised by being cut-off from Palestine and its hinterland, and jammed between Syria and the Mediterranean.

The journey of Lebanon grew rougher as time passed. During the conservative pro-Western era of President Camille Chamoun (1952-58), Lebanon became the commercial and banking centre for the Arabs Politically dominant, and more favoured than the Muslims, the Christians, while amassing great wealth, blocked social reforms (health care, public education and services and housing for the predominantly poor Muslims). This increasingly strained the political system and alienated the disadvantaged classes. The rich classes, notorious for tax evasion, emptied the state coffers leaving a weakened and impoverished central government. Revenues badly needed for public services, the armed forces and socio-economic development programmes were either lacking or mis-allocated. With few national institutions, many Lebanese identified more with their religious communities than with the nation as a whole. At the same time, discontent was brewing in the face of mounting disparities between the rising fortunes of the rich and the dismal plight of the poor. So, no sooner did Chamoun endorse the Eisenhower Doctrine in 1958, at the same time as he refused demands for reform after having rigged the elections trying to win another mandate, than civil war erupted in 1958. It was an instance of heightened international and inter-Arab rivalry and conflict combined with domestic malaise and inter-Lebanese jostling and politicking. This instance will become a recurring theme in Lebanese politics that augurs ill. Arab nationalists and left-wing rebels were supported by Nasser; right-wing Maronite militias backed Chamoun. US Marines landed in Ouzai near Beirut at the invitation of Chamoun after the successful 1958 coup d'état against the Hashemite Kingdom in Iraq. A negotiated settlement was reached in which General Fouad Chehab assumed the presidency. By now American influence, which started setting in during Chamoun's rule, had overtaken the British, especially after the 1956 Suez War.

The presidency of Fouad Chehab (1958-64), and less so his successor Charles Helou (1964-70), was a departure from the previous course. Leaning on the loyalty of the army and security apparatus and his support among the Lebanese, Chehab embarked on a programme of social and administrative reform. He built roads, overhauled the public educational system, spurred economic development and established important modern state institutions (Central Bank, Ministry of Planning, Public Service Authority, Central Inspection Authority, Court of Accounts, etc). He tried to move the economy in new directions, to build a strong executive and a sense of national identity that transcended sectarian loyalties. But neither Chehab nor Helou was able to break the power of traditional sectarian politicians or, significantly, undermine the sway of the confessional system.

One of the most important aspects of the Chehab era, however, was his tacit deal with Nasser in which Lebanon adopted a pro-Arab stance in foreign policy in return for internal pacification and stability. This was soon to change. With the defeat of Nasser in the 1967 war, the regional balance of power drastically changed. Nasser retreated from his active involvement in inter-Arab policies into a more passive inward-looking national policy of rebuilding the Egyptian army, and waging a war of attrition against Israel to redress the balance of power. This shift in the regional balance of power was soon reflected on the domestic scene in Lebanon.

Camille Chamoun, Raymond Eddé and Pierre Jemayel, old-time rivals, came together and formed the Tripartite Coalition (*Hilf Thoulathi*) to challenge the Chehabi regime (*Nahj*) that they perceived as a threat to their traditional sectarian power base. In the elections of 1968 they won a landslide victory in Christian areas, especially in Chehab's den in Kisrwan. This made possible the election of Souleiman Frangieh to the presidency in 1970 and the failure of the *Nahj* candidate Elias Sarkis. It also was a failure of one serious endeavour at state building and a return to the status quo of communal politics.

Frangieh's presidency (1970-76) was a period of turmoil. Rapid urbanisation, inadequate social services and rural migration combined to accentuate class disparities and to provoke a tide of protest strengthening leftwing forces, who demanded fundamental reforms and called for a non-sectarian democracy. Conservative and Maronite right-wing parties rejected reform as their militias prepared to fight off what they considered a foreign inspired radical challenge to the social and political order. The relocation of the PLO in Lebanon, after their forceful eviction from Jordan in September 1970, introduced a new regional force into the local scene. The internal immigration from the South either for economic reasons – relating to the decline of agriculture and the transformation of small land holding and its consolidation in the hands of few big land owners, or for security reasons – relating to Israeli military operations in response to PLO incursions – led to the relocation of tens of thousands to slum areas in and around Beirut. They were to become the fodder of the war and the fuel that kept it ablaze.

It was again an instance of the coming together and interplay of regional and domestic politics and rivalry, playing out dramatically in Lebanon. The coalition between the National Movement (*Harakat Wataniyeh*) and PLO forces were posed to take on the Lebanese Front (*Jabhat Lubnaniyeh*), a coalition of conservative Christian forces. But most importantly, this came at a time when, on grounds of its meddling in politics, the security apparatus (the *Deuxième Bureau*) had been dismantled, its officers and network dispersed leaving the national army exposed, vulnerable and at a great disadvantage during a critical period, thus rendering the state impotent and incapacitated.

By 1975 the pieces were falling into place. Lebanon was on the point of igniting; all that was needed was a spark, which presented itself in April 1975 when 27 Palestinians were killed by the Phalanghists in Ain Roumaneh, a Christian suburb of Beirut, heralding the start of the Civil War.

Studies on the history of modern Lebanon traditionally focused more on domestic issues and internal political realignments. This came at the expense of in-depth examination of the regional and international realities following the creation of the State of Israel in

1948, and its far-reaching effects on the fledgling and fragile Lebanese State and polity. The fallout of the settlement of hundreds of thousands of Palestinian refugees in Lebanon cannot be ignored. The medium and long-term effects of the Arab-Israeli conflict, the sharp polarisation of a pan-Arab axis and a pro-Western one following the rise of Nasserism in harness with the cold war, and East-West rivalry in the Middle East and its impact on the social and political fabric of the country, cannot be underestimated.

Indeed, the protracted military standoff with Israel, even after the ebbing of Nasserism, galvanised and radicalised the Arab youth, spurring the rise of the Palestinian armed resistance movement after the 1967 war and subsequently transforming South Lebanon into an open battleground with Israel, which, in turn, supervened the state building process. Much of this was not thoroughly gauged from the perspective of its repercussions on Lebanon and its various communities, and the huge strain it exerted on its delicate internal equilibrium, its political and communal configuration, and on its state building process.

But most importantly, one cannot be oblivious, from the perspective of the history of ideas, to the slow but steady corrosion of the idea of a diverse and plural Lebanon, in the face of the two dominant conflicting ideologies and their adverse appeal on the different communities in Lebanon.

Zionism, haunted by the trauma of the Holocaust, pushed to the limit the specificity of the Jewish minority which, they believed, could not be secured except in an exclusive Jewish state, albeit at the expense of the Palestinian Arabs and to the detriment of their most basic human rights. The appeal of this calling to the Christian minority in Lebanon, and its transformation into an alliance with Israel, was a matter of dire expediency. With the outbreak of the civil war of 1975, the collapse of the Arab-solidarity umbrella that had cushioned Lebanon, the forced retreat of the Christians into a canton of their own and threatened in their very existence, laid the foundations for the expedient realignment of the Lebanese forces with Israel against PLO forces, and their ultimate bid for a new

Christian-dominated Lebanon with the election to the presidency of Bachir Jemayel in summer 1982, in cahoots with the Israelis.

Contrary to Zionism, pan-Arabism, urged the subjugation of all the differences and specificities of the various constituents of Arab society – be it ethnic, religious or sectarian – to the supreme cause of fighting off the Israeli existential threat. This struck a favourable chord among the Muslims (who discovered its heavy cost later on), but alarmed the Christians who were very keen to protect their specificity and felt betrayed by the Arabs and abandoned to Syrian designs, as Syria gradually shifted towards the Muslims despite having been invited into Lebanon by the Christian Lebanese Front.

Furthermore, Christian fear for their status in Lebanon and their concern over their rights as a minority living next to a growing Muslim (especially Shia) population, within an overwhelmingly Muslim Arab world, were not assuaged by the insensitive practices of pan-Arab custodians. In the name of conformity and facing-up to Israel, not only were minorities marginalised and sidelined, but also basic human rights and liberties at large were sacrificed, national resources and fortunes were squandered in sustaining dictatorships and intelligence and security apparatuses of police states. In such a climate where even the basic rights of the majority were compromised, minority rights were a forlorn quest. This model alienated the Christians and forced them into a more isolationist mood. These two adverse appeals reignited the nascent mutual suspicion between the two communities.

With two antagonistic and conflicting ideologies at each other's throat, the Lebanese power-sharing formula – though more operational than ideological – by recognising the diversity and plurality within the Lebanese society and the apportionment of power between the different communities – albeit lop-sided and tipped in favour of the Christians – was a loud statement against both Jewish-minority and Sunni/Arab majority based regimes. It also served as a constant reminder of the inherent inconsistency in those two excessive and, seemingly, mutually-serving ideologies.

Such outside pressures and internal schisms were bound to influence the evolution of its political system, to unsettle its delicate internal balance, and to rock the Lebanese state. But the scene was not all that bleak. The brighter side was the process of modernity which had been put in motion in Lebanon since the 1950s. The modus vivendi and modus operandi between the different Lebanese communities, had led to a climate of liberal coexistence in which a free press and freedom of thought and expression flourished. The gradual accumulation of a judicial, constitutional and parliamentarian tradition, the emergence of non-sectarian and cross-community parties and syndicates, the rise of an assertive civil society and the inching-in of the idea of citizenship and of a secular society, testified to the vibrant Lebanese democracy. The *laissez faire laissez passer* and free market economy, a modern and successful private educational system served as positive indicators and stimuli for a growing and flourishing services-based economy. All of these were harbingers of modern statehood. Yet, they were not enough to spare Lebanon from its worst civil war. In 1975 the Lebanese edifice began to fall apart. The country was partitioned along communal lines, the state apparatus disintegrated, the army broke up and society divided into its constituent components.

Upheavals, turmoil, radicalisation and instability affected other Arab countries like Syria, Jordan and Egypt. None of them collapsed under such pressures as befell Lebanon. Jordan narrowly escaped a takeover by the PLO in 1970, despite the fact that the majority of its citizens were Palestinians; yet it did not slip into a civil war.

Why, then, was Lebanon the only Arab state and society that cracked in the face of such pressures, where other Arab states and societies did not? And is confessionalism to blame for that?

If one is to refashion the question and ask: Is confessionalism alone sufficient to engender a civil war? Or better, does it require more than confessionalism to do so? The answer will be in the affirmative. It does require other factors or elements to satisfy the requisites for unleashing a civil war. These other requirements are roughly the same ones enumerated above, which made possible, engendered, caused or accompanied the outbreak of the three episodes of civil war.

Another question follows: is any one of these other elements sufficient on its own, without the confessional constituent, to engender a civil war? The answer to that is in the negative. For these elements to engender a civil war, it is necessary to have the Lebanese people divided; for indeed, if they are not divided then the conflict will not be in the nature of a civil conflict, but rather a war waged by non-Lebanese against the Lebanese.

This raises another question: what, then, causes the Lebanese to be divided? Why do they not unite in the face of outside pressures, dangers and designs as, for example, did the Kuwaitis in the face of the Iraqi invasion and occupation of 1990, or as other nations or peoples normally do when confronted with serious outside threats? And why are they so vulnerable to outside pressures?

This brief and schematic narrative of modern Lebanon suggests an answer. By tracking the two interlocking processes, and analysing the paradigm that manifests itself as a result of this tracking, one can draw a lesson that points to a moral.

Firstly, the interlocked internal and external processes, in as much as they are facets of Lebanese history and politics, exhibit a tendency to interact and interlace so as to become cause and effect at the same time.

In that sense they show that the inherent predisposition of the Lebanese to split up in the face of such outside pressures stems from their confessional and sectarian identification, from their behaviour as members of a sect or a denomination and not as citizens belonging to a nation, and from the preponderance of the communal vision over the national one. But by the same token, and equally manifest, is the fact that outside pressures, in turn, emphasize and accentuate these divisions; divisions which in their own right invite such outside interventions, erroneously in the belief that they will reinforce this or that sectarian agenda, while, in fact, rendering the Lebanese unwittingly oblivious to the ascendancy of the hidden outside agenda over the open domestic one.

Since such pressures, dangers and designs are not perceived by all Lebanese through one and the same prism, and since each community or grouping usually tends to perceive such threats differently, so that what a community considers as a threat might be considered otherwise by another, a universal outlook accepted by all Lebanese, vis-à-vis external dangers and designs, is, therefore, paramount.

Secondly, this brings us to the paradigm ostensibly deadlocked in what might be labelled 'the External Pressures Versus Internal Divisions Equation'.

Since Lebanon will never be an isolated or insulated island and will always be under some sort of pressure from the outside, and especially its immediate surroundings, how best to neutralise the divisive abuse or interference by outside pressures so as not to rock the internal home turf? In other words, how best to cut this Gordian knot?

The obvious answer would be: if internal divisions are healed, bridged or resolved then they will neither invite outside pressures, nor will they be used (or abused) as a pretext to justify outside intervention. In fact, it will render the home front stronger to off-set such pressures or interventions. The contrary is equally true. If the outside has schemes against the inside, such schemes are more likely to achieve their goals if the inside is divided, than if the inside were united.

But how to arrive at a united home front? The answer is by the development of the Lebanese polity from the contract-nation (*nation-contrat*) – contracted by and between the various communities and the respective representatives – that exists now, into a nation-state (*nation-état*) built on the rule of law in which rights and obligations belong to all individuals in their own right, and not as members of their respective communities or clans. This will lend the Lebanese regime the clout and immunity necessary to off-set external pressures. The centripetal forces and the centrifugal forces in play on Lebanon will only be offset by the emergence of a strong state, able to exert its central authority by co-optation and, if need be, by coercion.

Thirdly, the moral to be drawn is: reform is long overdue and pressing. For such pressures not to engender a breakdown of the state, the task to remedy or redress these internal divisions is a matter of life and death for the Lebanese. To do so, reinforcing the home turf requires remedying such divisions by reforming the political system, so as to be able to offset the ramifications of such pressures.

But what reform? It is a reform that starts by abolishing confessionalism, in as much as it is a force that divides the Lebanese and invites outside intervention and lays the foundations for sedition. It is the Achille's heel of a strong Lebanese state that hamstrings its consolidation.

A strong state is imperative to ward off outside dangers. Again, confessionalism is a stumbling block to building a strong state. In any democracy, values like equality, justice and citizenship are important building blocks of the state's legitimacy which is the corner stone of a consensual and, therefore, a strong polity. Confessionalism denies the Lebanese such basic rights and, as such, impairs the evolution of a legitimate political regime by perpetuating inequality and injustice which, in turn, weakens the state.

Furthermore, accountability is a lynchpin for building the State of Law. Again confessionalism curbs proper accountability by affording sectarian protection to perpetrators of crimes or offences in the name of sectarian solidarity – the Amnesty Law of 1992 is a case in hand.

Confessionalism also stymies the natural political development of the individual, by overstating the rights and prerogatives of the community at the expense of the rights and prerogatives of the individual. This devious artifice penalises or ostracizes the individual who does not tow the community line. This, evidently, reinforces the system of sectarian apportionment (*muhasasah*) that holds the state and its apparatus captives in the hands of community overlords.

Since electoral laws are generally the foundation or the architecture of the political system, an electoral law based on proportional representation is of the essence. A proportional electoral system will allow for other political currents within every community to emerge and for different communal strands to be represented, thus ending communal monopoly. It will also encourage national-based coalitions laying the grounds for national and cross-community agendas and parties.

The Lebanese constitution enacted in section (H) of its preamble the gradual or staged abolition of political confessionalism lifting it to the rank of 'a basic national goal.'

It also enacted in Article 22 the establishment of a Senate 'in which all communities shall be represented', concomitant with electing a parliament on a non-confessional basis.

Furthermore, and as widely known, Article 95 of the constitution provided a mechanism for the gradual or staged abolishment of political confessionalism. Seventeen years after the ratification of the Ta'if Accord and the amendment of the constitution accordingly, none of these reforms were executed and for obvious reasons.

Lebanon is a part of a violent neighbourhood – a neighbourhood plagued with the Arab-Israeli conflict, one of the most intractable conflicts of the twentieth century and a root cause of radicalisation. This conflict, coupled with the rise of fundamentalist Islam, be it Shia or Sunni, will continue to exert pressure and threaten the unity of the Lebanese State and strain the political regime. The unfolding tragedy in Iraq does not help; nor does the Iranian-American stand-off on Iran's nuclear enrichment programme. The vendetta between Lebanon and Syria over its historical claim to Lebanon, the assassination of Rafiq al-Hariri and the ramifications of the International Special Tribunal the Security Council decided upon, as well as the lingering burdens of 30 years of Syrian hegemony over Lebanon will continue to poison the relationship between the two sister countries for a long time to come.

There is no salvation for Lebanon and the Lebanese except by reforming their political system through outgrowing their confessional loyalties, the most important impediment to building a strong modern state.

Lebanon is a small country. It is tiny in size and population. Had it been bigger in its area and more sizeable in population, then splitting it up would have been plausible. It is, therefore, destined to strive and toil to foster the coexistence of its constituent communities.

Defenders of confessionalism will argue that there are historical reasons for it. They will summon the 'specificity' of Lebanon as a 'mosaic of minorities'; they will also evoke 'the shelter-nation' theory. They are right, confessionalism is a historical phenomenon and its roots are deep in nineteenth and twentieth century Lebanese history. But it is no solace to attribute all this to historical reasons, albeit correctly, or to surrender to it as being historically inevitable. History is made by men and for men; it is animated by their will and their desire for progress. For Lebanon to best neutralise external pressures, designs and dangers, the urgency to reinforce its internal unity and cement it is self-evident.

What attests to that is that the sense of belonging first to the community and then to the state, is deeper now than ever before. This is not belied by the fact that in rare and exceptional circumstances the Lebanese can act as citizens of a state and not as members of a denomination or a sect. The example of the Lebanese joining ranks against the French mandatory authority in 1943 in defence of their newly declared independence is a case in hand. Another, is their coming together in 2005 in their quest to see Syria leave and to end its custody over Lebanon, in the aftermath of the assassination of ex-Prime Minister Rafiq al-Hariri. The fact remains, however, that those same Lebanese who are able to show such distinctive conduct under exceptional circumstances, are, sooner or later, as capable of regressing to an atavistic trait of prioritising their communal loyalty over their national allegiance.

This characteristic has proved a major challenge to the development of Lebanon from a contract-state (*état-contrat*) into a nation-state (*état-nation*). Another ancillary challenge was the turbulence that engulfed the Middle East in the wake of the declaration of the State of Israel in 1948 and the instability that followed, and which ultimately thwarted or, at best, stunted this development.

The causation here is not selective; it rather hinges on the question of 'how it happened'? (the functional approach) and not 'Why it happened'? (or the causal approach). It is in the tradition of what EH Carr has written relating to Causation in History: 'Every historical argument revolves round the question of the priority of causes'. It definitely is not a deterministic argument, for determinism is a problem of human behaviour and not of history. Neither is it inevitable, in the sense that: 'Determinism... means... that, the data being what they are, whatever happens happens definitely and could not be different. To hold that it could, means only that it would if the data were different'.

Is it then tautological? Maybe, but it definitely agrees with Friedrich Nietzsche when he says that the unhistorical and the historical are 'equally necessary to the health of an individual, a community, and a system of culture.' Or, to put my conclusion better, there is a degree of 'sleeplessness', of rumination, of 'historical sense', 'that injures and finally destroys the living thing', be it 'a man or a people or a system of culture'.

The Lebanese are imbued and possessed with an historical sense of confessionalism; they have to work hard not to be injured and finally destroyed by it.

References

Al-Sudairi, Abdulaziz A, *A Vision of the Middle East: An Intellectual Biography of Albert Hourani*, centre for Lebanese Studies, I B Tauris.

Baaklini, Abdo I, *Legislative and Political Development : Lebanon, 1842-1972*. No.2 in publications of the consortium for comparative legislative studies.

Carr, EH, *What is History?* London: Penguin, 1976.

Gordon, David C, *Lebanon: the Fragmented Nation*, London: Croom Helm, The Hoover Institution Press/Stanford, California, 1980.

Hobsbawm, Eric, *On History*, Abacus, Weidenfeld & Nicolson, London, 1997.

Hourani, Albert, *Great Britain and the Arab World*, John Murray, London, 1946.

———, *Syria and Lebanon: A Political Essay*, Oxford University Press, 1946.

———, *Minorities in the Arab World*, London, New York: Oxford University Press, 1946.

———, *The Emergence of the Modern Middle East*, Berkeley: University of California Press, 1981.

———, *Political Society in Lebanon: A Historical Introduction*. London: Centre for Lebanese Studies, 1986.

Nietzsche, Friedrich, *The Use and Abuse of History*, The Library of Liberal

Arts, Indianapolis – New York: The Bohles – Merrill Company, Inc., 1957.

Rabbath, Edmond, *La formation historique du Liban politique et constitutionnel, Essai de Synthèse,* Beruit, 1973.

Rabinovitch, Itimar, *The War for Lebanon 1970-1983,* Ithaca, London: Cornell University Press, 1986.

Tueni, Ghassan, *Lebanon: War of Others in and Over Lebanon,* An-Nahar.

Part II

Memories of War and Forgiveness

Chapter Four

Breaking the Vicious Circle! Contributions of the 25-35 Lebanese Age Group[1]

Pamela Chrabieh

On ne peut pas tout effacer et recommencer... Il faut continuer. Rentrer de plain-pied dans la fêlure et la transformer. De croire que je peux transmettre ma mémoire et la mémoire des miens est pure vanité. Il le faut pourtant. Ne pas me laisser broyer. La souffrance est partout, ici, là-bas, partout. La vie est partout, ici, là-bas, partout. On la tue par ignorance... Partout, à chaque instant. Ne pas nous laisser noyer. Rentrer dedans et en ressortir vivants. Écrire, pendant que je suis encore vivante (Farhoud 1997).

Amongst the lessons I learned in the past seven years while living in Canada is that once the war grabs hold of you, it never loses its grip. As Abla Farhoud puts it, we cannot erase it from our memory as if it never existed. And if we try to do so, motivated by a survival imperative or an instinct that requires pain to be 'relegated to oblivion' (Cooke 1998:21), it catches hold of us somehow and shapes our emotions, thoughts, attitudes and actions. It also leads many to despair, humiliation, denigration, and worst of all, it paves a nation with 'murderous identities' (Maalouf 1998). In *Le virus de la violence,* the Lebanese psychiatrist Adnan Houballah explains this 'state' or 'phenomenon' while arguing about the existence of a 'visible' war: combat, negotiations, treaties orchestrated by 'active fighters', and an 'invisible war': a gigantic symbolical and psychic conflict which involves the whole population. It is the war of fantasies and representations run by 'passive fighters' who fail to understand the nature of the national identity and their identities, which are not static or monolithic, but shifting composites of different allegiances and attachments, and who also fail to recognise the multiplicity and complexity of the Other. The visible and invisible war overlap and nourish each other, thus creating a vicious cycle and maelstrom into which all individuals within a society are dragged.

The case of Lebanon's recent civil war is a particularly relevant example. Although the war's physical or 'visible' form has been dormant for several years, its non-physical or 'invisible' form encompasses many dynamics: an unstable pattern of events with no tendency towards equilibrium, despite Lebanon's independent status following the withdrawal of the Syrian Army in the spring of 2005; tensions between and within confessions, between and within political parties, between partisans of regional and international powers; an inability to institute deeply needed reforms in the country's political structure and governing arrangement; impunity, selective and biased amnesty laws (1991, 2005); a collective temptation to forget the pain of the past or the suppression of war memories, that breeds personal and national maladies; and a deep sense of fundamental injustice reaching across generations.

In order to break this war's vicious cycle, guns have not only to be silenced – in other words, it is imperative to have a ceasefire, but this crucial step does not lead to a long-term peace. There is an enormous task left – to share mourning, heal wounds, bridge divisions, reconcile emotions, build stability and initiate a process of normalisation. One might think that this multi-levelled task has not yet begun to be accomplished, or that it devolves upon the Lebanese government and the political leaders and elites to undertake its theoretical strategies and their applications. This belief conceals the complex realities of Lebanon and diminishes the crucial role of Lebanese civil society (Dawahare 2000) and diaspora. In fact, since the early 1990s there has been an increasing number of speeches and practices developed by individuals and collectivities (groups of dialogue, social movements, NGOs, transnational organisations or networks...) towards constructing a war memory and implementing peace, reconciliation and conviviality. Rarely covered by the media either locally or internationally, they offer alternatives to conflicting religious identities, sectarianism, socio-economical disparities, feudalism, corruption, parochialism, regionalism, clannism, as well as to means of governance and to social strategies incompatible with human rights and with pluralistic opinions and beliefs. In this sense, the voices of the 25-35 age group constitute an important subset of many constructive attitudes and actions worth taking into account in the process of breaking the war's vicious cycle.

War memories, Peace-building and Reconciliation

Various aspects of the history of the Lebanese war in its 1975-90 period have been the subject of studies, especially research on the geo-political, military and economic aspects, as well as on how the former Prime Minister Rafiq al-Hariri rebuilt the Beirut Central Business District. On one side, the vision of Solidere, The Lebanese Company for the Development and Reconstruction of Beirut Central District s.a.l, a private real estate company established by the late Prime Minister Hariri, concentrates on the construction of a centre with a sanitised cosmopolitan character for international commerce, the 'Hong Kong of the Middle East'. On the other side, the vision of many researchers reflects an opposition to the demolition of old buildings as an unhealthy expurgation of the war (e.g. Khalaf and Khoury 1993, Rowe and Sarkis 1998). For example, the Lebanese sociologist Samir Khalaf explores the role of the *Burj* – Place des Canons, or Martyrs' Square – in encapsulating collective memory and national identity (Khalaf 2005). His study reflects on the nature of public space in Lebanon's 'post-war period' and identifies the effects of Beirut's reconstruction era. Kaelen Wilson-Goldie writes:

In his central thesis, Khalaf argues that the *Burj* has always reinvented itself as a site of political mobilisation and must be seized and activated again to stave off what he terms 'the false consciousness' of seeking refuge in either primordial religious affiliation or faddish, seductive commercialism. The real charm of the *Burj*, in Khakaf's view, is its perpetual use as a kind of exaggerated playground' (Wilson-Goldie 2005).

Many artists and novelists, like Daoud Hassan, criticize the new downtown as a cover for the country's war wounds. Through his latest project, *Transit Beirut*, a collection of literature and drawings, he tries to confront the past: 'I need to talk about the [war], to know more things about it', says Reine Mahfouz, a photographer (Farah 2004). But 'it's not very easy. Some people say we should never talk about it' (Farah 2004). In fact, very few studies have been devoted to the way the Lebanese themselves perceive the war. Elisabeth Suzanne Kassab writes:

> The perceptions and personal experiences of people are relevant for the study of such conflicts for two reasons. First, because people themselves are relevant. Conflicts and wars are not carried out in abstract political, economic or social systems, but in the concrete lives of people. They are their perpetrators and/or victims, and it is in their bodies and souls that the most devastating effects of armed strife are to be found. Second, the perceptions and lived experiences of people are also relevant because they play a major role in shaping their socio-cultural and political attitudes, actions and reactions, and thereby influence the military and political course of events. (Kassab, 1992.)

Based on what Kassab argues, the memory of the war in Lebanon cannot be summed up in one reality. It is a plural memory (*'une mémoire plurielle'*[2]) that reflects a diversity of experiences: individual, collective, national, transnational, thus a diversity of wars: confessional, civil, regional, international, and of expressions: commemorations, monuments (such as the Armand Fernandez war memorial outside the ministry of defence, an accumulation of used and discarded T-34 tanks, howitzers and armoured personnel carriers, all embedded in concrete), souvenirs, histories of individuals and/or collectivities: 'reconstructions under the pressure of society' (Halbwachs 1992, 51), personal perceptions and experiences, developed in 'intimate spaces of culture'. (Herzfeld 2005, 12).

Personal perceptions and experiences have been depicted in fiction, memoirs, diaries, music productions, paintings, novels (e.g. Elias Abou Haidar, *La fracture*, 1999; Selim Nassib, *Clandestin*, 1998; Jean Said Makdissi, *Beirut Fragments: A War Memoir*, 1999; Nadine Khoury-Aoude, *L'obus Siffla*, 200; Lamia al Saad, *Le Bonheur bleu*, 2002) throughout the 1980s and 1990s, and even after, by Lebanese from all sides, backgrounds and identities, appealing to all who are concerned with human survival. They have also been portrayed in documentaries and movies since the late 1990s. Ziad Doueiri's film (*West Beirut*, 1998) cleverly interweaves the facts with the emotions of ordinary people in the Lebanese capital torn apart by war in 1975. Tarek and Omar, two Muslim adolescents, have several adventures in the chaotic streets with May, a Christian girl who moves into their neighbourhood. Along with their parents, they struggle to keep their souls alive in the midst of war. In the end, Doueiri reveals the extent of what this family, and the Lebanese, have lost.

Josef Fares presents in his film (*Zozo*, 2005) the story of a boy, Zozo, who is living in Beirut during the war. Zozo and his family are waiting for their papers in order to leave Lebanon and seek refuge in Sweden. Caught in the crossfire, his parents, brother and sister are killed. Fares depicts the horrors of the war and the way it affects civilians. A similar depiction is found in Khalil Joreige and Joana Hadjithomas's film (*A perfect day*, 2005). 'A perfect day' is the day when a court will be asked to declare officially dead 17,000 men and women who disappeared during the Lebanese war and have been missing for two decades. This film depicts the agony of the families who have to choose between waiting and moving on.

These depictions and many more express a particular type of memory based on contrition and solidarity in facing up to the war

(Messarra 2004), commitments in favour of peace and reconciliation, courage and hope despite constraining conditions. I had the opportunity to participate in the organisation of a *Journey of Discovery, Understanding and Healing* in November 2005, which gathered a group of American people who lost loved ones at 9/11 Ground Zero in New York with a number of Lebanese individuals who suffered loss due to war. Based on this fruitful gathering, which culminated in an olive tree planting ritual and inter-spiritual prayers in the Garden of Forgiveness (*Hadiqat as-Samah*) in central Beirut, I learned that a conflict is recurrent as long as a reconciliation process is not implemented, a process that involves justice, recognition and healing. It is about helping each other move forward with a better understanding of the deep echoes of the past as well as providing a strong sense of how we define ourselves in our societies, and how we take responsibility for solving our own problems.

Thus the example of the public apology of Assaad Chaftari and Muhieddine Mustapha Chehab (Initiatives of Change 2002) for their wrongdoings as militants during the war, demonstrates the existence of significant commitments towards public awareness of reconciliation among the Lebanese Civil Society since the mid-nineties. Even before, during the years of combat, individuals and groups kept alive the idea of national reconciliation and worked to rebuild relationships with people of other communities.[3] Chaftari and Chehab carry powerful stories of transformation. Acts of forgiveness and reconciliation profoundly changed each of their lives. Chaftari was brought up in a Christian environment; he used to consider the Muslims as inferior and as traitors for looking towards a united Muslim World.

In his statement, Chaftari clearly admits that when the war started in 1975 he was ready to fight for his Christianity, his Lebanon. He was fighting a 'Holy War' (Initiatives of Change 2002: 4). But at some point, he had to seek asylum after other Christians considered him to be a traitor for negotiating a peace agreement with the Muslims in 1985. He discovered the Moral Re-Armament – MRA – which became Initiatives of Change, an international network of people who work towards far-reaching change locally and globally. Through this organisation, he discovered two things:

> Firstly, it was no use trying to change the world if I did not start changing my life, and what was in my heart; and secondly, if one listens, God speaks, and if one obeys, God acts. Unsatisfied with my whole world, I decided to start with inner personal change on more than one level. It is a long process that will never end.... I had to reconcile myself with God before reconciling myself with others. I also had to forgive before asking for forgiveness. The multi-faith dialogue meetings, which the MRA team was organising, helped me to encounter Muslims and discover, to my surprise, that they had their families, dreams, expectations – and grudges against me and my people. I discovered the human being in them that I had forgotten throughout the civil war. We did not have to become similar or agree on everything, but to know, respect and love each other. (Initiatives of Change 2002: 5.)

Chaftari decided to publish in the Lebanese press a public letter of apology. I will never forget his sayings in a peace conference last spring in Montreal as well as in the Silk Museum at Bsouss-Lebanon during that November's *Journey*: 'I cannot give life back to those I have killed, but I can ask [and work] for forgiveness'. In my opinion, those words are a key element in building a process of reconciliation and conviviality, especially in a wounded society and nation that need to be healed. Otherwise this society will inevitably collapse again in violent persecution and victimisation. In this sense, Chehab, *mokhtar* (Notary Public) of Ras Beirut, states:

> I cannot talk about how I arrived at reconciliation with myself and others without mentioning how hatred starts to infiltrate our hearts and minds, to take control of our lives and actions. There is no doubt that hatred towards the 'other' exists in our lives. It exists in mosques, churches, the family, the community and the educational system that depicts the world as rotating around a particular community and strives to reshape the world in its own image. When we were teenagers, we Muslims were told that the Christians

intended to slaughter us, throw us into the sea, and found a Christian state similar to Israel and allied with her, to spearhead the war against the Arabs and Muslims. Those ideas mobilised us to fight against the Christians. But I discovered later that the Christian youth were told that the Muslims wanted to establish a Muslim state, oust all the Christians, and join the Arab countries in their fight against Israel. Hence, neither of the two versions of the 'conspiracy' was true. (Initiatives of Change 2002: 6).

Chehab founded a social committee in 1992 to promote dialogue instead of violence as a way to solve conflicts. His work shows that 'one should forget but remember still and break the chain of hate', so that the cry of 'Never again!' ('*Plus jamais!*') would not be uttered again.

Contributions of the 25-35 Lebanese Age Group

My research has enabled me to discover that men and women between more or less 25 and 35 years of age, who survived the 1975-90 combat period and who live in Montreal and/or in Beirut, are increasingly involved in the construction of war memories towards a long-term reconciliation and conviviality, based on their personal perceptions and experiences. Their kind of activism and engagement is less characterized by demand-making movements than non-violent direct, individual or collective, informal, underground, or even institutional action. (Bayat 2000, Karam 2000). They are journalists, poets, novelists, artists, psychologists, movie and documentary producers, activists in NGOs[4] (e.g. Nahwa al-Muwatiniya[5]), in transnational organisations (e.g. Art of Living[6], Tadamon,[7] Helem[8]), in groups of interreligious and intercultural dialogues (e.g. Le Cercle Interreligieux de Montréal[9], Chrabieh 2003). They publish articles (e.g. Michel Hajji Georgiou, a young journalist in *L'Orient-le-Jour*, a well-known Lebanese French newspaper; Natacha Sikias, an independent journalist), books (e.g. Lebanese poets Nadim Bou-Khalil's *Mal de Terre*, 2005, and Rita Bassil's *Beyrouth ou Le Masque d'Or*, 2005), launch alternative web sites (e.g. caricaturist Wassim Mouawad's weblogs: 'Shlon' and 'Les niouzes: des infos du Liban'; *Electronic Lebanon,* a project from the *Electronic Intifada,* that offers commentary, analysis, human rights and development information, and voices from Lebanese Young activists) and radio programs (e.g. Tadamon's 'Lebanon: Poverty, War and Globalisation' on CKUT 90.3 FM, Montreal), produce short films, documentaries, independent media reports, trauma plays or dramas of survival (e.g. Wajdi Mouawad's *Journées de Noces Chez les Cromagnons,* 1994, *Littoral,* 1999) , organise artistic exhibitions (e.g. Paola Yacoub's *Garden of Eden, Monument for Beirut,* 2001; Taghrid Darghouth's *Parties Tombantes,* 2006)[10], round tables and debates (e.g. Nahwa al-Muwatiniya), home movie screening events (e.g. Helem).

Since September 2006, I have contacted most of these individuals and collectives and asked them basic questions that can be summarized as follows: how do they remember and memorialise the war in Lebanon? How do they use the war memory to define their identity and citizenship? The data collected from this fieldwork's first stage allowed me to construct my conceptual and methodological research framework, as well as to identify many characteristics of the contributions of this 25-35 Age Group. The second stage aims at expanding the research in order to profile these contributions as the work of important private and public war memories' agents, thus national reconstruction voices and mediums. It also aims at showing changes in the topography of social and political contest over issues of memory, identity and citizenship in Lebanon.

Most of the depictions of war that I studied within the 25-35 Age Group dramatize the disruption of normal life in Lebanon, the devastation of cities and villages, the decimation of the population, and the forced emigration. These individuals and collectivities witnessed as children or adolescents war raids, car explosions and falling bombs. They have seen their houses destroyed, armless and legless people, people knifed and splashed across walls. They have slept in basements, hallways or stair-wells. Many used to play games that reproduced the war of adults. Many have lost family members and friends and were forced to flee with their families to safer places, secluded destinations, whether in Lebanon or abroad. They usually do not identify the underlying origins of the war, whether internal, external, geo-political, economical, religious or cultural. They do not attempt to produce emblems of facts to support the assertion of history – on the contrary, they show that facts of war are transformed into myths that condition later responses to war (Calder 2004) – but rather strange structural links between what is known to be true and what is needed to be believed.

An interesting example is found in the installations of Rayyane Tabet, a young Lebanese artist and architect living in New York, whose main inspiration is his own biography and childhood in a Beirut tormented by war: he sublimates everyday objects like mattresses, soap or suitcases to surreal symbolic codices. Another example is the case of director Danielle Arbid's movie *In the Battlefields* (2004), in which she tells the story of twelve-year-old Lina in East Beirut during the 1975-90 war that includes autobiographical elements, feelings and emotions. In this film, truth and fiction intermingle. Similarly, Wassim Mouawad's original multimedia drawings and burlesque cartoons serve as symbolic and phantasmagoric emblems of individual war memories that fight both amnesia and hypermnesia.

These individuals and collectivities try to testify to what they have experienced as children and/ or adolescents, overcoming the silence and desire to forget that frequently accompany the horror of war. Their projects, expressions and initiatives denounce violence at the same time they memorialise the victims (the displaced, the disappeared, the dead, children, women, refugees). As Danielle Arbid puts it, the war becomes a metaphor for the interior war between people. *In the Battlefields* shows that this 'interior war' is much more cruel and tough than the 'war outside', waged against girls and women. It also shows that digging into the manner in which history has been written and communicated, expressing unexplored dimensions of the war, as well as working through the trauma, are essential steps to ensure that grief does not lead to despair.[11] In *Alone with War* (2000), Arbid wonders about the collective amnesia that seems omnipresent in

Lebanon. She visits soldiers, widows and fugitives, interviews killers from both the Muslim and Christian militias, searching for the story of her country. She knocks on doors, asks questions: Who was killed? How? Why? Is the history fading? Did the massacres happen after all?

Other questions are also asked by activists whom I encountered in Nahwa al-Muwatiniyya, Art of Living and Tadamon: 'What about responsibility? Are we all responsible? Are we alien to each other in spite of having endured a similar fate? Where did I stand? Where do I stand? What can I do? What can we do? Can we create common grounds to transcend our barriers, recognise each other and live in peace?' Their response is simple: breaking the war's vicious cycle is the concern and the responsibility of all generations and identities. War is a human experience, a tragedy that marks all age groups and affiliations. Everyone should therefore bear witness to the loss caused by war, construct and reconstruct a personal memory, then share it with others through a diversity of means in order to build a collective memory that manages different kinds of memories – *A chacun sa guerre, son histoire, sa mémoire* – and takes into account people's sufferings on all sides, in particular, the suffering of the youth.

Needless to say, the collection of contributions of this 25-35 Age Group is just a small subset of the many civil society and diaspora efforts to break the war's vicious cycle, many of which remain invisible or unrealised. (Habache, Bousquet 2000; Amin, Kenz 2003). Maybe one can say that these efforts are limited and they present uncertainty and contradictions. Furthermore, there are difficulties in conceptualising the role of young adults in peace-building and reconciliation processes. (Kemper 2005). One of the obstacles is finding a common definition for them, because in reality, they constitute a very heterogeneous group. Also, the temporality of the 'past' itself changes from one individual to another, and it grows more complex as memories of the more recent conflicts begin to overlap with the previous ones. Moreover, non-financial contributions of the diaspora tend to be less tangible, and therefore, difficult to address in the context of public policy; little information is known on conditions for the engagement of the young Lebanese diaspora in home country development, on modes and channels of transfer for their various contributions, and on the extent to which these impact development in Lebanon.

Despite all obstacles and limits, these efforts provide a needed supplement to mainstream representations of the Lebanese war, and they are somehow filling a part of the gap that government, leaders, elites and silent parents could not fill, by disturbing the ambient amnesia – whether willed or not – fighting against the Historical Mythology (Hobsbawn 2003), thinking the unthought and the unthinkable (Arkoun 1995-96, 2002), and by standing against state alienation, the confessional socio-political system, youth unemployment, and the enslavement of a large part of the Lebanese society, in particular a part of the younger generation driven into the recurrent political parties' rivalries.[12] I believe their contributions constitute a welcome addition to the study of the larger problem of engineering war memory, especially in the Lebanese political culture where the identity of the nation-state is in a considerable state of flux.

Recommendations

Raising questions about the war and trying to understand the personal perceptions and experiences of the war that set up the foundations of these interrogations, are important steps towards a more constructive remembrance. In that sense, a first requisite for breaking the war's vicious cycle is to look backwards while focusing on individual and collective experiences, not only institutional dynamics, chronology of combats, and biography of participants. Therefore, collecting stories, covering them more effectively in the press and television, and analyzing war representations of various social actors – in particular within the 25-35 Age Group – is a must. These testimonies would allow the Lebanese to nourish their diverse narratives and their dissimilar ways of interpreting the war, to open up their wounds to themselves and to one another, to reach a level of common understanding of their previous predicament and to become 'less vulnerable to the demons of collective aggression and collective suicide.' (Kassab 1992).

In that sense, academic research, round tables and conferences are needed, but a series of civil forums, debates, artistic exhibitions and cinematographic events on the war – such as Tadamon's in winter and spring 2006, Montreal – its effects and the lessons learnt from the past could also be organised in Municipalities' Cultural Centers, Youth groups, political parties, community organisations, schools and universities. For example, Nahwa al-Muwatiniya organises once per week, since January 2006, a debate on topics of political, social and economic interests. More than 40 individuals participate in each debate: young professionals, activists in diverse NGOs, and university students. One of their main objectives is to move from ancient and recent wounds to their most important duties as responsible citizens: mutual respect, dialogue, exploring and understanding similarities and differences, and working for democratic development and reform.

From this perspective, a second requisite for breaking the war's vicious cycle is probing the organisation and articulation of war memory as an integral part of the socio-political process. Thus, it is about building a social and political culture of reconciliation, conviviality and human rights. Comprehensive awareness programs for schools and universities, for the curricula of teacher training institutions, and for teachers currently teaching could, therefore, be deployed. For example, Nahwa al-Muwatiniya is implementing a project for secondary school students 'Baddi koun mas'oul' – I want to be responsible – that seeks to teach them the mechanism and intricacies of the Lebanese electoral process, their rights and duties as responsible citizens, as well as the ethical standards required for the integrity of the electoral procedure. Such a project could be pursued on a larger scale and integrate other notions and practices in reconciliation, conviviality and Human Rights.

However, this culture can neither be established by one force, nor on a vertical integration basis where the communitarian leaders try to preserve their own communal influence. Therefore, the second requisite is to establish bridges between all forces within Lebanese civil society and diaspora, along with the state, political leaders, elites, official and unofficial religious institutions, regional and international organisations, willing to engage in dialogue, to cooperate and make concessions in order to become efficient agents of reconciliation and conviviality. These bridges would distribute in a more equitable way the political power with a particular emphasis on diversity, give the most marginalised a voice, and would allow diverse strategies and tools to reach a wider audience which is not confined to elites, leaders' partisans, narrow activists' circles, and underground channels. Breaking the vicious cycle is not only a matter of 'pressure from below', which is requisite for meaningful policy change and for institutional reform conducive to social and political development. It is a matter of breaking the *Tours d'ivoire* – Ivory Towers – and building networks of interactions between the diverse identities and memories that would allow the emergence of a new *Nahda* – Renaissance in Lebanon.

A third requisite for breaking the war's vicious cycle is to implement transitional Justice Strategies (Walgrave 2003; Kieran McEvoy, Tim Newburn 2003)[13] adapted to the Lebanese context, that do not require vengeance nor retribution: trauma clinics (De Jong 2002) which provide a professional counselling service and outreach programmes to overcome ordeals; self-help groups and unofficial truth-seeking projects[14] that consist of either victims or the families of victims – or even perpetrators – that could share common experiences and solutions, and build support structures between victims or the families of victims. These strategies do not consist of policing the past, nor allowing war 'closure' to become a convenient 'end', but of seeking catharsis and reconciliation through a restorative justice process.

In the vein of Chehab and Chaftari's work, contributions of the Lebanese 25-35 Age Group show that achieving reconciliation and conviviality must begin with individual acts of confession and extend from the most basic unit of socialisation to the most expansive relationship between citizens and the state. Furthermore, they show that real peace-building and reconciliation in Lebanon in the decade ahead resides in the ongoing endeavour of Lebanese individuals and collectives in Lebanon and abroad to act for marginalised voices, to re-craft the relations among themselves and with others, to work on implementing a long-term 'positive peace' process, and not only to try living in the absence of criminal or political violence.

Building that 'positive peace' is not an elusive goal, and it is not a question of adopting drastic security measures aimed at reducing the risk of conflicts. It is not about proposing solutions to a 'post-conflict' situation that could 'explode again' – it is not a matter of prevention and of putting forward *early warning* ('*des mesures d'alerte*'). It consists of crafting a durable Democracy by dealing with this tremendous heritage of trauma instead of denying it, by capitalising on the small gains earned so far in order to tackle difficult issues, and by recognising the essence of what the Dalai Lama called 'the human nature' in his acceptance speech of the Nobel Prize in 1989. From this perspective, despite all our differences and regardless of what part of the world we come from, 'we are all basically the same human beings', seeking happiness, trying to avoid suffering and doing our best 'to cultivate a universal responsibility for one another and the planet we share'.

References

Amin, Samir and Kenz Ali, *Le monde arabe. Enjeux sociaux, perspectives méditerranéennes*, Paris: L'Harmattan, 2003.

Arkoun, Mohammad, 'Clarifier le passé pour construire le futur', *Confluences Méditerranée*, no.16, hiver, p.12, 1995-96.

———, *The Unthought in Contemporary Islamic Thought*, London: Saqi Books, 2002.

Barash, David P. (ed.) *Approaches to Peace: A Reader in Peace Studies*, Oxford: Oxford University Press, 1999.

Bayat, Asef, *Social Movements, Activism and Social Development in the Middle East*, UNRISD, 2000.

Brodeur, Patrice, *Building the Interfaith Youth Movement*, with co-editor Dr. Eboo Patel. Walnut Creek, CA: AltaMira Press, 2005.

———, 'Pour faire place à l'étude critique appliquée de la religion', *Religiologiques*, 29, Québec, p.61-78 (a), 2004.

———, 'From Postmodernism to 'Glocalism': Towards a Theoretical

Understanding of Contemporary Arab Muslim Constructions of Religious Others', in *Globalisation and the Muslim World*, ed. by Birgit Schaebler and Leif Stenberg. Syracuse: Syracuse University Press, p. 188-205 (b), 2004.

Calder, Angus, *Disasters and Heroes: On War, Memory and Representation*, University of Wales Press, 2004.

Chrabieh, Pamela. Janvier, *Pour une gestion médiatrice des diversités au Liban. Une théorie du plurilogue, au-delà du confessionnalisme*, Thèse doctorale, Bibliothèque des Lettres et des Sciences Humaines, Université de Montréal, 2006.

————, 'Dialogues islamo-chrétiens contemporains dans les sociétés proche-orientales: Enjeux actuels et perspectives d'avenir', *Studies in Religion/ Sciences Religieuses,* Canadian Corporation for Studies in Religion/Corporation Canadienne des Sciences Religieuses, 32/3, p.243-259, 2003.

Cooke, Miriam, *War's Other Voices: Women Writers on the Lebanese Civil War,* Cambridge: Cambridge University Press, 1998.

Cullell, Jorge Vargas, 'Democracy and the quality of Democracy: Empirical Findings and Methodological and Theoretical Issues Drawn from the Citizen Audit of the Quality of Democracy in Costa Rica', in *The Quality of Democracy. Theory and Applications,* ed. by Guillermo O'Donnell, Jorge Vargas Cullell and Osvaldo M. Iazzetta. Indiana: University of Notre Dame Press, p. 93-162, 2004.

Dawahare, Michael, *Civil Society and Lebanon: Toward Hermeneutic Theory of the Public Sphere in Comparative Studies,* Universal Publishers, 2000.

De Jong, Joop, *Trauma, War, and Violence: Public Mental Health in Socio-Cultural Context,* New York: Springer, 2002.

Farah, Samar, 'Beirut's artists confront legacy of civil war', *The Christian Science Monitor*: www.csmonitor.com, 2004.

Farhoud, Abla, *Jeux de patience*. Montréal: VLB éditeur, 1997.

Habache, Iskandar and Bousquet Michel, *Avoir 20 ans à Beyrouth,* Paris: Alternatives, 2000.

Halbwachs, Maurice, *On collective Memory,* Chicago: University of Chicago Press, 1992.

Herzfeld, Michael, *Cultural Intimacy: Social Poetics in the Nation-State,* revised edition, New York: Routledge, 1997.

Hobsbawn, Eric, *Interesting Times. A Twentieth Century Life,* London: Pantheon Books, 2005.

Houballah, Adnan, *Le virus de la violence,* Paris, Albin Michel, 2003.

Initiatives of Change, *Breaking the Chain of Hate,* London: Agenda for Reconciliation, 2002.

Jodelet, Denise, 'Aperçus sur les méthodologies qualitatives', MOSCOVICI Serge et BUSCHINI Fabrice (dir.), *Les méthodes des sciences humaines.*

Paris: Presses Universitaires de France, p.139-162, 2003.

Karam, Karam, 'Associations civiles, mouvements sociaux et participation politique au Liban dans les années 90', dans Colloque international *ONG et Gouvernance dans les Pays Arabes*, UNESCO, IRD, CEDEJ et CEPS al-Ahram, Le Caire, 2000.

Kassab, Elisabeth-Suzanne, *The Paramount Reality of the Beirutis: War Literature and the Lebanese Conflict*, in *The Beirut Review*, Beirut: The Lebanese Center for Policy Studies, no. 4, 1992.

Kemper, Yvonne, *Youth in War-to-Peace Transitions. Approaches of International Organisations*, Berlin: Berghof Research Center for Constructive Conflict Management, 2005.

Khalaf, Samir and Khoury, Philip S, *Recovering Beirut: Urban Design and Post-War Reconstruction*, Leiden: Brill, 1993.

Khalaf, Samir, *Heart of Beirut: Reclaiming the Burj*, London: Saqi Books, 2004.

Maalouf, Amin, *Les identités meurtrières*, Paris: Grasset, 1998.

McEvoy, Kieran and Newburn, *Criminology, Conflict Resolution and Restorative Justice*, UK: Palgrave Mcmillan, 2003.

Messarra, Antoine (dir.), *Monitoring Civil Peace and Memory in Lebanon (From the Remembrance of War to a Peace Culture)*, Beirut: Lebanese Foundation for Permanent Civil Peace – Ayia Napa Conference Center, Cyprus – Konrad Adenauer Foundation – Librairie Orientale, 2004.

Rowe, Peter G and Hashim, Sarkis, *Projecting Beirut: Episodes in the Construction and Reconstruction of a Modern City*, Munich, 1998.

Walgrave, Lode (dir.), *Repositioning Restorative Justice*, UK: Willan Publishing, 2003.

Wilson-Goldie, Kaelen, 'Sociologist Samir Khalaf takes the city's pulse', *The Daily Star*, Beirut, 21 December 2005.

Notes

1 This article is a summary of the preliminary work I conducted so far for my post-doctoral research - entitled 'Voix de reconstruction nationale au Liban. Contribution des jeunes de 25-35 ans' – from September 2005 to May 2006 mainly in Montreal and lately in Beirut. This work was financed by the Canada Research Chair of Islam, Pluralism and Globalisation (University of Montreal) and consisted of   Literature Analysis, participation in many encounters and events organised by Lebanese and transnational NGOs – Nahwa al-Muwatiniya, Tadamon, Helem, Art of Living, Islamic-Christian groups of Dialogue…, as well as of contacts with young activists, artists and journalists in Lebanon and Canada. The second phase of my research will be pursued at the same

Chair and at the Institute of Islamic-Christian Studies (Université Saint-Joseph, Lebanon), from June 2006 to May 2008. This phase is financed by the Social Sciences and Humanities Research Council of Canada (Government of Canada). Given the lack of data, this second phase is based on qualitative analysis of field interviews – individual, collective, group focus (Jodelet, 2003; Cullell 2004; Brodeur 2004 (a), (b); 2005), field notes and different material collected during fieldwork (press reviews and articles, multimedia reports and documentaries, electronic material, educational material, reports of meetings and workshops, statements and reports designed for fund-raising, unpublished documentation...).

2 I describe the war memory in Lebanon as 'an ongoing process of interactions between individual and collective readings of the diverse pasts and presents; a plural and dynamic process in which the constructions-representations-expressions of all actors of the Lebanese civil society and Diaspora contribute' ('processus en devenir d'échanges-interactions entre des relectures individuelles et collectives des divers passés et présents; un processus pluriel et dynamique auquel contribuent les constructions-représentations-expressions de tous les acteurs de la société civile et de la diaspora libanaises' (Chrabieh 2005, 12-13).

3 It is also the case since the Israeli offensive against Lebanon in July 2006, whereas political and civil society organisations and movements are helping people to deal with the effects of the offensive. See: http://pchrabieh.blogspot.com

4 Other Lebanese NGOs, groups and movements dealing with the issues of war, conflict resolution, peace building and dialogue will be contacted throughout this year: Permanent Peace Movement, Amam 05, Haya Bina, Kafa, Sawa Group.

5 Nahwa al-Muwatiniya is a non-profit organisation founded by young individuals in 2005 in Lebanon – 15 permanent members and 70 supporters – seeking a progressive and forward-looking democratic society. This organisation empowers and mobilises citizens towards active participation in governance through research, publication, education, and lobbying.

6 The Art of Living Foundation is the largest volunteer based Non-Governmental Organisation in the world. The Foundation's service projects, programmes on yoga, meditation and stress elimination have benefited over 20 million people representing all walks of life, religions, cultures and traditions. In Lebanon, amongst its diverse initiatives, Art of Living organises trauma relief and peace building projects.

7 Tadamon ('Solidarity' in Arabic) is a new Montreal-based collective of social justice organisers and Media activists, working to build relationships of solidarity with grassroots political movements for social and economic

justice between Montreal and Beirut. Amongst the diversity of their activities, the members of Tadamon produce radio programmes about the Lebanese war, organise ciné-clubs and events addressing issues such as war memory, immigration, racism, poverty, labour rights, human rights, Palestinian refugees.

8 Helem, a group previously known as Club Free, has been working on LGBT (Lesbian, Gay, Bisexual and Transgender) issues in Lebanon for the past four years (as well as in Ottawa, Montreal, Sydney Paris and San Francisco). Its activities have included social and cultural events to bring the gay community together, extensive work on HIV/AIDS related issues, advocacy for prosecuted LGBT individuals and lobbying with other human rights organisations for the advancement of human rights and personal freedoms in Lebanon (i.e. Huriyyat Khassa – Private Liberties – Rassemblement Canadien pour le Liban, Nouveaux Droits de l'Homme, Foundation for Human and Humanitarian Rights…).

9 Le Cercle Interreligieux de Montréal is a Montreal based group of Islamic-Christian Dialogue, founded in 2003. This group of 15-20 permanent members which include young Lebanese activists, organised in 2004 and 2005 peace building projects and conferences about war and reconciliation in Lebanon, as well as producing and animating several radio and television programmes (Radio Canada, Radio Ville-Marie, Canal Vox).

10 Being an artist, I often refer in my writings to the role of arts in the Middle East, especially contemporary arts in calling existing situations into question. Various Lebanese artists are socially or politically committed, akin to a thirst for meaning after experiencing tremendous crisis. According to Christine Tohmé, Chairperson of the Lebanese association for Plastic Arts *Ashkal Alwan*:

'It is not a matter of analyzing the war. From a historical point of view, that is behind us. But in fact it still surrounds us, and raises questions that we have to look at…. The war affected our lives so massively in every regard that it is simply always present' (see: Tania Förster. *Faces of Truth. The Ayloul Festival in Beirut in September 2001*: http://www.springerin.at/dyn/heft_text.php?textid=746&lang=en).

11 Another example is the independent music production and song writing that contains powerful critiques of Lebanese society and government such as Nadine Khoury's *Cuts from the Inside* (2006) – commenting on her tired generation in 'Wail', the struggles of the youth to believe in a strong future, and her 14 March 2005 inspired 'All this Violence'; rappers Kitaayoun, The New Government, Soap Kills, Scrambled Eggs and Lumi whose stand out tracks on *Lebanese Underground* (2006) reflect a fearless young generation who chose music as their weapon.

12 See: Universities' Students Elections in 2005, Appearances on television

talk-shows (Marcel Ghanem, LBC; *Hadan yessma'na*, NTV...).

13 According to the *Restorative Justice Consortium* (London), 'Restorative Justice is a process whereby:

(i) All the parties with a stake in particular conflict or offense come together to resolve collectively how to deal with the aftermath of the conflict or offense and its implications for the future.

(ii) Offenders have the opportunity to have their harm or loss acknowledged and amends made'. (http://www.restorativejustice.org.uk).

See also: 'Dealing with the Past in Lebanon: Various Approaches to Transitional Justice', workshop organised by The Lebanese Center for Policy Studies along with the International Center for Transitional Justice and the Sustainable Democracy Centre organised, on 2 and 3 December 2005; (http://www.lcps-lebanon.org/web04/english/activities/2005/transitionaljus/report.doc).

In this workshop, Paul van Zyl, the Programme Director of ICTJ, discussed current trends in transitional justice; prosecution, truth-seeking through commissions, reparation programmes, institutional reform, reconciliation and peace-building, and memorialisation. After detailing these strategies he underscored the interconnected nature of all six and the importance of utilising all to achieve successful progress in the reconciliation process. He also discussed the importance of truth commissions, suggesting that they can change the nature of discourse on the topic, create an awareness of the importance of individual responsibility and making amends, and create a domino effect whereby action is taken after the recognition of the events. Van Zyl emphasized the importance of civil society, particularly victims' groups, in the reconciliation process. It is the case of the Committee for the Relatives of the Kidnapped and Missing in Lebanon who has been involved in processes to create public awareness and also pressure the government to establish a committee to investigate what happened to the disappeared from the war.

14 See: Nordic Commission. *Witness of War Crimes in Lebanon* (testimony given to the Nordic Commission, Oslo, October 1982). London: Ithaca Press for EAFORD, 1983.

Chapter Five

Breaking the Cycle of Violence in Lebanon and beyond

Alexandra Asseily

Introduction

Theories abound about the cycle of violence in Lebanon and how to end it. The perception of what drives and perpetuates this violence defines the approach taken to defuse it. There are two general modes of perception and corresponding prescription.

The first is the structural or institutional mode whose pure form views political, economic or social constructs and disparities as the root causes of conflict. As a result, solutions are only given at this level, (e.g. fixing political formulas or alleviating external interferences, religious differences or socio-economic grievances). One could term this a top down approach to conflict resolution. Find the right framework and conflict will disappear. The second bottom up mode looks at the primordial bases for conflict. Its proponents point out the limitations of structural theories for explaining the real emotional drivers, the brutality, or the way the conflict takes on its own persona once commenced. Here, the role of interpersonal dynamics and the individual's psychological status and background provide the reasons for, as well as the solutions to, the problem.

Both these modes provide analysis critical to an understanding of the many factors involved in igniting, accelerating or merely tempting violence. Neither is sufficient to explain why these conflicts repeat in cycles across generations despite changes in structure and despite differences in educational levels or material well-being. They do not resolve pent-up grievances that provide the source for renewed conflict. Thus, they serve only to delay or repress violence. My approach is complementary to these two modes. It seeks to explain existing personal and structural relationships in an alternative light and offers a path to break cycles of violence at both levels. What can be instigated at the level of the individual can then be applied to groups of individuals and by extension to political formulas between such groups in order to make feasible otherwise doomed structural options.

Current as well as past, or more historic, conflicts affect us psychologically as individuals and in our relationships, especially with loved ones (not just 'others' or enemies). They shape our beliefs and patterns of behaviour. This contributes to our propensity to participate in the next wave of strife or pass it on to the next generation thereby creating a cycle of violence. Thus, each one of us plays some role in this cycle – either actively or passively. We each therefore bear some responsibility for it. The responsibility becomes clearer when, through our beliefs and behaviour, we pass on traumas and grievances to our children. Similarly, we can see ourselves as receivers of inherited patterns and traumas from conflicts rooted before our time.

By addressing these issues and tackling them at the level of the individual and then the group, I believe we can diffuse the emotional charges against the 'other' that perpetuate these cycles. Central to transcending these emotional fuses is the concept of forgiveness. Where there is a lot of pain through conflict, addressing these emotions and forgiving can be one of the hardest challenges for a person to undertake. I do offer, however, some prescriptions for the individual and my hope is that decentralised networks of such like-minded persons who can work through this pain can then act as a source of encouragement for each other and for groups to create a political space for real reconciliation. This will then help in specific instances of violent disagreement and eventually, I hope, even at the structural political level.

Since I am talking at the level of the individual, I will start with my own personal story to illustrate how I came to explore these questions of cycles of violence and inherited grievances. I will also offer some examples from my professional work to show how I have put these theories into practice and how they have been reinforced by the work of others. I will then provide some tools that can enable the individual to address his or her personal stories and change behaviour that leads to conflict. Finally, through an explanation of the power of forgiveness at healing root causes of strife, I will offer some suggestions that I believe can help us break the cycle of violence in Lebanon.

My story

Like so many millions of others, wars are part of my history. I was brought up in the Second World War; my father grew up in the First World War and lost a brother. My mother fled the Russian Revolution, losing family members and grew up as a refugee. This familiar pattern has continued. I discovered Lebanon and my future husband in 1966. We enjoyed a few carefree years before the cataclysm of the civil war in Lebanon uprooted us all. It was in my own life that I began to see the concept of patterns between generations and repeating cycles.

What I felt instinctively, I learned that many others had formalised through extensive analysis: the concept of recurrence in conflict and the impact of trauma across generations. Anne Schutzenberger in *The Ancestor Syndrome*, for example, has looked at cancer, car accidents and war trauma and their effects on the descendents of the victims - in terms of their both experiencing and *repeating* the original incidents.[1]

In early 1984 a group of Lebanese living between Lebanon and London met regularly in our house to attempt to make a difference to what was going on in Lebanon, to try to understand what had brought us to this point and what could take us out of it – and be lasting. Of course, we didn't know the answers. So we set up the Centre for Lebanese Studies as a way of looking more profoundly at ourselves – our past, present and future.

In parallel to looking at historical facts and figures at the CLS, I reflected about the war in Lebanon and my own part in it. How can a country implode so quickly and so violently? I felt helpless. I later realised that I too must be part of the war. I questioned: what part do I play in war? How can I contribute to peace?

I began to explore. What stirs such inhumanity? How do we create personal and collective hells? For years I took courses in various therapeutic disciplines. I also attempted to reconcile my spiritual life and personal 'beyond the brain'[2] experiences with a more scientific, psychological understanding. I believed this would help me communicate these experiences more effectively to myself and others. I learned how fear is used internally and externally to separate us from one another and from our inner instincts of loving others and indeed ourselves. Fear also acts as a vehicle for anger, pain and vengeance. This process of exploration led me to become a psychotherapist.

Examples of ancestral influence in creating 'cycles' of violence

One of my first clients was a young French teenager who came to see me in London. His goal was to become a general. That's odd, I thought, in the France of today. I then discovered that he also had a driving belief: 'In order to be honourable, I have to die for my country.' A catch-22 situation. I won't describe all the extraordinary details of the case, but I later found out that this boy's ancestors had been connected with the Crusades and with the Levant for generations. His young cousin had also run away to fight in the Lebanese civil war. Two lives today were being tragically and unconsciously driven by beliefs created in the Crusades by long dead ancestors.

Since then, time and again, my work as a psychotherapist has shown me the interconnectedness between present conflicts and deeply held, out of consciousness, ancient group grievances. I work to heal pain in the individual caused by events in his or her life and/or echoed from earlier generations. Such patterns can extend to groups of individuals with common grievances. Schutzenberger uses the example of the Balkans to show the links throughout history of a particular conflict:

> During the Middle Ages, Ottomans (Muslims, Turks) and Serbs (Christians, Orthodox) fought for leadership in the Balkans. The Battle of Kosovo Fields (Kosovo Polje) ended with the defeat of the Serbs by the Ottomans on 28 June 1389 (cf. Volkan 1997). Serb leader Milos Kobolic assassinated the Sultan Murati; then in turn, Milo's brother-in-law Prince Lazar (later canonised) was decapitated by the Turks. With the fall of Constantinople (1453) to the Turks and the end of the great Serbia (1459) the Kosovo Fields 28 June defeat became an historical trauma for the Serbs.
>
> When on the anniversary of the Kosovo defeat, 28 June 1914, Archduke Franz Ferdinand, heir to the Austro-Hungarian Empire, entered Sarajevo; he was assassinated by a Serb activist, Gavrilo Princip, for the humiliation of Serbia. This act sparked the First World War.
>
> On 28 June 1989, Slobadan Milosevic, the Serbian leader, made a speech at the newly erected monument to the recently returned remains of Saint (Prince) Lazar at Kosovo Fields (with its inscription 1389-1989). He recalled Lazar's call to arms: 'Never again will Islam subjugate the Serbs'.[3]

Another topical example of history reflecting, some would say driving, current tensions can be observed in the state of dialogue today between Christianity and Islam. The last Pope, Jean Paul II, not long before his death, asked forgiveness in Bosnia-Herzegovina for the Catholic Church's past sins against humanity, human dignity and freedom. His successor, Pope Benedict XVI has offended many Muslims by quoting a fourteenth century Christian Emperor.[4] Pope Benedict later repaired some of this damage when, on his journey to Turkey in December 2006, he prayed in the Sultan Ahmet (aka the Blue) Mosque, facing Mecca. This symbolic act helped the reconciliation process between Christians and Muslims. It would appear that the previous Pope understood the 'live-wire' historical roots of grievances, as he persistently asked for forgiveness on behalf of the Catholic Church's past mistakes.

On a lighter note, Michael Henderson, author of several books on Forgiveness, recently moved to Cornwall from the United States. I enquired 'Cornwall must be nice and peaceful, I suppose'. He said 'well, I have just met a farmer here and he asked me 'do you know why my village Bideford is not talking to Barnstaple?' 'No', I said. He answered, 'They didn't send enough ships to fight the Spanish in the Battle of the Armada!'(In 1588).[5]

At the Centre for Lebanese Studies Conference in Beit Meri, on 8 June 2006, after a talk I gave on this subject, a gentleman in the audience (Yahya Hakim) stood up to tell the following story of an inter-generational memory link coming up at a corporate level. He recounted how in Germany he was attempting to discover the reason for a marketing puzzle. Why did the internationally successful French company called Eminence not sell well in Germany? Market research over six months revealed that the name 'Eminence' reminded the Germans of the hugely powerful Catholic French Cardinal Richelieu who was known as l'Eminence and dominated French policy between 1624-42.

Recently, whilst talking with an Ismaeli colleague, she told me this story. Her daughter, Sara, aged 8, was attending a school in the UK. She had a best friend whom she wanted to invite home. Her friend was delighted and both little girls were happy – until the grandmother of her friend stepped in and said 'No, you cannot go to Sara's house.' 'Why?' 'Because the Muslims killed Hindus' (in India 150 years ago). Sara was distraught and puzzled. She asked her mother, 'Are Muslims bad people?'

All of the above were what I call the memory 'puppet master' – a puppet master who lives in and feedds off the active pain of a memory hundreds of years old, and who manipulates the present and the future, until the pain in the memory can be released, thereby destroying the food of the puppet master, whose power comes from the active pain still held in the memory – however old it might be.

The role and influence of events and beliefs from previous generations that perpetuate cycles and receptivity to hate is obvious to some, preposterous to others. Such thinking evolved early on in the field of psychology, as explained by Carl Jung in *Memories, Dreams, Reflections*.

> I feel very strongly that I am under the influence of things or questions which were left incomplete and unanswered by my parents and grandparents and more distant ancestors. It often seems as if there were an impersonal karma within a family, which is passed on from parents to children, it has always seemed to me that I had to answer questions which fate had posed to my forefathers, and which had not yet been answered, or as if I had to complete, or perhaps continue, things which previous ages had left unfinished. It is difficult to determine whether these questions are more of a personal or more of a general (collective) nature. It seems to me that the latter is the case. A collective problem, if not recognised as such, always appears as a personal problem, and in individual cases may give the impression that something is out of order in the realm of the personal psyche. The personal sphere is indeed disturbed, but such disturbances need not be primary; they may well be secondary, the consequence of an insupportable change in the social atmosphere. The cause of disturbance is, therefore, not to be sought in the personal surroundings, but rather in the collective situation. Psychotherapy has hitherto taken this matter far too little into account. [6]

Towards the end of his life Jung used the term 'ancestral unconscious' in his correspondence with the Jungian Erio van Waveren.[7] On this topic, modern psychotherapy has advanced beyond the boundaries set by Jungian analysis[8] because it does account for ancestral influences as opposed to mere archetypal assimilations during the subject's life.

Many non-western cultures have always maintained a leading role for ancestors and their deeds in the present lives of their descendents. As Some, rooted in the Dagara culture argues, this provides an active link between the living and the dead in terms of behavioural inheritance.

> It is my belief that the present state of restlessness that traps the modern individual has its roots in a dysfunctional relationship with the ancestors. In many non-Western cultures, the ancestors have an intimate and absolutely vital connection with the world of the living. They are always available to guide, to teach, and to nurture, They represent one of the pathways between the knowledge of this world and the next. Most importantly—and paradoxically—they embody the guidelines for successful living—all that is most valuable about life. Unless the relationship between the living and the dead is in balance, chaos results. When a person from my culture looks at the descendants of the Westerners who invaded their culture, they see a people who are ashamed of their ancestors because they were killers and marauders masquerading as artisans of progress. The fact that these people have a sick culture comes as no surprise to them. The Dagara believe that, if such an imbalance exists, it is the duty of the living to heal their ancestors. If these ancestors are not healed, their sick energy will haunt the souls and psyches of those who are responsible for helping them.[9]

If it is indeed the case that the link between living and dead is not static then there is a capacity to resolve 'sick energy'. Indeed, there is a responsibility to do so by those who can act, i.e. the living.

At the other end of the scientific spectrum, new work is now being done to look at these phenomena at a genetic level – how our genes are affected by trauma. Last year, biologists including Professor Wolf Reik[10] of Cambridge, have found that genes have memory and this can be switched on or off. This gives a new biological dimension to what psychotherapists working with ancestral memories have known for some time. Their work represents a significant shift in scientific thinking and ties it up with much larger philosophical questions of personal and collective identity. Many philosophers have tried to understand what constitutes a person in his/her uniqueness (numerically and qualitatively) either by calling upon somatic principles (i.e.

genetics) or psychological analysis (i.e. memory), and found both answers unsatisfactory.[11] However, one proposal, by D Mackie[12], came close to Reik's suggestion of marrying memory and genes. Mackie postulated that it is an 'embodied memory', extending 'before and after' our life span, that is central to understanding the identity of a person and consequently this person's unique predispositions and behaviour[13]. Also, Reik's discovery is changing the way the causes of disease are viewed as well as the importance of lifestyles and family relationships. As the biologist Marcus Pembrey in this new field of epigenetics says: 'we are all guardians of our genome'[14].

In some parts of India they train baby elephants by tying one leg to a large chain and post for the first few years. When the elephant is large it then doesn't go anywhere. It stays a prisoner of its memory. We too are prisoners of old memories and are chained to the past. We act today because of deeply rooted grievances which haven't been dealt with; sometimes for generations. Not only, therefore, do we have to face and deal with the consequences of conflict in our own lives but we also have to deal with the effects of what has been passed down.

How to break the cycle? How to become 'good' ancestors?

Jonas Salk, the famous polio vaccine biologist is often quoted as saying: 'our greatest responsibility is being good ancestors'[9] Yes, but how? How do we become good ancestors and refrain from passing on trauma or negative beliefs to future generations? How do we stop being the prisoners and the puppets of the stinging memories of strife that we can still feel today as though we ourselves were present at that first event? How do we clean up what I call our 'ancestral arteries' so that our children are free to act in the now, free from the blocks which echo from the past, and clog up our todays and our tomorrows? When working with the past, Madie Gustafson makes a good point: 'The goal is to let our history inform us, not control us.'[16]

In order to break free from these inherited patterns and thereby end unhelpful or destructive cycles, we must undergo a process that falls broadly into three steps. Each step can occur sequentially or simultaneously. The process can apply to specific issues of conflict or to broader parts of our lives. The first step is to take responsibility for the active or passive role we play in propagating a conflict. The second involves creating a space for self-reflection so that we can become aware of nocuous behaviours and beliefs that reinforce that role. The third is to release the source of grievances we hold on to so that we can be free to replace old habits and thinking with new life-affirming ones thereby creating 'positive cycles' around us and for our children. Releasing the source of grievance that would otherwise compel us to repeat and pass it on can only be done through a process of understanding and forgiveness.

We cannot force nor be forced to undertake the process that leads us to understanding and forgiveness. We can become willing to do so; to allow ourselves to bring about this change in the perceptions that underpin our attitudes. I have observed through my work that it is when individuals choose to take these three steps that patterns which might otherwise seem immutable or pre-destined can be dissolved.[17]

Step 1 – Taking responsibility

By taking responsibility for our own choices, for our own lives and for the part we may be playing in any conflict, imbalance, tension, grievance or problem, we learn that we have a way out from existing patterns. We discover that we do certain things or think in certain ways quite 'unthinkingly' – because that is the way they have always been done or thought about. It takes courage, honesty and humility to see the role we play in the different conflicts around us. Ironically, as we begin to look at the conflict from a more reflective position in relation to ourselves, we may suddenly feel that we are not as personally or directly involved even while accepting our role in it for the first time. This reflective distance can also serve as a space within which alternative perceptions can be entertained. It leads us to the second step: altering our behaviours and beliefs about a conflict.

Step 2 – Changing our behaviour and beliefs

I have seen time and again that as individuals learn to deal with their personal grievances within families, they can break a cycle of repetitive pain, anger and violence which has been there for generations – thereby endowing theirs and their children's future with a new behavioural inheritance. This does not mean we all have to go into therapy, but it does require us to be *self reflecting* and as we do that, we are less likely to hold onto our own mindsets or to be predisposed to project blame on to everyone else for mistakes in our own life situations.

Once we are ready to take advantage of, and actively enter into, this new personal space for reflection, we can begin to transform our behaviours and actions. We can become aware of the behaviours and beliefs that reinforce the negative patterns of the past and keep us stuck in the cycle. This awareness may come to us in quiet moments of reflection, in dreams, intuitively, or through the feed-back from others and sometimes through accidents or illness, when we realise we have to change in order to choose a life-enhancing path.

Although some of the paths to becoming aware and changing behaviour may seem obvious, they may be quite hard to follow. Here is a sample of what we can undertake to help ourselves:

- Become aware of what motivates our actions and reactions – specifically towards those with whom we are in conflict. This entails digging under the surface for a candid assessment of our driving beliefs and desires. (Writing them down, so we do not forget or glide over them can help us confront difficult issues about ourselves.)
- Move beyond thinking of ourselves as a 'victim', a 'persecutor' or a 'saviour' – all these aspects are fuelled by anger/fear/guilt. As we become more accepting, forgiving and more compassionate with ourselves, and others, we can let go of and dissolve these

negative energies and cease to project them on others. 'A person should never be reduced to his or her trauma.'[18]

- Notice what we feel: whatever the feeling is (sadness, happiness, love, anger, fear, pain) we need to allow ourselves to *feel it without judgement.* We must remember that we hold 99 per cent of the same genetic code as chimps; all our territorial and fight/flight/freeze responses are activated from the animal areas of the brain – not our reflective human ones. We therefore need to learn to minimise fear-activated knee-jerk reactions by practising the human qualities of choice and reflection. This helps us to take responsibility for our own emotional life and also allows us to deal with painful feelings. Mind-body techniques to lower the stress and bring the body back to centre are useful tools when the anxiety is intense.[19]

- Notice the grievances in our lives. This includes those we feel towards others or that we perceive they feel towards us. Grievances lead to endless cycles of revenge. As Gandhi remarked 'an eye for an eye makes the whole world blind.' We need to observe those grievances that come from deep in the past of our family or group, religion and nation; how they affect or drive us today. We also need to address current gripes and grievances with others, even though there may not be 'justice' or an apology. This includes listening to others' grievances and complaints about us with an open mind.

- Notice when we ignore or avoid, do not listen to, or exclude 'the other' and vice versa. This will be a guide to something deeper that needs addressing. Engage the other by staying open and moving towards talking with 'the other' rather than closing up and running from them, as well as stepping into the shoes of 'the other' and seeing ourselves from the other's perspective

- Notice how we judge or blame or hate 'the other', and perhaps deny our own part in a conflict. The easiest way to become self aware is to realise that what we reject in ourselves, or have not forgiven in ourselves, we may be projecting onto others. When we accept this realisation, we are taking a positive step to remove our participation in the most common cause of bickering, fights and wars.[20]

- Notice fear and how we use it or it uses us. Fear of losing control leads us to try to take greater control – usually control of the future, in order to feel that we will be safer. The need to dominate comes from fear. Become aware of old wounds connected with power struggles both within and without. Become aware of feeding fears with guilt and the self-attack of 'not being strong enough, good enough, acknowledged enough, powerful enough, nice enough, brave enough, rich enough, beautiful enough etc.' – all of which keep us in 'victim mode'. Victims usually feel helpless. To escape endless self-attack we strive to get free and to feel more powerful by attacking someone else who is weaker. We build walls within ourselves against the justice of forgiving. And so the cycle goes on. Also notice fear-mongering and the feelings connected with it, whether it is our own or others who are doing the fear-mongering (including our leaders and the media).

- Notice any signs of despair then make another choice, a commitment towards life. Despair is possibly our greatest enemy. Many people, including great leaders, have survived the most incredible hardships by keeping a sense of faith and hope.[21]

- Notice humiliating, shaming, dominating and bullying actions. Those who are humiliated and bullied, in their turn humiliate and bully others, particularly when they find someone who appears weaker. We also bully ourselves and become self-created victims, using the voice internally of whichever authority figure originally dominated us, (until we can forgive that person or persons).

- Be aware that every time we humiliate someone, we risk setting off a chain reaction; a time bomb thrown into the future.

Humiliation is a particularly strong cause of vengeful behaviour. Indeed it is not hard to see from our own lives, from school, family and war. People, tribes and nations, who have been humiliated, humiliate. The memory stays live, if it is not healed.

Most of the dictators and despots of the world were humiliated as children: Napoleon, Hitler, Stalin, Saddam Hussein etc. And as groups: Germany was humiliated after the First World War, which led to the Second World War. The list is endless: Israelis and Palestinians, Hutus and Tutsis, Sunnis and Shi'ites in Iraq, colonialists and the colonised, blacks and whites in South Africa and in the USA. Not to mention the 286 different militias in the Lebanese civil wars enumerated by Samir Khalaf.[22] In Lebanon the deep memories of humiliation and domination of and by different groups is at the root of many of the difficulties we have today in creating a country. I suggest that we shall not be able to bridge our differences until we have dealt healthily with these recent, old and ancient wounds.

This list of behaviour awareness and change is in no way exhaustive. It is a sample of what is needed to help us to become more compassionate and understanding and therefore more capable of facing our fears and pain.

There are many different methods to reach this same goal, whether by working with groups of like-minded people, reading books or other spiritual practices. There are now many thousands of non-violent communication groups worldwide as well as hundreds of others working on Truth and Reconciliation techniques that can assist individuals and families in this step of behavioural change.[23]

As we uncover the nocuous patterns and reinforce helpful ones, we become more open and capable of resolving the fundamental sources of the fear/pain/anger/vengeance that we may hold on to so dearly. In order to cover this last step, we also need to learn how to forgive.

Step Three – Forgiving

I thought that the only hope for the world lay in an all-embracing attitude of forgiveness of the people who had been our enemies. Forgiveness, my prison experience had taught me, was not mere religious sentimentality; it was as fundamental a law of the human spirit as the law of gravity. If one broke the law of gravity one broke one's neck; if one broke this law of forgiveness one inflicted a mortal wound on one's spirit and became once again a member of the chain gang of mere cause and effect from which life has laboured so long and so painfully to escape.

Laurens van der Post, *The Night of the New Moon*[24]

The only thing that will bring us closer to lasting peace is a different way of facing our memories than we have used before. This requires leveraging the formidable power to change in the human heart in order to forgive. It does not mean forgetting, or brushing things under the carpet. Nor does it mean continuing the lies and betrayals that characterise war and which can fester for decades, or denying and covering up memories that are painful or shameful.

Hewitt and Wheeler[25] provide a succinct review of the current academic definition of forgiveness:

Although there is no consensual definition of forgiveness, most researchers in forgiveness agree with the definition proposed by Enright and Coyle.

'In genuine forgiveness, one who has suffered an unjust injury chooses to abandon his or her right to resentment and retaliation, and instead offers mercy to the offender'[26]

Enright and Coyle follow North's[27] notion of forgiveness. Forgiveness begins with hurt and pain. The injured has a moral right to anger and resentment but chooses to give up this right and desire for revenge. Instead he or she shows compassion, benevolence and love to the offender. This notion of forgiveness stresses the importance of the forgiver's free and unconditional choice, and requires the forgiver actively to involve in the process of changing either attitude or behaviour. Forgiveness is regarded as an interpersonal process which occurs only between people but not between a person and an inanimate object or an event. Most researchers also concur with the views of Enright et al.[28] that forgiveness is to be distinguished from pardoning, condoning, excusing, forgetting and denying. It is related to, but different from, reconciliation. McCullough [29] further suggests that the essence of forgiveness is the prosocial motivational change on the part of the offended. In forgiving, the offended becomes less motivated to harm but more motivated to do acts that will benefit the offender.

Where I differ with some of the above is that I find that the term 'offers mercy to the offender' can seem patronising. I think of forgiveness as a self healing process, which results in benefits for one and all. Forgiveness therefore is ultimately an act of self preservation, not a gift to be bestowed on others by us, (or by others on us), but received as a grace by surrendering our pain and offered to ourselves and others, and even to events beyond our control, with a willing and open heart. Our freedom comes when we realise that in order to thrive and survive and to break out of our prisons of resentments and hate, we do not have another choice, but to forgive and live our true purposes – fully alive. It is in this way that we become good ancestors.

In his book *The Art of Forgiving*, Lewis Smede gives six simple statements of what forgiveness is *not* about:

1. Forgiving someone who did us wrong does *not* mean that we tolerate the wrong he or she did.
2. Forgiving does *not* mean that we want to forget what happened.
3. Forgiveness does *not* mean that we excuse the person who did it.
4. Forgiveness does *not* mean that we take the edge off the evil of what was done to us.
5. Forgiveness does *not* mean that we surrender our right to justice.
6. Forgiving does *not* mean that we invite someone who hurt us once to hurt us again.[30]

I believe that forgiveness begins with a choice to become free. It is a supreme grace. We cannot manipulate grace, but we can make a space for it. That space, I believe, comes from a willingness to understand and to let go of that which holds us in pain and resentment. It is not easy, though it can be spontaneous. We may think we should forgive someone else, or ourselves, or an event, but pressurising ourselves will often make us resist. So I suggest that we do not force anything, either on others or on ourselves.

When we think of forgiveness, the fear may arise that evil will remain unpunished. It is as if forgiving might mean to give up the right to punish evil. Despite all of this, I have to see what evil does to me; it makes me want to react to evil with evil. Then I see everything with dark glasses of evil. It paralyses me and alienates me from life. Forgiving means bidding goodbye to evil, in order not to be guided by it any more.

A process of reconciliation may take some time, as the other side has to recognise its faults also. With forgiveness, however, I don't have to wait and waste time. Forgiveness gives me the freedom to love now. When we attain this freedom, we realise that those who have done evil are themselves its victims.

In forgiving we do not lose anything, rather we receive a gift.
Father Adrija Vrane, Bosnia 1998[31]

Sometimes we feel we will let someone 'off the hook' by forgiving them, that they do not deserve to be free of our righteous judgment of them. The problem is that *we* are the ones who remain bound. We may spend a whole lifetime subjugated to this righteousness, enslaving our own lives and the lives of those around us to the same cause.

Scilla Elworthy and Gabrielle Rifkind state in their book *Making Terrorism History* that 'the power of change in the human heart is formidable. It is what can transform violent activists into statesmen.'[32] Mandela, together with Tutu, courageously stepped out of the cycle of violence and terror to save South Africa and millions of lives, by taking a road to forgiveness, via truth and reconciliation, not revenge. As Tutu famously said '*There is no future without forgiveness.*'[33]

Why forgiveness?

We need to remember with passion what has happened in the immediate or distant past but above all we need to release what I call the 'sting' in that memory. It is when the 'sting' remains

105

entrenched in the memory that the memory becomes so destructive, triggering us to repeat the same thing over and over again, *whenever our safety seems threatened.* Through forgiveness we remove that sting (but not the memory). My work has shown me time and again that forgiveness is an effective process that frees us of the burdens of anger, guilt, fear and hate. It is essentially therefore a self-preserving act.

We are not alone in tapping into the healing effects of forgiveness. Forgiveness is being used in a host of therapies to deal with pain. According to Hewitt and Wheeler, 'recent literature on counselling and psychotherapy reveals an increased interest in the application of forgiveness.[34]' They state that in the United States, for example, forgiveness has been used as a brief therapy[35], as intervention for people hurt in relationships,[36,37,38] as psychological healing for adult incest survivors[39], and as therapy to heal intergenerational pain[40]. In the UK, recent research has seen the use of forgiveness in therapeutic contexts by counsellors and psychotherapists as well as by spiritual directors[41]. Stanford University's Center for Research (SFP) in Disease Prevention, oversaw the Stanford Forgiveness Project set up by Dr Fred Luskin. The SFP then evolved into an umbrella organisation for numerous Stanford research projects addressing forgiveness.[42] These projects documented how forgiveness can enhance not only psychological health, but reduce anger, blood pressure, depression and stress.

In spite of all the above studies, the West is seen as a newcomer to forgiveness. Using traditional forgiveness methods, many Ugandans have decided that they do not wish to continue to fight the war against the rebels from The Lord's Resistance Army. The LRA is reputed to have abducted more than 20,000 children while the war itself has killed over 100,000 with 1.5 million displaced. Now Ugandans are using their own forgiveness ceremonies to welcome back the rebels into society and to 'cleanse the sins'. Rwot Acana, chief of the Acholi population of northern Uganda has declared that through 'stepping on the egg', the former rebels are being forgiven. Almost all the rebels in the LRA were abducted as children and forced to carry out atrocities on their own communities. These same communities are now forgiving them- even though 'justice' has not been seen to be done. [43]

Of all the approaches available to break the age-old cycle of violence and counter-violence so endemic to Lebanon I believe none is more potent than forgiveness. Forgiveness is, in its essence, a spiritual force with boundless therapeutic virtues. It is upheld by all the great religions and wisdoms. In the Koran alone there are about 200 references to forgiveness in various forms. The New Testament is rich in forgiveness teaching and you only have to search the word, to find thousands of wise quotes on forgiveness from those who have tested it. In Lebanon today, education, economic prosperity, social welfare and all efforts at integration can do much to quell fears and clear misconceptions between different and segregated communities. They nonetheless need to be consolidated by forgiveness, in order to transcend painful memories and grievances and redirect this energy into genuine venues for peaceful and creative coexistence.

Battles reverberate throughout history. Every act has a resonance in time: warlike actions create waves that affect our lives, our children's lives, and the lives of those we may never meet. We create cycles of violence and grievances that are self-perpetuating, until we develop the ability to use the key of forgiveness in the present and connect with the understanding that the roots of grievances often lie deep in the past.

The concept of forgiveness is therefore an essential key to reconstruction and rehabilitation. Without it, the impressive projects underway in Lebanon may well be eclipsed by the same forces which razed their predecessors. Friends can live in the same shack and remain friends but enemies, embittered by the feelings of enmity and revenge, cannot share even a palace in the hope of becoming friends.

Forgiveness is an internal journey. It can be one of the hardest things to allow ourselves to undertake and requires real courage. It cannot be imposed: it must be undertaken by each individual because every person has his or her unique relationship with their memories and ancestry. I believe it begins with being willing to take responsibility for finding a way to heal our *own* grievances – even when we wish to blame others and feel we have a right to do so. In this way we free ourselves and our children from great burdens.

Extending the three steps to break the cycle of violence at the structural level

Though it must encompass the internal journey, avenues towards forgiveness can be created and reinforced at the structural level as well. Committed individuals can also create bridges to other members of their group or community. Approaches can then be made at the inter-communitarian level. This has already happened in many parts of the world including Lebanon, where there are several groups working towards peace, reconciliation and forgiveness. Through an act of leadership, forgiveness can take whole groups beyond the traps of past wounds and grievances and into a creative future.

For example, at the Religions for Peace eighth World Assembly in Kyoto entitled 'Confronting Violence and Advancing Shared Security' in August 2006, hundreds of committed religious and community leaders from all over the world, representing all religions, participated in commissions on conflict, reconciliation and healing. The policy resolutions from almost all the group discussions highlighted forgiveness as a means to solve and prevent further conflict.

In addition to working on behaviour awareness and forgiveness at policy conferences and in community discussions, there are many other ways in which society can teach children self-reflection and learn about their behavioural patterns as well as providing opportunities for the public at large to engage in these practices. Here is a shortlist of examples:

• Investing in skills and understanding of new approaches connected with war prevention. Especially exploring how to transform the dangerous 'stings' from the past to enable individual and group healing to take place.[44]

- Bringing into our educational curriculum psychological know-how for dealing with grievances and learning to understand and respect the 'others' point of view. In Lebanon the stark need for this was highlighted by Dr Shuayb's empirical research.[45]

- Such training in self-reflection should be introduced into the curriculum during the years of high brain development. Modern neuroscience shows that the frontal lobes of the higher cortex do not start to develop until the teenage years and continue to develop into our 20s; i.e. from ages 12 to 22.[46]

- Providing opportunities for different groups to learn about one another through joint activities, everyday tasks and family interactions. Groups demonise 'the other' so as to sanctify their brutality. I spoke to an ex-sniper who said he found it easy to kill 'the other' until one old lady he was targeting in his sights, reminded him of his grandmother. After so many deaths this at last brought home to him that 'the other' was not so different, but a human with the same emotions and fears.

- Understanding 'the other' with compassion acts as a barrier to violence. Therefore we must move away from segregation and create more avenues to share our human selves more fully with each other. Public and private institutions can help by creating public spaces and architecture which encourage healthy pluralism and mixing of groups. The Garden of Forgiveness in Beirut, for example, envisages such a public space in a setting that engenders self reflection. In this way, it can provide a structural setting to encourage the individual down the path of self awareness and forgiveness.

Conclusion

I have come into this world to see this: the sword drop from men's hands, even at the height of their arc of anger, because we have finally realised that there is only one flesh we can wound.

Hafiz, Persia, fourteenth century

My inner and outer journeys have led me to understand that I do indeed play a part in war and peace. I have realised how important it is for me to take responsibility for the parts of myself that can contribute to fear and war-like acts or feelings in me and around me. The alternative to real healing is bleak: the memory of war, like the harrowing events themselves, may be trivialised, forgotten, buried, or denied and hence, prone to reappear suddenly, as they did in the Lebanon of our lifetime.

I believe that breaking the cycle of violence starts with personal accountability and responsibility from each one of us. This entices us to make space for reflection and thereby allows us the chance to be more compassionate and understanding towards ourselves and others. We can therefore transform our behaviour and thereby break with patterns of conflict and violence based on fear and anger that may have been handed down unwittingly to us over generations. Forgiveness is the most powerful process available to us for getting at the root causes of these destructive emotions without repressing or forgetting them. It is not an easy path but the cycle can be broken.

The cycle itself starts inside each of us. But it extends itself naturally to groups and can take on a political dimension. The psychological definitions used to explain behaviour within the self can also be extended to explain the actions and reactions between groups. Example: A father bullies his child; the child bullies himself and the weakest one nearest to him. A group acts in the same way. Therefore, addressing the psychology of the self also affects the actions of the group.

As we begin to address our own cycle of fear and anger, we also create a new momentum of transformation around ourselves, in the lives we touch and within our group or community. We can build on this momentum to create new avenues that help us to reinforce and accelerate the process of healing and through that to break the cycles of violence. Each one of us is therefore a vital part of the whole. We are all responsible as individuals for creating a new and viable and peaceful Lebanon.

In conclusion, I quote a few words written in 1998 by a young medical student at the American University of Beirut:

'Forgiveness is an expression of tolerance and love. It is the subordination of hatred and vengeance. Forgiveness is, above all, a human necessity and a means to live. Without forgiveness friendships end, love terminates, and eventually the beauty of life ceases to refine our senses. Without forgiveness no one will ever learn from a mistake or bad luck but will be blinded by retaliation and killed by pride.'

Notes

1 Anne Ancelin Schutzenberger, *The Ancestor Syndrome*, Appendix 8, Routledge, 1998. (Originally published in French as *Aie Mes Aieux!* in 1993).

2 'Beyond the brain': A term used by the Scientific and Medical Network for an annual series of conferences exploring the frontiers of applied spirituality and consciousness research. It refers to what can be traditionally called a 'mystical' experience or one which is not derived from rational thought alone. It is called 'beyond the brain' because it is a state where the feeling of consciousness is powerful yet beyond any linguistic articulation derived from the human brain. The Scientific and Medical Network is an international group based in the UK and consists mainly of qualified scientists, doctors, engineers, psychologists, philosophers, therapists and other professionals. The conferences are supported by the Royal College of Psychiatrists and the British Psychological Society.

3 Anne Ancelin Schutzenberger, *The Ancestor Syndrome*, p.28, 1998.

4 During a lecture in Cologne, 15 September 2006.

5 Conversation with Michael Henderson, April 2006. (Author of *The Forgiveness Factor*, Grosvenor Books USA, 1996; and *Forgiveness: Breaking the Chains of Hate*, Arnica Publishing 2003).

6 Jung, CG, *Memories, Dreams, Reflections*, p.233-244, Pantheon, New York, 1963.

7 Personal communication from Roger Woolger PhD, Jungian Analyst, June 2006.

8 Jung, CG, *The Archetypes and the Collective Unconscious*, Routledge, 1991.

9 Some, M, *Of Water and the Spirit*, p.9-10, Penguin, 2005.

10 Dr Wolf Reik, based at the Babraham Institute, and his team published the report in *The Journal of Biological Chemistry 2004*, www.jbc.org. It establishes Epigenetics and proposes a control system of 'switches' that turn genes on or off – and suggests that things people experience, like

nutrition and stress, can control these switches and cause heritable effects in humans.

11 Wiggins, D, *Identity and Spatio-Temporal Continuity*, Oxford: Blackwell, 1967; Olson, E., *The Human Animal: Personal Identity Without Psychology*, Oxford University Press 1997; Thomas Nagel, 'Brain Bisection and the Unity of Consciousness', *Synthèse* 22: 396-413, 1971and reprinted in Perry, 1975 and in Nagel, *Mortal Questions*, Cambridge University Press, 1979.

12 Mackie, D, 'Personal Identity and Dead People', *Philosophical Studies* 95: p.219-242, 1999.

13 Ibid.

14 http://www.bbc.co.uk/sn/tvradio/programmes/horizon/ghostgenes.shtml

15 See for example: http://www.nsf.gov/news/speeches/lane/slsmef.htm

16 Conversation with Madie Gustafson, September 2004.

17 All this presupposes, in the words of Sartre, that as individuals we need to choose the Fundamental Choice of *life*, of a world free from conflict and must achieve it through a state of authenticity. In other words, we are more than the sum of our inheritance, memories and experiences. Furthermore, we are transcendent beings capable of change even in the face of pernicious influences that might seem irreversible. Knowing that we can break free of even the heaviest weight of behavioural predisposition can lead to a certain freedom to act. In the case for breaking the cycle of violence, that action needs to work through forgiveness. Otherwise, we are assuaged only for a short while from the boulder of predisposition.

18 Interview with neuropsychiatrist Boris Cyrulnik, *Humanities*, No 45 December 2001.

19 'Brain Gym' refers to a series of mental exercises developed by Dr. Paul Dennison and Gail E. Dennison. It develops the brain's neural pathways the way nature does, through movements.

20 See Levy, P., *Shadow Projection: The Fuel of War, 2006*.

21 For example, Nick Yarris, a prisoner on death row after 22 years was vilified for a crime for which he was proved innocent by DNA testing in 2004. When asked if he felt revengeful, he answered 'what's the point in leaving hell if you take it with you'. (BBC Radio 4, 26 September 2006).

22 Conversation with Samir Khalaf, June 2006.

23 There are also many people and groups working on the power of forgiveness: a few of the ones I know personally are: Dr Fred Luskin at Stanford, Dr Enright at University of Wisconsin-Madison, The Templeton Foundation, Harvard Medical School, The Scientific and Medical Network, Brandon Bays 'Journey' work, Chuck Spezzano's Psychology of Vision, The Course in Miracles Network, Initiatives for Change, Carolyn Myss and Marianne Williamson, Deeprak Chopra,

Jampolsky. There are many other authors on forgiveness who include techniques that have been tested and proven to touch all areas of an individual's life and health.

24 Van der Post, L, *The Night of the New Moon*, Hogarth, 1970, pp.153-4. 'The Night of the New Moon' is August 6, 1945, the end of the day on which the world's first atom bomb was dropped on Hiroshima. At that time Laurens van der Post was in a Japanese prison camp in Java. For him and for the thousands of prisoners in the hands of the Japanese in South-East Asia, the bombing of Hiroshima was not the remote and localised act of war that distance would suggest, but an event which had a direct and profound influence on their fate. In his account of their ordeal, Laurens van der Post tells a story that goes beyond the confines of their captivity into the whole human tragedy of Hiroshima and its significance for the history of our time.'

25 Hewitt, E and Wheeler, S, *Counselling in higher education: the experience of lone counsellors*, p.1, January 2004.

26 Enright, RD and Coyle, CT researching the process model of forgiveness within psychological interventions, *Dimensions of Forgiveness*, Worthington E.L. (ed.) Templeton Foundation Press. Pennsylvania, p.140, 1998.

27 North, J. 'Wrongdoing and Forgiveness', *Philosophy*, 62, p. 499–568, 1987.

28 Enright, RD, Gassin, EA and Wu, C, Forgiveness: a developmental view, *Journal of Moral Education*, 21, p.99–114, 1992.

29 McCullough ME, 'Forgiveness: who does it and how do they do it?' *Current Directions in Psychological Science*, 10, p.194–197, 2001.

30 Smede, LB, *The Art of Forgiving*, Ballantine Books/Random House, April 1996.

31 As recounted by Michael Henderson in *Forgiveness: Breaking the Chains of Hate*, preface XVIII, Arnica Publishing 2003.

32 Elsworthy, S and Rifkind, G, *Making Terrorism History*, p 90, Rider, London, 2006.

33 Tutu, D, *No Future Without Forgiveness*, Rider & Co. 2000.

34 Hewitt, E and Wheeler, S, *Counselling in higher education: the experience of lone counsellors*, p.1, January 2004.

35 McCullough ME and Worthington EL, 'Promoting forgiveness: a comparison of two brief psycho education group interventions with a waiting-list control', *Counselling and Values*, 40, p.55-68, 1995.

36 Al-Mabuk R, Enright, RD and Cardis, P, 'Forgiveness education with parentally love-deprived college students', *Journal of Moral Education*, 24, p.427–444, 1995.

37 Coyle, CT and Enright, RD, 'Forgiveness intervention with post-abortion

men', *Journal of Consulting and Clinical Psychology*, 65, p.1042–1046, 1997.

38 Hebel, JH and Enright, RD, 'Forgiveness as a psychotherapeutic goal with elderly females', *Psychotherapy*, 30, p.658–667, 1993.

39 Freeman, SR and Enright, RD, 'Forgiveness as an intervention goal with incest survivors', *Journal of Consulting and Clinical Psychology*, 64, p. 983–992, 1996.

40 Murray, RJ, 'The therapeutic use of forgiveness in healing intergenerational pain', *Counselling and Values*, 46, p.188–198. 2002.

41 West, W, 'Issues relating to the use of forgiveness in counselling and psychotherapy', *British Journal of Guidance and Counselling*, 29, p.415–423, 2001.

42 Examples of such research papers are: *'Effects of group forgiveness intervention on perceived stress, state and trait anger, self reported health, symptoms of stress and forgiveness'* F Luskin, C. Thoresen, A Harris, S Standard, S Benisovich, J Bruning and S Evans 2001; *'The art of forgiveness'* F Luskin 2001; *'Forgiveness, physical health and disease: what's the relationship?'* C. Thoresen, A. Harris and F Luskin, 2000; *'Science and forgiveness interventions: reflections and recommendations'* C Thoresen, F Luskin and A Harris 1998.

43 Will Ross, BBC Uganda, 25 October 2004.

44 Alexandra Asseily has developed a simple way in which individuals and groups can personally contribute to the peace in the World. Copies of the process can be obtained from the Centre for Lebanese Studies. An example of this is in the Appendix.

45 See her chapter in this book.

46 A team led by Dr Deborah Yurgelun-Todd at Harvard's McLean Hospital has been using MRI scans to follow development of teen brains (National Institute of Mental Health: 'Teenage Brain: A Work in Progress', 2001; and 'Inside the Teenage Brain', PBS 2002.

APPENDIX

What is my Responsibility For?

Peace in the World?

Steps towards a Peace Process

To encourage peace, harmony, and understanding between peoples
Regardless of their ethnic origin or religion.

The following five steps are for all who desire to develop a greater awareness of peace in their own life and acquire more skills to apply around them. They can be used for all three stages of conflict: prevention before conflict, resolution during conflict and reconstruction after conflict.

What is normal is the ebb and flow of tensions that form part of a healthy interaction among the life forces which influence us in this world. Conflict need not be the norm, but the exception. When tensions rise high, conflicts can erupt and we often blame others for our grievances instead of taking responsibility for the part which we may have played in fuelling the tensions.

These five steps can be experienced individually by anyone, with ample time to explore and share their experiences and emotions with others in this exercise. The practice of open communication, which includes compassionate listening among individuals and actively facilitating group dynamics, is helpful to the process.

This peace process encourages a general spiritual awakening and awareness of our divine inner voice.

STEP ONE: Taking Responsibility

The first step towards a peace process is to take responsibility for one's own part in any conflict/imbalance/tension/grievance/problem with courage, honesty, and humility, even if one does not feel personally involved in conflict.

STEP TWO: Asking and Reflecting

The second step is to ask a number of questions, examples of which are found on the following pages of this leaflet.

A few guidelines about the Asking and Reflecting process:

– Sit or stand quietly, relaxing for 15 – 20 minutes. Allow thoughts to come and go to clear the mind of daily events and to become quiet.
– Ask each question internally and wait patiently – the reply may come in a variety of ways: a picture, a series of pictures, words in the head, words written on an internal screen, a feeling, thoughts, and a combination of all or some of these responses.
– Reflect for a few moments on what has been received and get an inner understanding.
– Pause, relax and clear your mind, before asking the next question.

STEP THREE: Forgiving

The third step is to understand the power of forgiveness. By allowing for forgiveness of oneself and others, including our ancestors, we can let go of guilt, shame and fear. We then no longer need to uphold the same grievances from one generation to another. As we forgive others, we forgive ourselves and vice versa. (Many of us resist forgiveness because of the feeling, conscious or unconscious, that in so doing we are letting a significant 'other' off the hook and/or betraying our obligations to ancestors if we let go of their negative beliefs and grievances. This resistance blocks us from fully expressing our giftedness.) *Asking for forgiveness can be done at any time in this peace process.*

STEP FOUR: Releasing

The fourth step is to release within ourselves all obstacles that prevent each one of us from promoting peace in us and around us at this time. *Asking for release can be done at any time in this peace process.*

STEP FIVE: Sharing

The fifth step is to share and experience this peace process with others. Practising this process transforms both us and our environments towards peace.

Peace Asking and Allowing:

At this time...
1. What is peace for me?
2. In what way am I preventing peace in and around me?
3. What is the special gift (spiritual or physical) I am not yet fully using to bring peace in me and around me?
4. In what way am I preventing peace in my body?*
5. What is the gift that I am not yet using to bring peace to my body?
6. In what way am I preventing peace with [name of the person/s with whom I have the greatest conflict]?

   * Questions 5 and 6 to be repeated replacing the word 'body' with other key words, such as: self, family, work, group, nation, world

Forgiveness Asking and Allowing:

A) At this time ...
– What stops me from forgiving myself?
– How do I forgive myself?
– Can faith allow me to forgive myself?
– What is forgiveness when it comes from grace and faith?
– What is my gift for peace when I have fully forgiven myself or allowed myself to be forgiven?

B) At this time ...
– Who is the 'victim' in me?
– Who is the 'persecutor/victimiser' in me? (The 'racist', the 'enemy', the 'terrorist', the 'other', etc.)
– Who is the 'saviour' in me?
– How can I enable these aspects in myself to be forgiven?
– How can I be enabled to forgive these aspects in others?

C) At this time ...
– How may I fully accept the 'other' to bring unity to myself?
– What is the potential for world peace when I fully accept the 'other'?
– How is it when all parts of me are fully in harmony?

Ancestors:

The following questions related to family history, experiences, ancestral beliefs and patterns are essential to understand the deeper roots of present conflicts:

At this time ...
– What do I model or inherit from my father's *family line*, which is no longer appropriate?
– What do I model or inherit from my father, which is no longer appropriate?
– What do I model or inherit from my mother's *family line*, which is no longer appropriate?

– What do I model or inherit from my mother, which is no longer appropriate?

Ask for the grace of an inner awareness of forgiveness for ourselves, our parents, and our ancestors.

At this time ...
– What is the gift from my father's *family line* which I am not yet fully using in my life at this time?
– What is the gift from my father, which I am not yet fully using in my life at this time?
– What is the gift from my mother's *family line* which I am not yet fully using in my life at this time?
– What is the gift from my mother which I am not yet fully using in my life at this time?

Ask for an inner awareness of gratitude for ourselves, our parents, and our ancestors.

Chapter Six

Memory as Representation and Memory as Idiom

Sune Haugbolle

In this short chapter I want to contribute to the debate about Lebanon's past and present wars by making two general points about memory of the Lebanese Civil War (1975-90). My first point is to show how certain narratives of the war have been privileged in what I call memory culture, meaning the people involved in debating, expressing and producing memory of the war for public consumption. I argue that over the last ten years, memory of the war has become an idiom for political change, and recapturing history a means of recapturing influence. My second point is that memory as idiom often sits uncomfortably with the details of memory as lived experience, in Lebanon and elsewhere. This problem has particular influence on the question of how Lebanese society can come to terms with the war experience on a collective level, and how such an evaluation may prevent a new civil war.

Memory as cultural representation

It has been said that the absence of a collective response to mass atrocity leaves victims with either too much memory or too much forgetting (Minow 2002: 16). Too much forgetting can lead to amnesia or repression. The lack of a basic acknowledgement and explanation is confusing and essentially dehumanising to victims because it deprives them of a contextual language with which to express their pain. Alternatively, victims may be left with too much memory: paralysed with memories of victimisation, they block out alternative voices of victims from other sides in a conflict. Such a situation often sustains animosities and hinders post-conflict reconciliation.

Through art, media, activism and public debate, Lebanese intellectuals have since the mid-1990s, some even earlier, come to the conclusion that their country suffers from both these ills: at once too much and too little memory. This conclusion emerged in reaction to the scarce efforts by successive post-war governments in Lebanon to promote public debate and commemoration of the civil war. In the vacuum of what many critics have called 'state-sponsored amnesia,', political groups and parties recreated hardened memories from the war within closed-off discursive and physical realms, such as particular media and neighbourhoods. Consequently, the burden of creating and sustaining civilian memory has fallen squarely on civil society. Their challenge has been to break the silence and involve the population in 'memory work' that would show how similar the war experience had actually been for ordinary people. In sharp contrast to these efforts, large parts of the Lebanese population through the 1990s and the early 2000s seemed to prefer letting the past be past and focussing on the present and the future. As the artists, activists and intellectuals involved with memory culture repeatedly argued, this sluggish attitude of *laissez-faire* proved that the regime, for large parts made up of veterans from the war, protected and promoted by the general amnesty passed in 1991, had failed to help the Lebanese people overcome their sense of confusion vis-à-vis the war. Instead, the 'muted anguish of the Lebanese' had made them 'wrap themselves in their suffering' and perpetuated the pain and guilt of the war under the surface of normality in post-war Lebanon (Makarem 2002: 39; Khalaf 1993).

Most people living in Lebanon will be familiar with this confusion. Exactly because memories of the war are intrinsically multifaceted and confusing, people struggle to find words to express them. Therefore the unmediated voices of war memories have rarely appeared in public. War memories are in need of interlocutors, which is where the agents of memory culture step in. Their approach to this task ranges from the artistic twists often applied by artists, novelist and filmmakers, to the reportage of journalists and other artists. In artistic renderings the focus is often on the victim, either in form of the classic war-victim subjected to flight and suffering, or in the form of perpetrators who were duped into fighting by sectarian leaders. The little man, the typical Lebanese, and the Lebanese people generally, we are led to believe, were victims of circumstance. Of course there are exceptions, such as Randa Sabbagh's controversial film *Civilisée* from 1999 which points an accusing finger at certain aspects of the Lebanese mentality that led to the war (Haugbolle 2005).

In the reportage genre, the same approach dominates, again with notable exceptions. Generally, interviews about war-memory published in the Lebanese press aim to portray ordinary Lebanese as double victims: victims of war and victims of post-war amnesia. A typical example of the reportage was printed in the newspaper *al-Balad*, which ran a series of twenty feature articles on the lived memory of the war in April 2005. Here, a variety of ordinary Lebanese spoke about their memories and their understanding of the war. Many of these civilian memories are characterised by an inability to grasp the political context of the events. They appear as broken bits and pieces of the past, what Peter Van der Veer has called memory fragments (Van der Veer 2002). Some interviewees attempt to explain the war by blaming outside forces. Others simply refuse to construct wholesome narratives from their accounts, like an old woman from Dikwaneh in East Beirut who first related the details of her personal travails but then, stopping to ponder the war, asked her interviewers: 'What happened? To this day we still don't know if it was a civil war, a war of the others, or the war over Lebanon.' This quote is interesting because she recognises the common explanations of 'a civil war, a war of the others, or the war over Lebanon,' but fails to make sense of the array of interpretations. Unlike the agents of memory culture who are motivated by national redemption in their confrontation with the war, civilian memories are often characterised by scepticism and confusion. This suggests that people need collective histories in which to situate their private stories. Without a context, personal pain overshadows and precludes collective memory. Many victims of the Lebanese Civil War lack a narrative that corresponds meaningfully to their personal experience and their often conflicted memories.

It is therefore the job of cultural agents to provide a context. The tale that they privilege corresponds (unsurprisingly, if we follow Halbwachs's dictum about the social construction of memory) with their own experience of the war as well as that of their social group (Halbwachs 1992). For the people involved in memory culture, that experience is overwhelmingly one of civilian resistance to the war and the sectarian militias. Many of them belong to the secular Left. Some even fought with leftist organisations during the civil war. Others have their roots in the milieu of the war-time peace movement, which was particularly active towards the end of the war. This correlation of interests has privileged a particular memory of the war, namely that of civilian resistance to the sectarian militias, or, pacifism and anti-sectarianism. In other words, most representations of the war are motivated by particular visions of Lebanon and the Lebanese which privilege cross-sectarian nationalism and often play down sectarian affiliation and certainly sectarian violence.

Sectarian violence was an integral part of the civil war. From the late 1960s, the presence of armed Palestinian groups provoked deep schisms in the Lebanese population, which was already divided over the nature of Lebanon's political system and Arab/Western allegiance as well as economic inequalities. As a result, sectarian groups and parties armed themselves in anticipation of hostilities, and in realisation that the Lebanese state was unable or unwilling to solve the crisis. The ensuing civil war saw two forms of sectarian violence: one spontaneous and popular and the other a direct result of centrally organised militias which incorporated young restless men and trained them in sectarian exclusiveness and violent coercion of the enemy (Salmon 2006: 110-126). It is the latter form of violence, the enforced tyranny of sectarian militias, which war-memory tends to confront. The other violence, the violence of popular participation which manifested itself most clearly in the 'two-year war' of 1975-76, remains much more difficult to approach. However, it was part of the war and is therefore also part of people's memories, even if these memories do not lend themselves easily to a constructive narrative applicable to constructive memory culture.

In these and other aspects of Lebanese memory culture, the underlying strategy stems from the idea that healing is possible through revelation, which in Michael Humphrey's words has become 'an 'article of faith' for personal therapy and social redemption in the secular world' (Humphrey 2002: 111-112). Despite this ultimate valorisation of memory over forgetfulness, certain intellectuals like Fawwaz Traboulsi and Elias Khoury have also noted that at least some of the violence must be repressed in order for people and society to live sanely (Peleikis 2006: 145). The question is: how does one reconcile the need to forget with the need to remember? Ultimately, tough choices of exclusion and inclusion must be made.

The absence of any authoritative national interpretation does not mean that there are no explanations on offer in the broader population. On one hand, defensive, apologetic narratives persist within the confines of regions, sects or political parties, expressed through the cult of dead leaders, through commemoration in spaces of local remembrance and through socialisation in sectarian confines of family, sect, neighbourhood or village (Peleikis 2006; Haugbolle 2006). On the other hand, there is the vague but popular notion of 'the war of the others' mentioned by the woman in *al-Balad*. This explanation, which is a vulgarised version of Ghassan Tueni's original thesis, externalises the guilt of the war, albeit in different ways (Tueni 1985). In effect, the expression applies to various quite different historical memories, depending on the 'other' in question. Some blame Syria, some Israel, some the Palestinians, some the US and the West, and some blame the militias. All these different narratives blend into the generic explanation of 'the war of the others' and make the war digestible as a collective, national experience.

Thus, the viability of this explanation depends on people's ability to block out alternative narratives of the war and of culpability. In that respect Lebanon is hardly unique. Fitting the past in a common frame is a conventional, some would say indispensable, part of forging a national identity. Constructions of nationalism always entail a list of omissions that inform collective memory. In the 'homogenising discourse of nationalism,' certain events and perspectives that complicate national myths are necessarily forgotten or deliberately excluded (Burke 1998: 4). It would seem that, in what Malinowski called the 'functional application of myths' to reinforce group solidarity, public debates have a tendency to develop self-censoring mechanisms (Malinowski 1960). My point here is that certain cultural elites dominate the making of these myths disproportionately to other social groups. While this is hardly surprising or novel, it should influence the way we study and refer to national memory. In particular, it is important to examine the intentions and motivations of cultural elites rather than, as it is often done, uncritically reproducing their representation as 'the memory of the people.'

Memory as idiom for political change

Through public discourse and action, cultural producers, artists, activists and others involved in the business of bringing the de-contextualised narratives of civilian victims out in public, are trying to give them a voice and humanise their memories by resisting collective amnesia for the sake of national healing and, eventually, in order for Lebanon to be able to forget and move on. This is evident in literature, film and the plastic arts where the war has been *the* theme at least since the mid-1990s (Haugbolle 2005). The Lebanese press has also more and more frequently returned to memory of the war in the same terms of memory as a means to national healing, reconciliation, peace 'with the truth and with the self,' particularly around 13 April and the anniversary of the outbreak of the war. The notion that a 'collective amnesia' is plaguing society has become so popular that most attempts to make the memory of the war public in Lebanon today are formulated in response to this so-called 'collective amnesia.' '*Tandhakir ma tan'anad*' (remember so that you don't return) is the campaign slogan of one movement and 'Memory for the Future' the name of another. In both cases the basic idea is to create lasting memory, so that future generations do not repeat the mistakes of the past.

Without being dismissive of the good intentions behind memory culture, I think there is reason to question how well this self-proclaimed universal road map to reconciliation adapts to the Lebanese context. Simply put, memory is contested terrain and essentially political. As Fawwaz Traboulsi has put it, a constructive role for public memory necessitates a common understanding that certain things should be remembered and certain things forgotten. As long as memories focus on suffering, on the fact that all Lebanese in one way or another were victims, the logic of healing through revelation makes immediate sense. But when memories of violence are expressed in strictly political terms, victimisation fails to suffice as *the* overarching tale of the war.

Unfortunately, it is very hard to say anything meaningful about the war without mentioning politics, *even* for victims and *particularly* for perpetrators. The war may have been characterised to some extent by unrepresentative coercive control by militias, but it was also fought over actual political and ideological differences which run through Lebanon's history. In the pre-war period, competing nationalist narratives struggled to achieve a hegemonic position on the political scene. The main schism in this competition was over Lebanon's past and national character, which some claimed was primarily Arab while others emphasised the idea of Lebanon as a refuge for sects characterised by multi-confessional power sharing. The war transformed this competition into violent struggle and even created ideologies of sectarian separatism. In the course of fifteen years of fighting, the moral legitimacy of the various nationalisms was undermined by the militias who fought in their name, and the war ended with a 'burn-out stalemate' when all sides realised that they had no chance of achieving superiority (Reinkowski 1997: 494, 508). After the war, a new public consensus stressing coexistence, tolerance and, more implicitly, Syrian tutelage effectively effaced the strident ideologies from public discourse. The war essentially became a taboo because it endangered this public consensus. A comprehensive break with this strategy, therefore, necessitates a comprehensive new political and social contract to replace that of the Ta'if Accord that ended the civil war. Whereas some activists are very explicit about their revolutionary intentions, others seem unaware that they are partaking in a political project. But memory is not just culture; memory is politics. And in Lebanon, the politics of memory revolves around a frontal attack on the 'culture of sectarianism' – of sectarian affiliation and authority as the basis for national and local political power – that has dominated Lebanese politics since Independence and particularly since the end of the war (Makdisi 2000).

Another reason why memory culture has failed to penetrate effectively to the wider population is a tendency to speak of memory in abstract terms, as a fashionable and worthy topic for concerned debate. There have been several colloquia on memory, plenty of editorials on memory, plays and films about memory, etc. But in the rare cases when people's voices are actually heard, the raw nature of their war memories inevitably makes it clear that probing the violence and its root causes is much trickier, uglier and more painful than the teleological narratives of memory culture – from trauma through memory to redemption – imply. It is true that certain aspects of the war as, for example, the resistance against Israel and popular coexistence in spite of the boundaries imposed by militias, are capable of creating a positive and constructive memory and can therefore, free of any risk, be shared in public.

But other aspects of the war inevitably point to more complicit participation by the Lebanese population. If anything, the history of the war is complicated; indeed, so complicated that it defies attempts to simplify the complex by grouping its different periods and aspects into bracket explanations. There are many ghosts if one wants to raise them, and several of them sit very uncomfortably with a benign national self-understanding. Hence, a selection must be made, a selection which is natural and common in post-conflict situations, but a selection which cultural producers often fail to recognise that they are making.

It is, therefore, hardly surprising that variations on the theme of the fight against outsiders dominate most public renderings. Nor was it surprising that this particular theme dominated the way in which demonstrators and politicians utilised the memory of the civil war during the series of demonstrations known in Lebanon as the Independence Intifada and in the West as the Cedar Revolution. In February, March and April 2005, elements in the broad coalition known as *al-mu'arada* (the opposition) confronted powers inside and outside Lebanon who, in their view, were to blame for the civil war. These elements counted youth organisations, the Democratic Left Movement and groups and individuals from civil society. Their confrontation was somewhat complicated by the fact that the *mu'arada* itself also counted wartime leaders like Walid Jumblatt. Nevertheless, a distinct part of the revolutionary discourse of the anti-Syrian opposition revolved around the idea that a showdown with political mismanagement, violence and amnesia would, in turn, buttress national unity and finally pave the way for 'a second independence.'

The Bristol Declaration and the Independence Intifada

The use of memory of the civil war as idiom for political change became gradually more apparent in the years leading up to the death of Hariri and the Independence Intifada. From being primarily involved in a 'cultural' movement, the agents of memory culture now increasingly influenced politics. A defining moment in the period that went before the Intifada was a meeting at the Bristol Hotel in December 2004 attended by political parties representing the Druze and Christian communities, as well as some leftist groups. The Declaration produced by that meeting is a remarkable document which clearly shows the way in which memory culture managed to leave its stamp on political narratives. It presents the crisis of post-war Lebanon as a moral crisis connected to the failure to deal with the legacy of the civil war. The document claims that the Lebanese are haunted by their corrupt state officials, are unable to govern themselves, and that the state uses fear and separation as a means to perpetuate its control over society; the state is a relic of the civil war and a source of collective shame. However, the current situation offers an opportunity to overcome the perpetuated national crisis of the post-war period. This should be done by assuming responsibility for the Lebanese' own role in their civil war and their 'common guilt.' The war was a war of the others, but also a war of the Lebanese, who sought the assistance of others. Furthermore, the document states that a political programme for the new Lebanon should be based on independence, *rafd al-tawtin* (rejection of nationalisation of Palestinian refugees in Lebanon), commitment to Arabism and a new role for Lebanon as a sort of groundbreaker for Arab democratisation.

From the Bristol Declaration and through to the landmark '14 March demonstration' that filled downtown Beirut with over a million protestors after Hariri's death, the anti-Syrian opposition became increasingly coloured by ideas of coming to terms with the war that had existed in society and had been propagated in memory culture since the end of the war and particularly gained ground after 2000. The conflation of Christian and Muslim symbols, the insistence on national symbols over sectarian party symbols, and the public refutation of the theory that Lebanon is too weak to contain its differences, all drew on the idea of a common civilian memory of the civil war. Through a mesh of signs and slogans, the demonstrators made it clear that the Lebanese 'have learned', the Lebanese 'will never go back to the war' and the Lebanese 'want unity.' Some of these slogans emerged more or less spontaneously. Others were invented or spun by media and political groups who sought to co-opt the populist sentiments in the heat of the events. The alliance between the Hariri family's Future Movement and the centre-right newspaper *An-Nahar* proved particularly decisive in allying Christian and Sunni parties around the ideas of national rebirth through memory, learning the lessons of the past and wide-ranging political reforms.

The Independence Intifada had three more or less clearly stated ambitions: Syrian withdrawal, the regaining of full sovereignty and establishment of the truth about Hariri's murder, or in slogan form: 'Freedom, Truth and Independence' (Safa 2006). Syria did withdraw, but that remains the only tangible political result of the Intifada. In late 2006, the truth about Hariri's murder is still pending. For those in the *mu'arada* who saw the Independence Intifada as a means to break with the past and establish a new political class with no connection to the civil war, the revolutionary promises failed to deliver. In that sense, the Intifada remained 'unfinished' and unity a slogan more than political reality. Before the parliamentary elections in June 2005, the *mu'arada* split over questions of the presidency and Hezbollah. The unfinished Intifada in turn stalled political progress and landed Lebanon in an open-ended political deadlock (Leenders 2006).

My point is not to ridicule any of this with the cruel wisdom of hindsight. There is enough in the Independence Intifada and in Lebanese memory culture to make one hopeful of the Lebanese people's resolve to overcome imposed and self-imposed divisions. Certainly, the civil war should be remembered and more should be done to ensure that people overcome their overload of memory and make up for their lack of it. But it is important to maintain that memory as idiom for political change tends to exclude certain aspects of the war experience, and that the discourse of memory as healer fails to take account of memory as political contestation. This is important exactly because the discourse of healing through revelation is so pervasive with the group of organisations and individuals who are concerned with memory of the war and may in the coming years influence political decisions to be taken on what to do with Lebanon's 'memory deficit.' Should Lebanon have a truth and reconciliation committee? A truth report? A war museum, new monuments? If any of these plans materialise, the Lebanese state and the people involved will have to take a principled stand on whether memory as idiom for national unity or memory as the naked reflection of lived experience – in other words, truth – should guide its expression. Given Lebanon's latest travails in 2006, the question remains when the right moment will materialise for a head-on confrontation with Lebanon's ghosts as long as new human tragedies keep piling up.

References

Burke, Edmund III, Orientalism and World History: Representing Middle Eastern Nationalism and Islamism in the Twentieth Century. *Theory and Society* 27 (3):589-607, 1998.

Halbwachs, Maurice, *On Collective Memory*. Chicago: University of Chicago Press, 1992.

Haugbolle, Sune, Public and Private Memory of the Lebanese Civil War. *Comparative Studies of South Asia, Africa, and the Middle East* 25 (1):191-203, 2005

————, Spatial representation of sectarian national identity in residential Beirut. In *Secular Publicities: Visual practices and the transformation of national publics in the Middle East and South Asia*, edited by M. Yahya. Ann Arbour: University of Michigan Press, 2005.

Humphrey, Michael, *The Politics of Atrocity and Reconciliation: from Terror to Trauma*. London: Routledge, 2002.

Khalaf, Samir, *Beirut Reclaimed: Reflections on Urban Design and the Restoration of Civility*. Beirut: Dar an-Nahar, 1993.

Leenders, Reinoud, How UN Pressure on Hizballah Impedes Lebanese Reform. *Middle East Report Online* May 23 2006. http://www.merip.org/mero/mero052306.html.

Makarem, Amal, ed., *Mémoire Pour l'Avenir, Dhakirat lil-ghad, Memory for the Future: Actes du Colloque tenu à la Maison des Nations Unies, ESCWA (Beyrouth)*. Beirut: Dar an-Nahar, 2002.

Makdisi, Ussama S, *The Culture of Sectarianism: Community, History, and Violence in Nineteenth-Century Ottoman Lebanon*. Berkeley: University of California Press, 2000.

Malinowski, Branislaw, *A Scientific Theory of Culture*. New York: Galaxy Books, 1960.

Minow, Martha, *Breaking the Cycles of Hatred: Memory, Law, and Repair.* Princeton: Princeton University Press, 2002.

Peleikis, Anja, The Making and Unmaking of Memories: The Case of a Multi-Confessional Village in Lebanon. In *Memory and Violence in the Middle East and North Africa,* edited by U. Makdisi and P. Silverstein. Indianapolis: Indiana University Press, 2006.

Reinkowski, Marius, National Identity in Lebanon Since 1990. *Orient* 38:493-515, 1997.

Safa, Oussama, Lebanon Springs Forward. *Journal of Democracy* 17 (1):22-37, 2006.

Salmon, Jago, Militia Politics: the Formation and Organisation of Irregular Armed Forces in Sudan (1985-2001) and Lebanon (1975-1991), Politics, Humboldt, Berlin, 2006.

Tueni, Ghassan, *Une Guerre Pour les Autres.* Paris: JC Lattes, 1985.

Van Der Veer, Peter, The Victim's Tale: Memory and Forgetting in the Story of Violence. In *Religion Between Violence and Reconciliation,* edited by T Scheffler. Beirut: Ergon Verlag, 2002.

Part III

The Politics of Reform:
An Agenda for the Future

Chapter Seven

Managing Political Change in Lebanon: Challenges and Prospects

Michael Johnson

Lebanon's political system faces many challenges and, at the time of writing, its prospects are not particularly promising. An understanding of the current state of affairs requires a consideration of developments since Syria ended the civil war in 1990, because problems over a continuing conflict with Israel, relatively poor economic growth and increasing public debt were all exacerbated by the Syrian occupation of Lebanon. These challenges, however, continued even after Syrian troops withdrew in 2005. Damascus still exerted pressure on the Lebanese polity, both directly by assassination and indirectly through its Lebanese Shi'ite clients; and the Sunni Prime Minister and his allies sought countervailing help from the United States and Europe – in effect creating a local proxy conflict in the American-led 'war on terror'. What makes Lebanon so vulnerable to these external pressures are the sectarian divisions within civil society and the delicate balance of power in its confessional system of government. Thus of all the challenges facing Lebanon, managing a move away from confessionalism is perhaps the most pressing.

Confessionalism and romantic nationalism

Although Syria suppressed the militias in 1990-91, it had, like Libya, Iraq, Israel, the United States and others, done much to prolong the warfare at different times since 1975. It would be naive to think that Lebanese fighters were innocents manipulated by outside forces. They were equally adept at manipulating their backers and were even capable of inflicting defeats on foreign forces in Lebanon. But the fighters were a minority of the population. An overwhelming majority of Lebanese in the 1980s wanted a liberal-democratic end to the war, and an antiwar movement had developed in civil society (Hanf 1993: 519-34, 639-40). The militias became increasingly unpopular and it is clear they could not have fought for as long and as fiercely as they did without material and political support from outside.

External interference not only prolonged the war but was also the main cause of its starting in 1975. Whatever sympathy we might have for the plight of the Palestinian refugees, it cannot be denied that their armed liberation movement – along with associated interferences by Arab and Israeli governments – contributed more than any other factor to the militarisation of Lebanese politics. We should not idealise the pre-war political system. Prominent politicians or 'zaims' (zu'ama') had co-operated with, and often encouraged, a violent culture of honour and feuding. But the feud was a limited and mediated form of conflict. It was not conducted at a level of violence comparable with the ethno-confessional warfare in the 1970s and 1980s (Johnson 2001: 25–69). Also, governmental reformism in the 1960s had demonstrated that, at a time of relative regional stability, groups as different as Kamal Jumblatt's Progressive Socialist Party and the Maronite Phalanges could co-operate with an astute president in an essentially liberal project to create a united Lebanese nation.

In the 1970s a potential partnership between a liberal state and the organisations of civil society was massively undermined by the violent activities of Palestinian commandos and a minority of the Lebanese people who received material aid and encouragement from their external sponsors. However, in the latter half of the 1980s, liberal society reasserted itself. A movement called 'Women Against War' marched on parliament; the secular and multiconfessional confederation of trade unions, the *Confédération Générale des Travailleurs Libanais* (CGTL), led a series of mass protests against the war; and the professional associations of lawyers, doctors and engineers excluded representatives of the militias from their governing bodies (Hanf 1993: 639-40). Such developments demonstrated the strength and vitality of civil society, auguring well for any post-war settlement and demonstrating that significant sections of that society could live together in confessional harmony.

Lebanon's civil society was in many respects highly developed with its independent schools and universities, hospitals and clinics, its trade unions and professional organisations. Nevertheless, many of these organisations were divided each from the other by confessionalism; and schools and hospitals, in particular, were funded by religious foundations that were often closely linked to the patronage networks of confessional *zaims*. Had it not been for external interference, the separation between such organisations could have been overcome, but if we are interested in a stable future for Lebanon it would surely be sensible to encourage the promotion of inclusive, as opposed to confessionally exclusive forms of organisation. It is therefore worrying that the new Lebanon has been constructed along the same confessional lines as the old.

Under the terms of the Ta'if Accord negotiated in Saudi Arabia in 1989, the political imbalance in favour of Christians was changed. The powers of the Maronite president were circumscribed, the remits of the Prime Minister and the speaker of the parliamentary assembly extended, and the ratio of Christian to Muslim members of parliament was changed from 6:5 to an equal representation of the two communities. But the presidency was still reserved for a Maronite Christian, the premiership for a Sunni Muslim, the parliamentary speakership for a Shi'ite Muslim, and the seats in parliament for the different sects according to their rough size in the population. There is thus a continuance of the confessional principle in political representation, which many would say weakens a sense of Lebanese national identity and encourages parochial forms of leadership and the sorts of divisions that contributed to 15 years of civil war.

The secular organisations and trade unions at the forefront of civil society's antiwar movement were virtually ignored in a *pax Syriana* that for most of the 1990s seemed intent upon incorporating into Lebanon's 'Second Republic' the sectarian confessional warlords who had done so much to destroy the country in the 1970s and 1980s. While some Christian opposition leaders remained in exile, other warlords who were prepared to co-operate were elected to parliament and recruited to ministries. Elie Hobeika, the former Phalangist and mastermind of the 1982 massacres of Palestinians in Sabra and Shatila, had switched his loyalties to Syria in 1985, was elected to parliament in 1992 and 1996 and served as minister for electricity; the Druze *zaim* Walid Jumblatt was elected from a carefully gerrymandered constituency in all four elections between 1992 and 2005, and in the 1990s served as minister for displaced persons; and Nabih Berri, the leader of the Shi'ite Amal, was also successful in all elections and served as speaker of the parliament for most of the 1990s and continues to hold the office today.

Perhaps the local power of the militia leaders made such an incorporation a pragmatic necessity, and in the immediate aftermath of the civil wars it might well have been sensible to opt for a continuation of confessional representation, just as Michel Chiha, the architect of Lebanon's 1926 constitution, had felt it was a temporary necessity to heal divisions and create the conditions for a truly liberal and inclusive nationalism. But in the longer term it would surely be advisable to move to a secular system.

Confessional representation inevitably favours strong communal leaders and warlords. Even those pre-war *zaims* who had worked hard to contain communal conflict were in effect confessional leaders, and they had certainly laid great emphasis on communal honour when it came to managing their clienteles.

Because values of honour and violence were built into the clientelist structures of the pre-war state, some young men had been encouraged by the political establishment to assert their masculinity in an heroic culture of pride, feuding and vengeance (Johnson 2001: 47-54). It is oversimplified to see a direct link between political feuding and confessional war (Johnson 2001: 60-9, 122-31). Nevertheless, the values of personal honour and vengeance, coupled with ideas about authoritarian and patriarchal leadership, are characteristics of romantic or ethnic nationalism which, when they are combined with notions of common ancestors and a shared blood, can encourage extreme forms of ethnic identity and hostility (Johnson 2001: 132-223).

Whether it took the form of Maronite particularism, Muslim Arabism, or Islamic militancy, ethnic nationalism in Lebanon was an exclusive and nostalgic reaction against modernity, as compared with an inclusive and forward-looking liberal nationalism that embraced the modern with enthusiasm. An inclusive form of Lebanese nationalism was central to the ideas of the National Pact, which paved the way to independence in 1943, and it was also a normative theme during the reformist regimes of the 1960s. Given that liberal nationalism was so influential in modern Lebanon, and that a network of effective civil-society groups operated even under Syrian tutelage (*LCPS* 1999), it is perhaps surprising that patriarchy and romanticism remain so prominent in the political culture. While, for example, some new and secular leaders (including women) were elected to the Lebanese parliament in the post-war elections of 1992, 1996, 2000 and 2005, many of the most successful politicians were communal militants. Despite the growth of a sense of Lebanese nationalism in civil society in reaction to the confessional warlords and their violent depredations, there is still considerable electoral support for the former militias that have now become influential political parties in the Second Republic.

There is obviously a continuing tension in Lebanese civil society between the values of liberal and romantic nationalism. A sample survey of 1987 (Hanf 1993: 523-34) suggests that while a minority of the population was fully committed to political reform and a thorough secularisation, a larger group gave support to a confessional system. The majority, however, was prepared to accept some form of secular government so long as there were confessional safeguards. This solution was suggested by the Ta'if agreement that talked of the eventual establishment of a bicameral parliament, with a lower house elected on a secular basis and a senate selected by confessional representation. The agreement stated that 'the abolition of confessionalism' was 'a vital national objective' and should be achieved 'in stages' (Hanf 1993: 585-8). However, no timetable was set for a new political system; and although there was some popular support for the idea, there has been little sign of any governmental momentum towards it.

Reconstruction and the economy

Initially, the recovery of Lebanon after the civil war was impressive. A considerable amount of economic activity was generated by reconstruction. Electricity and water supplies were repaired and enhanced, telecommunications expanded, old hotels like the Phoenicia were renovated and new ones built, and the Beirut property company, Solidere, embarked on an ambitious programme to rebuild the city's central business district. Even banking made a recovery through money laundering, currency speculation and subscribing to treasury bills.

After the 1992 elections, a new cabinet was formed under an extra-parliamentary Prime Minister, Rafiq al-Hariri, a billionaire with Saudi as well as Lebanese citizenship. His appointment stimulated confidence, particularly because he was prepared to invest much of his personal fortune in reconstruction. The currency stabilised, rates of inflation and unemployment fell, and impressive economic growth rates of Gross Domestic Product were achieved at 9 per cent in 1994 and 6.5 per cent in 1995 (Perthes 1997). Based on the expectation that Lebanon would regain its pre-war status as a centre of business and tourism, this period of construction-led growth was severely curtailed by fighting between

Hezbollah and Israel in 1996 leading to Israeli air raids and artillery bombardments in April. Annual growth rates declined to 4 per cent in 1996 and 1997, and GDP actually contracted by 1 per cent in 1999, only making modest improvements in the early years of the new millennium (*MENA* 2006: 708).

In 1997 the budget deficit rose to 59 per cent of state expenditure and the government came to rely on heavy borrowing requirements (*MEED*, 19 June 1998). As a result, interest rates were high and this meant that lending to the private sector was squeezed, delaying the start of revenue-earning projects and contributing to the lower rate of economic growth. Some argued that the government should raise taxes – income and corporation tax had been lowered to a flat rate of 10 per cent, and there was certainly a case for an increase. But for many, including the government, the answer lay in foreign aid, concessionary finance, and private investment. The problem was that these would not be as forthcoming as expected while the security situation in relation to Israel was so uncertain.

The refusal to raise taxes was seen as an example of the government's intention to favour the economic elite at the expense of the poor. It was estimated that more than 25 per cent of the population lived below the poverty line in 1996 (Perthes 1997), while those close to the regime made fabulous profits from an extraordinarily corrupt and politicized economy (Leenders 2004). A UN study claimed the government lost over US $1,000 million annually to corruption in public administration (*MENA* 2006: 710), and stories of bribes and kickbacks were legion. It was estimated, for example, that the successful tender for the southern extension of the coastal motorway was overpriced by millions of dollars, and much was made of the fact that the firm that had the contract was run by the wife of Nabih Berri, the leader of Amal and speaker of the parliament (Perthes 1997: 17).

In 1998, President Elias Hrawi's extended period of office came to an end, and Emile Lahoud, the commander of the Lebanese armed forces, was elected in his place with a commitment to stamp out corruption and deal with the budget deficit. The new president worked closely with a technocratic government under the premiership of Salim al-Hoss, and in April 1999 a reformist budget was presented to parliament. Although the deficit had decreased in Rafiq al-Hariri's last year of office to 43 per cent of government expenditure, it was still large, and the new finance minister announced his intention of reducing it much further from its current level of 14 per cent of GDP. The budget raised income and corporation taxes to a rate of 15 per cent, and announced an indirect 'value-added' tax (VAT) on a wide range of goods and services. Along with plans to privatize government holdings in utilities, these measures stimulated a degree of confidence and the growth rate of GDP was predicted to rise in the new millennium (*MEED*, 11 December 1998 and 23 April 1999).

A year later there was no improvement. Indeed, the situation was worse than ever. Total public debt was estimated at 130 per cent of GDP, and the budget deficit had increased to nearly 52 per cent of government expenditure or about 15 per cent of GDP (*MEED*, 16 June 2000). The prospects for lifting the economy out of recession in 2000 were very limited so long as investors were discouraged by the lack of progress in a peace agreement between Israel and Syria. In addition, Hoss's government was too politically weak to carry forward its fiscal adjustment programme: parliament refused support for a value-added tax, and proposals for the privatisation of public utilities were not implemented.

Rafiq al-Hariri returned to the premiership after defeating Salim al-Hoss in the 2000 elections. With a stronger control of the parliament, the new government was able to introduce VAT and start the process of privatisation and the reduction of the public-sector payroll. Nevertheless, the continued reliance on domestic and foreign borrowing meant that the national public debt continued to increase. In 1996 public debt was 79 per cent of GDP, by the end of 2000 it was 135 per cent, and in February 2006 it had risen to 186 per cent. In July and August 2006, the destruction of infrastructure and public and private buildings during another war between Hezbollah and Israel amounted to an estimated cost of US$2,500 million. This could only add to

Lebanon's debt problems, but with the public debt amounting to well over US $30 billion the greater threat to the Lebanese economy was the way the continuing conflict with Israel was preventing the previously expected development of business and tourism (*MENA* 2006: 707, 710, 717-18).

Hezbollah's war with Israel

With funding from Iran, Hezbollah was able to provide extensive educational, welfare and health services to its clientele. Coupled with its militant stance against Israel this made it immensely popular within the Shi'ite community. But resentment was periodically expressed in other communities – and among some sections of the Shi'ites themselves – about Hezbollah's guerrilla war against Israeli forces in southern Lebanon. A regional peace settlement would have ended the fighting, but Damascus was in no hurry to achieve this and the warfare was interpreted as a ploy by the Syrian president, Hafez al-Assad, to strengthen his hand in any negotiations with Israel. Entirely subordinate to Damascus, the Lebanese government could not negotiate with Israel in its own right, and meanwhile Israeli reprisal raids undermined the prospects for foreign investment and job-creation in the Lebanese economy. Thus, although Hezbollah was seen by some as part of the opposition movement in civil society, others saw it as a collaborator with an occupying power that was using the Lebanese people and their political integrity as pawns in a dispute with Israel.

Israel launched a massive air and artillery reprisal in April 1996. 'Operation Grapes of Wrath' involved some 600 air raids against Hezbollah and civilian targets in a little over a fortnight. 400,000 people were displaced from southern Lebanon, and many were killed or maimed. In the most horrific incident of the operation, Israeli artillery fired on a United Nations observation post at Qana where a number of civilians had taken shelter. Over a hundred people were killed in the UN compound and a similar number wounded. Such carnage, accompanied by the influx of frightened and exhausted refugees to Beirut, prompted an upsurge of national feeling throughout Lebanon. Individuals and non-governmental organisations provided help to the homeless, there were demonstrations of solidarity with the south, and a national day of mourning was declared for the victims. (Harris 1997: 319; Hollis and Shehadi 1996).

Once more, when faced with adversity, large sections of civil society revealed a significant sense of unity. Nevertheless, attitudes toward Hezbollah remained ambivalent and Rafiq al-Hariri eventually complained of the militia's 'boastful behaviour and its logic of constantly defying the state' (*MEED*, 21 June 1996). This reflected a wider Lebanese opposition to an Iranian-backed militia that threatened political stability. Despite moderating its theocratic stance, Hezbollah still represented militant Islamic values that were alien to Lebanese culture, and this was a matter of concern to Nabih Berri's Amal as well as Sunnis and Christians.

Overall, however, Hezbollah was seen by many as a force committed to the restoration of Lebanese territory, a reputation that was considerably enhanced when, after more fighting in February 2000 between the militia and Israel, and more reprisal bombing raids, Israel unilaterally withdrew from southern Lebanon in May. As members of the South Lebanese Army militia and their families fled to Israel, and their prisoners were freed from the notorious Khiam torture and detention centre, crowds gathered all over the country to celebrate a liberation brought about by the tenacity and bravery of the Hezbollah fighters (*MEED*, 18 February 2000 and 2 June 2000). Hezbollah's victory generated tensions with Amal as both groups competed for the leadership of the Shi'ite community, and there were armed clashes between them in June and July after Amal had sought to claim some of the credit for the Israeli withdrawal (*MEIB*, 1 July 2000; *MEIB*, 'Intelligence Briefs', 5 August 2000).

Repression of civil society

No one could stand for election to parliament without Syria's blessing. Some candidates whose loyalty to Damascus was not enthusiastic were tolerated, but any critic of the Syrian occupation who commanded a significant popular vote was excluded. Thus while the pro-Syrian members of the Frangieh clan were guaranteed that one of their number – Suleiman Frangieh, the son of the murdered warlord Tony Frangieh – would be elected to parliament, other Maronites such as the Jemayels and Chamouns were excluded, with Amin Jemayel and Dory Chamoun deciding their security could only be guaranteed abroad.

The self-imposed exile of these leaders reflected a widespread Maronite disenchantment with the Second Republic. Many Christians had supported General Michel Aoun's failed attempt to unite the Lebanese against the Syrians in 1989-90. Shortly after the defeat of Aoun's forces in October 1990, one of his lieutenants, Dany Chamoun, the leader of the Liberal National Party's militia and son of the former president, Camille Chamoun, was assassinated along with his wife and two children in their home near the general's headquarters. Suspicion fell on another Maronite warlord, Samir Geagea, who had led his faction of the Lebanese Forces (LF) against Aoun in favour of an accommodation with the Syrian-sponsored Ta'if Accord. Geagea's apparent collaboration with Damascus meant he was unpopular in his community, but he soon demonstrated he was not prepared to accept a permanent Syrian rule. His relations with the post-war government deteriorated, and he began to articulate a Maronite opposition to the continued occupation of Lebanon by Syrian troops.

Then, in February 1994, when Geagea's LF was transforming itself into a political party, a bomb exploded in a Maronite church, killing ten people. Many Christians blamed the Syrians and Lebanon's security forces, arguing that the bombing was an attempt to terrorize the Maronites and justify further repression. The Syrians, on the other hand, claimed a Maronite conspiracy. The LF was banned and Geagea was arrested and charged with organising both the bombing and the murder of Dany Chamoun. The bombing charge came to lack credibility, but Geagea was found guilty of the Chamoun assassination and sentenced to life imprisonment. (Harris 1997: 277, 290 and 300-1). Further charges were brought against Geagea in later years and, at different trials, he was sentenced to life imprisonment for the attempted murder of Michel al-Murr in 1991, life for the assassination of the Lebanese Prime Minister, Rashid Karami, in 1987, and life again for the murder of an LF official in 1989. At his trial for the assassination of Rashid Karami, Geagea complained of 'selective justice' (*MEIB*, July 1999). He pointed out that although it possessed intelligence about their identities, the government had not charged those who had killed the Lebanese president René Mouawad in November 1989, the Lebanese *mufti* (Sunni juriconsult) Sheikh Hassan Khalid in May 1989, and the Druze leader Kamal Jumblatt in 1977. The implication was clear: the assassins had all been agents of Syria and were therefore immune. Why were some warlords and other killers granted an amnesty and not the leader of the Lebanese Forces?

The allegiance of the largest Christian confession to the post-Ta'if regime remained problematic. The Lebanese Forces produced a hagiography of Samir Geagea on their website alongside a similar treatment of another victim of the Syrians, Bachir Jemayel, the LF leader and Lebanese president-elect who had been murdered in 1982, and whose assassin had been freed from prison when the Syrian army took control of East Beirut in 1990. This and other websites talked of a plucky and tenacious Maronite resistance to Syrian hegemony, and provided details of political prisoners, torture and other abuses of human rights. Maronite rivals of the LF were also active. In Paris, General Michel Aoun, Dory Chamoun (Dany's brother) and Amin Jemayel (the former president of Lebanon and Bachir's brother) formed an alliance to press for Syrian withdrawal and the re-establishment of Lebanese sovereignty. Although this group and Geagea's LF were unable to exercise any significant influence over events in a Lebanon so much under the control of Damascus, they did represent a considerable degree of privately expressed hostility within the Maronite community.

Opposition persisted in all communities to the occupying power. Although there were some Syrian troop withdrawals, the

Syrian and Lebanese security services continued to maintain a police state. Throughout the 1990s, there was little action on the part of Lebanese governments to trace the whereabouts of Lebanese and Palestinians, Christians and Muslims, who had 'disappeared' and were thought to be imprisoned in Syria; and opponents of the regime were arbitrarily arrested, tortured and held incommunicado (Sherry 1997).

Popular protest in civil society was ruthlessly suppressed, and even opinions remotely critical of the regime were censored. In February 1996, for example, when the CGTL unions organised a general strike in pursuit of higher salaries, it was put down by the Lebanese army and a curfew imposed in the major towns and cities (*MENA* 1998: 752). Then in November, the army was deployed again to prevent demonstrations demanding the rescinding of legislation that would restrict Lebanese broadcasting to six television and 12 radio stations. There was no doubt that the civil war had contributed to a chaotic state of broadcasting, with many small stations representing narrow sectarian interests. But the government's intention to license only a limited number of companies was seen as an attempt to restrict freedom of expression in the political and financial interests of the regime. Of four private television networks granted licences under the new law, one belonged to Rafiq al-Hariri, one to Nabih Berri, and another to the brother of Michel al-Murr, the Greek Orthodox minister of the interior. Only eleven private radio stations from an estimated total of 150 were granted licences; and of the three allowed to broadcast news, one was owned by Hariri and another by Berri. More attacks on the independent media came in late December 1996 when, after a mysterious machine-rifle attack on a bus carrying Syrian migrant workers, some fifty people were arrested, including a journalist for the prestigious daily newspaper *An-Nahar*. Concern was expressed that these arrests were part of a pattern of excessively heavy clampdowns by the government and Syrian authorities. (*MEED*, 11 October 1996 to 17 January 1997).

The annual reports of Amnesty International (1997-2006) suggest there was some improvement in the government's human rights record toward the end of the 1990s. For example, although each year dozens of people were arrested on political grounds, most were released without charge after a few hours or days. Some long-term prisoners were freed as well. But despite encouraging signs, there were still many abuses of human rights. The practice of the judicial process in political cases fell short of international fair-trial standards, students were arrested during demonstrations, political activists were tortured, and some simply 'disappeared', all with the aim of terrorising the Lebanese into accepting the new order. Meanwhile, Syrians and Lebanese close to the corrupt regime enriched themselves, with apparently little regard for the rest of the population. Large numbers of people eked out a living below the poverty line, forced to compete with a massive influx of migrant workers from Syria who had flooded the labour market. Representing some of the poorest members of its community, Hezbollah became increasingly oppositional, participating with the trade unions in anti-government protests, and winning widespread Shi'ite support in the poverty-stricken suburbs of Beirut (*MEED*, 19 June 1998).

Removing the Syrians

When General Emile Lahoud took over as the new president of Lebanon in November 1998, he gave a warmly received speech to the parliament, pledging his 'intent and determination' to address issues of governmental corruption and what he called the 'sectarian' or confessional 'protection' of those who abused their offices (*MEED*, 11 December 1998: 2). This was a thinly veiled attack on the way the 'troika' of President Hrawi, Premier Hariri and Speaker Berri – along with long-serving and favoured ministers – had divided public works contracts, kickbacks and other spoils of office among themselves and their confessional clients in what became known as the 'allotment' (*muhassa*) system (Leenders 2004).

Hariri made his displeasure known and was replaced as Prime Minister by Salim al-Hoss, a highly respected member of parliament for Beirut. A former banker, Hoss was a technocrat in the

'Chehabist' mould who had established his political reputation when he first served as premier (1976-80) during the regime of President Elias Sarkis, a man who had run Fouad Chehab's presidential office in the 1960s. It seemed appropriate that Hoss should now be Prime Minister to a president who, like Chehab, had previously been commander-in-chief of the armed forces. In place of Hariri's 30-member cabinet, Hoss formed a government of 15 ministers, none of whom had been a militia leader. (*MEED*, 18 December 1998).

Rafiq al-Hariri, Walid Jumblatt and others were investigated on charges of corruption and, in 1999, 23 administrative officials – most of them appointed as clients of Hariri or Jumblatt – were removed from office (*MENA* 2006: 687). Many Lebanese had turned against Hariri's corrupt and repressive government, and so Emile Lahoud's regime, with its promises to root out corruption and deal with the budget deficit, was greeted with a sense of public optimism. There was also considerable Christian support for a president who was seen as a much stronger Maronite leader than Elias Hrawi had ever been. But there was still a clear recognition that the government was ultimately subservient to Syria. Lahoud was apparently close to Bashar al-Assad, Hafez al-Assad's son, who had been given charge of Lebanon as part of a process to prepare him for succeeding his father as president of Syria. Lahoud and Bashar, it was said, shared a determination to stamp out governmental corruption. There were also suggestions that Bashar had wanted to remove Hariri from the premiership in 1998 because he was closely associated with a Syrian old-guard that might have posed a threat to Bashar's presidential ambitions (Gambill 2000: 2-3).

It is clear that the gradual distancing between Damascus and Rafiq al-Hariri started when his Syrian patrons were removed by Bashar al-Assad, as indeed it is also clear that Walid Jumblatt's growing opposition to the Syrian presence began at the same time. Jumblatt lost his ministerial portfolio when Hariri was forced from power, and in 1999 the Druze *zaim* became a spokesman for those politicians who had been marginalised since Emile Lahoud became president. At a time when power seemed to be slipping away from the former warlords to Lebanese security and intelligence officers appointed by Lahoud, Jumblatt even complained of a 'neo-military regime' (*MEIB*, August 1999).

In the event, the succession of Bashar proceeded smoothly after Hafez al-Assad died in June 2000. But although the new presidents of Lebanon and Syria seemed close, they were not able to prevent Hariri's comeback in the 2000 parliamentary elections. President Lahoud and Prime Minister Hoss had promised to end corruption and promote economic recovery. Instead public debt had increased, the recession had deepened, and in consequence people turned against a failed technocratic government – some of them presumably encouraged by payments from the millions of dollars allegedly spent by Hariri on his election campaign (*MENA* 2006: 689). Despite an attempt to weaken him by dividing the large Beirut constituency into three – thus providing Hoss with a supposedly safe seat – Hariri and his allies won the overwhelming support of the electorate and took 18 of the city's 19 seats, even defeating Hoss in his gerrymandered constituency. In October 2000 – apparently back in favour with the Syrian government – Hariri formed a new cabinet.

Opposition to the Syrian occupation grew after the withdrawal of Israeli forces from southern Lebanon and the death of Hafez al-Assad. Newspaper editors and human rights activists became more outspoken, and in September 2000 the council of Maronite bishops explicitly called for the Syrians to leave Lebanon. Chaired by the Maronite patriarch and cardinal, Nasrallah Sfeir, the council issued a document (translated in *MEIB*, 5 October 2000) condemning the corrupt parliamentary elections, the dire state of the economy and the coercive political system. This remarkably critical declaration spoke of citizens who 'feign loyalty' to the government, but who in reality were 'full of resentment', and who if they protested openly would be 'tracked down' and imprisoned in Syria. President Lahoud immediately accused the bishops' council of 'encouraging sectarian bigotry', but the Lebanese and Syrian regimes felt unable to act any more severely against a body protected by the Catholic church and the Vatican. Instead, they encouraged Muslim spiritual leaders to condemn the council's declaration. The Sunni *mufti* and other Sunni, Shi'ite and Druze sheikhs spoke of their 'astonishment' and reminded their people of the sacrifices made by 'sisterly Syria' to preserve a united Lebanon (Gibreel and Gambill 2000: 2). In so doing, of course, they encouraged the confessional tension and enmity that Lahoud had earlier condemned.

Increasingly open criticism of the Syrian occupation provoked more confessional division and even some violence. In 2001 university students supporting the exiled Maronite leader, Michel Aoun, demonstrated, and perhaps as many as 100,000 Christians lined the streets to welcome Cardinal Sfeir back from a visit to the United States where he had again called for Syrian withdrawal. Rival groups threatened to mount demonstrations, with Christians supporting withdrawal and Muslims – and especially Shi'ites – dominating the pro-Syrian group. Under increasing international pressure, the Syrians withdrew troops from parts of Beirut and Mount Lebanon, and in August 2001 Cardinal Sfeir and Walid Jumblatt met in the Chouf to mark a reconciliation between the Maronite and Druze communities. Soon after this, many Christian activists were arrested and, in the mass protests that followed, more were taken into custody, members of Aoun's Free Patriotic Movement and Dory Chamoun's Liberal National Party being particularly targeted. (*MENA* 2006: 695).

Angered that he had not been consulted over the security crackdown, Prime Minister Hariri found it increasingly difficult to work with President Lahoud, and relations worsened as they and the other member of the troika, Speaker Nabih Berri, quarrelled over the distribution of top civil service posts, the privatisation programme, and the awarding of development contracts. Then in 2003, to Hariri's exasperation, Lahoud began to canvass support for renewing his term of office which was due to expire in November 2004. Lahoud and Hariri visited Damascus to put their case, but the Syrians eventually backed Lahoud, allowing him a three-year extension which was ratified in September 2004 by the required two-thirds majority in parliament.

Syria justified the extension in terms of a need to maintain governmental continuity at a time of considerable regional and internal instability. There was warfare in Iraq and Palestine, and the

Arab-Israeli conflict threatened regional security. Elie Hobeika, the former Phalangist had been killed by a car bomb in January 2002, possibly by Israeli agents or a rival Christian group; and another probable victim of Israel, Jihad Jibril, a leader of the Popular Front for the Liberation of Palestine (General Command), had been assassinated by a car bomb in May 2002. Severe fighting between rival Palestinian factions later in the year and the discovery of arms caches had led to exchanges of fire between Lebanese army units and Palestinian fighters in which at least one soldier and three Palestinians were killed. In June 2003 Hariri's television station in Beirut was attacked by rockets fired by Palestinian Islamists, and in May 2004 a strike called by the CGTL led to rioting in the Shi'ite suburbs of southern Beirut during which army units opened fire, killing three protesters and wounding thirty. (*MENA* 2006: 695–98).

Hariri went along with the Syrian diktat on Lahoud's renewal, but he resigned from the premiership in October 2004. While he did not speak openly against the Syrians, he was now seen as lined up with the anti-Syrian faction grouped around Walid Jumblatt and the recently formed Qurnet Shehwan Gathering, named after the town in the Metn district of Mount Lebanon where a group backed by Cardinal Sfeir and mainly composed of Maronite politicians had established a movement to oppose the Syrian occupation. Anti-Syrian sentiments – mainly Christian and Druze, but with some Sunni support – were encouraged by UN Security Council resolution 1559, sponsored by the USA, France, the UK and Germany, and calling for an immediate Syrian withdrawal, free elections and the disbanding and disarming of all militias.

Agents of Syria responded with a campaign of what appeared to be state-sponsored terror. Marwan Hamadeh, a Jumblattist Druze who had resigned his ministry in protest against Emile Lahoud's extension of office, was severely injured and his driver killed by a car bomb in October 2004. A few months later, in February 2005, Rafiq al-Hariri and 14 others were killed when a huge bomb exploded as his motorcade passed near Beirut's seafront. Mass demonstrations of protest against this outrage were held across the country, and counter-demonstrations were organised in support of the Syrian presence by Hezbollah and Amal. On 14 March, hundreds of thousands of anti-Syrian demonstrators – mainly Christians, Sunnis and Druze – gathered in Beirut's Martyrs' Square and, now under immense pressure, Damascus ordered a phased but complete withdrawal of its troops by the end of April.

As the Syrians were leaving Lebanon, Walid Jumblatt opened talks with representatives of Hezbollah and later with Nabih Berri, the leader of Amal. It seemed Jumblatt was repositioning himself, maintaining close relations with Rafiq al-Hariri's son Saad but mending his bridges with the pro-Syrian Shi'ite parties (*Daily Star,* 14 June 2005). When it was announced that the 2005 parliamentary elections would be held under the 2000 electoral law, many Christians were angry. The constituency boundaries were drawn in such a way that most of the 64 seats reserved for Christians in the 128-seat parliament were in Muslim majority areas, thus lessening the likelihood of strong Christian champions being elected. Christians complained that the 2000 law was a Syrian device designed to weaken Maronite and other Christian opposition to the occupation. Now the Syrians had gone, what were Saad al-Hariri and Jumblatt doing with pro-Syrian Berri? Was this another Muslim alliance against the Christians?

In the first round of elections in May 2005, Saad al-Hariri and his allies won all the seats in Beirut's three constituencies, nine of them uncontested, including seven of the nine Christian seats. Some relatively popular Christian candidates were included on Hariri's lists, such as Gibran Tueni, the Greek Orthodox editor-proprietor of *An-Nahar,* and Solange Jemayel, the Maronite widow of the warlord Bachir Jemayel. But most of the Christians elected were seen as token representatives, their potential opponents knowing they could not win against the Hariri electoral machine. A week later, the combined lists of Amal and Hezbollah swept the board in South Lebanon, six of the 23 members of parliament elected unopposed, including Rafiq al-Hariri's sister in Sidon and three of the four Christian members. (Details of the 2005 elections are from the Lebanese press May-June 2005, and *LibanVote,* www.libanvote.com).

The third round of elections saw Amal and Hezbollah victories in the Bekaa, but a surprise result in the Mount Lebanon constituencies of Jbeil-Kesrouan and Metn where Michel Aoun's Free Patriotic Movement and its allies won 15 seats, and in Zahle where Elias Skaff's bloc won five. Aoun had only recently returned from exile and this was a remarkable success. His alliance with the Greek Catholic *zaim*, Elias Skaff, won in those constituencies with a majority of Christian electors, Aoun winning one of seven Maronite seats in Jbeil-Kesrouan. By contrast, in the constituencies of Baabda-Aley and the Chouf, Walid Jumblatt and his allies were elected with Druze, Shi'ite and Sunni votes. Clearly Aoun represented the Christian ethos in the Maronite heartlands of the Mountain. But he was not able to carry his success through in North Lebanon where, in the final round of voting, lists allied to Saad al-Hariri – including the Christian Qurnet Shehwan Gathering – were overwhelmingly successful.

This produced a parliamentary majority for the so-called 'Rafiq al-Hariri Martyr bloc', which controlled most of the key ministries in the new government formed in July 2005 under the premiership of Fouad Siniora, a close associate of Rafiq al-Hariri who had

Distribution of seats in the Lebanese parliament after the 2005 elections	
Bloc	*Seats*
Rafiq al-Hariri Martyr bloc*	72
Resistance and Development bloc**	35
Free Patriotic Movement bloc***	19
Total	128

* Saad al-Hariri's Future Movement (36 seats), Walid Jumblatt's Progressive Socialist Party (16), Lebanese Forces (6), Qurnet Shehwan Gathering (6), Tripoli bloc (3) and others (5).

** Amal (15), Hezbollah (14), the Syrian Social Nationalist Party (2) and others (4).

*** Michel Aoun's Free Patriotic Movement (14), Elias Skaff bloc (3) and Michel al-Murr bloc (2).

Source: MENA 2006: 730.

served as finance minister in all Hariri's cabinets.

All major blocs in parliament except Michel Aoun's Free Patriotic Movement were represented in the 24-member cabinet – including for the first time Hezbollah. Despite Aoun's omission and some residual Maronite unease, there was general support for the new regime, especially when, the day before Siniora formed his government, parliament voted overwhelmingly to pardon Samir Geagea and free him from prison. His wife Strida Geagea and five other members of the Lebanese Forces party had already been elected to parliament as part of Hariri's alliance, and it was hoped that Geagea's release would now pave the way for a wider national reconciliation

The security situation, however, remained tense. There had been a number of sectarian incidents during the elections and, after the announcement of the vote on Geagea's release, one man was killed and 14 wounded when Christian and Shi'ite gunmen fired at each other across the civil war's 'Green Line' in Beirut – apparently Geagea's supporters had first shot in the air to celebrate their leader's impending freedom (*The Daily Star*, 20 July 2005). More worrying were a series of bomb attacks and assassinations, mostly, it seemed, the work of Syria or its agents. Just after the first round of the parliamentary elections, Samir Kassir, a leading anti-Syrian journalist was killed by a car bomb in Beirut. Two days after the final round of voting, Georges Hawi, former secretary-general of the Lebanese Communist Party and another outspoken critic of Syria's role in Lebanon was killed by another car bomb in Beirut. Three weeks later, in July, the deputy Prime Minister and defence minister, Elias al-Murr, survived a car bombing in a suburb of Beirut. This was mysterious as he was the son-in-law of President Emile Lahoud and considered close to the Syrians. A few days later, a car bomb exploded in a Christian district of Beirut, wounding 12 people. Then in September 2005 one person was killed and 22 wounded in a bomb attack on an apartment block in a Christian district of Beirut and, later in the month, May Chidiac, a prominent journalist and anchorwoman of a leading anti-Syrian TV station, lost an arm and a leg in a car bombing just north of

Beirut. At the end of a violent year, in December, Gibran Tueni, a member of parliament and managing editor of *An-Nahar*, was killed by a roadside bomb in a suburb of Beirut. (Details of the assassinations are from the Lebanese and international press, and from *MENA* 2006: 701).

Despite the uncertain security situation, there was some optimism in the first half of 2006. The Syrians had gone, free elections had been held, and a reasonable distribution of power had emerged in parliament and government. A commission was established to design a new electoral law, President Lahoud did not have much more of his extended term to serve, and there were signs that a truly independent Lebanon might be attractive to investors. The sheer size of the demonstrations against the Syrians had encouraged students, members of non-governmental organisations, trade unionists and members of professional associations that they rather than the old elites might soon come into their own. The sense of an exciting new beginning was palpable.

Nevertheless, there were two significant communities outside this consensus. The Palestinian refugees remained a demographic and political problem, particularly as some Palestinian 'camps' or districts were home to armed militias. The latter were not a great threat and seemed to be more concerned to fight each other than the Lebanese or Israeli armies, but of much greater concern were the growing ties between Palestinians and the other excluded community, the Shi'ites. Hezbollah militiamen continued to fight Israeli troops in and around the Sheba Farms on the southern border. This was a small area of territory Israel had captured from the Syrians in 1967, but its ownership had been contested and Syria had conveniently 'gifted' it to the Lebanese in 2000 when Israel withdrew from Lebanon. An excuse to maintain a Lebanese armed resistance against Israel, the Shebaa Farms had been used by Damascus as a ploy. Now the Syrians had left, many Lebanese asked why Hezbollah continued to fight. Even here, a solution seemed to emerge: the Lebanese government would seek a determination of the ownership of the Shebaa Farms in international law. If they really were Lebanese, then Israel would withdraw from them; if they were Syrian, then there was no justification for Hezbollah to fight to liberate them. In either event, Hezbollah could be persuaded to disarm.

As if to prevent this solution, a Hezbollah unit crossed the Israeli border in July 2006, capturing two and killing three Israeli soldiers. In reprisal, Israel launched massive air and artillery strikes and then a ground invasion into southern Lebanon, while Hezbollah launched rockets into northern Israel and engaged the Israeli army in guerrilla warfare until the conflict ended with a ceasefire in August. The war killed around 1,500 people – mostly Lebanese – and caused widespread destruction of roads, bridges and other infrastructure. This was a disaster for the Lebanese economy, and for those who wanted to see Hezbollah disarmed. While there had been considerable criticism of the militia's provocative actions in July, public opinion had once again swung behind Hezbollah as Israel punished the Lebanese and as the militia fought bravely and effectively to defend the Lebanese homeland.

Not long after the end of the fighting, the dreadful threat to the safety of Lebanese politicians and journalists was illustrated again when Pierre Jemayel, a member of parliament and minister for industry (and son of Amin Jemayel), was shot dead by gunmen in a Beirut suburb in November 2006. Some politicians had chosen to live abroad, others stayed at home with electronic security and retinues of bodyguards, while all of them lived with a growing sense of insecurity. That democratically elected members of the Lebanese parliament could be treated in this way by agents of a Syrian dictatorship was of course intolerable. Nevertheless, as the UN security council approved plans for a special tribunal to try those high-ranking Syrians and Lebanese suspected of plotting the assassination of Rafiq al-Hariri, Hezbollah and Amal pulled their five ministers out of the cabinet. They demanded a government of national unity – to include representatives of Michel Aoun's bloc, which had entered into an opportunistic alliance with the Shi'ite parties – and most observers thought Hezbollah and Amal wanted greater ministerial representation so they could veto and block the

UN tribunal.

A Christian minister also resigned, claiming he could not serve in a cabinet without Shi'ite representation. The resignations of six ministers and the death of Pierre Jemayel meant the government needed to lose only two more ministers before it became inquorate. The implication was not lost on many Lebanese who thought the Syrians might just remove two unfortunates by killing them.

Sheikh Hassan Nasrallah, Hezbollah's secretary-general, continued to pile on the pressure by calling his followers out on the streets, and in December 2006 downtown Beirut witnessed more massive demonstrations – this time made up of an unlikely alliance of Shi'ite militants and Maronite Aounists. Rocks were thrown in sectarian incidents, and in one clash between Hezbollah demonstrators and Sunnis in West Beirut a man was shot dead (*The Guardian*, 4 December 2006). The national unity generated during the war with Israel in the summer had given way to the confessional divisions of an earlier period. The fact that Michel Aoun's Christian supporters were demonstrating alongside their former Shi'ite enemies was not a reason for optimism: this was merely an alliance of convenience in which Aoun jockeyed for leadership of the Maronite community and presumably for the Lebanese presidency that would be vacated when Emile Lahoud left office in 2007. Much more significant – especially in view of the communal conflict in Iraq – was the growing hostility between Shi'ites and Sunnis, with the Shi'ite leaders backed by Iran and Syria and such Sunni leaders as Fouad Siniora and Saad al-Hariri drawing support from the United States.

Once more, Lebanon's confessional groups were acting as proxies for a wider global conflict.

The confessional challenge

The main political challenges facing Lebanon are the corruption of public life, an associated lack of public accountability, the continued state of war with Israel and the interference of external forces bidding for influence. Woven into all of these are perhaps the greatest challenges of confessional identity and politics (Beydoun 2004).

Lebanese administration has always been corrupt, but prior to the civil war corruption remained within 'reasonable' limits in that budget deficits were usually low (Gaspard 2004: 124). In the early 1990s Lebanon had one of the lowest levels of government debt in the world as measured as a percentage of GDP. By the early years of the new millennium it had one of the highest, and meanwhile reconstruction and economic growth were actually rather modest in extent, too much of the fiscal deficit funding corruption instead of development. The heightened levels of corruption in the Second Republic were due in large part to the lack of any accountability of the government to the electorate. Indeed until 2005 the client government was only really accountable to its Syrian patrons who enriched themselves by taking substantial cuts from the money passing up through the clientelist hierarchy.

Clearly a reformed political system that can hold the government to account is essential, and a fair and broadly accepted electoral law will no doubt help. But the peculiarities of Lebanese corruption are not confined to the political elite's relationship with external patrons. It is also structured by and through confessionalism, with such institutions as the troika and its allies ensuring that each community gets its share. In the 1990s, the Council for Development and Reconstruction was used for the benefit of Prime Minister Hariri's Sunnis, the Council for the South was controlled for his Shi'ite clients by the speaker, Nabih Berri, and the funds and resources attached to the ministry of displaced persons belonged to Walid Jumblatt's Druze (Mattar 2004: 181). Clearly, confessionalism encouraged clientelism and corruption, and in turn it increased public debt as each community vied with the other to increase its share.

Any attempt to hold corrupt politicians or officials to account was almost certainly bound to fail as anyone prosecuted for corruption could be portrayed as a victim of confessional prejudice. In the late 1990s, attempts to prosecute highly placed officials of the Council for the South were vetoed by Nabih Berri; and while Sunni clients of Rafiq al-Hariri, such as his finance minister Fouad Siniora, were initially pursued because with Salim al-Hoss as Prime Minister there was no one to protect them, eventually charges were dropped under an avalanche of Sunni sectarian protest (Mattar 2004: 180).

Confessionalism affects many aspects of Lebanese politics. Very importantly, it distorts and becomes muddled with the issue of Lebanon's relationship with Israel. There can be little doubt that left to themselves after the civil war, freely elected politicians in Lebanon would have negotiated a peace settlement with Israel. Instead Hezbollah was allowed to fight a war and develop an image of itself as the saviour of Lebanon – an image that was coupled with a sense of victimhood on the part of its Shi'ite constituency which encouraged it to make an essentially confessional bid for power in 2006 on behalf of its Syrian (and Iranian) sponsors. The continuing conflict with Israel and periodic government crises, stimulated at least in part by wider regional or global conflicts, in turn discourage foreign investment and deepen public indebtedness, driving Lebanon into a confessional vortex of economic stagnation.

It is almost as if nothing has changed since an American Protestant missionary wrote of Lebanon in the nineteenth century:

> The Sunnites excommunicate the Shi'ites – both hate the Druze. The Maronites have no particular love for anybody, and in turn are disliked by all. The Greek Orthodox cannot endure the Greek Catholics – all despise the Jews. They can never form one united people and will therefore remain weak, incapable of self-government, and exposed to the invasions and oppressions of foreigners. Thus it has been, is now, and must long continue to be – a people divided, meted out, and trodden down.
>
> (Thomson 1858: 168-9)

A notion of common descent, of a shared blood, lies at the root of ethno-confessional identity. One is born a Sunni or a Maronite and one has no choice in the matter. Even if a Muslim converts to Christianity, or a Christian to Islam, the convert can never be a 'proper' Christian or Muslim, and the natal confession can still claim the convert as its own. Marriages between Maronite

Catholics and Greek Catholics, for example, are acceptable, between Maronites and Orthodox Christians less so, and between Christians and Muslims virtually anathema (Hanf 1993: 81, Johnson 2001: 161-2, Khlat 1989: 44). On the rare occasions when Christian-Muslim marriages occur outside the small liberal elite, the offending couple are often ostracized by their respective communities and there are cases of young women being killed by their male relatives to prevent such an abhorrent stain on the family's honour (Younes 1999).

Until endogamy is challenged, ethnic identities can always be reproduced in any socio-political conjuncture. It is thus a matter of concern that there continues to be a powerful resistance to civil marriage in Lebanon. It is not simply the problem of a strong norm of confessional endogamy in civil society. Even if two people from different confessions want to marry and would be allowed to do so by their families, they are unable to be legally married unless one converts to the other's faith. When, in March 1998, President Elias Hrawi proposed to his government that they draw up a civil marital code, he was opposed not only by virtually all the religious authorities in Lebanon but also by the Prime Minister, Rafiq al-Hariri, who said he was afraid of offending confessional values and interests (*MENA* 1998: 754-5). Although some Lebanese saw Hrawi's proposal as a welcome step in the direction of a secularisation that might help to bridge sectarian divisions, there was no sense of any widespread disapproval when Hariri refused to submit legislation to parliament.

Civil marriage would at least start a process away from the ethnicisation of confession by facilitating mixed marriages. It would also undermine the political power of religious authorities, help promote gender equality in personal law, and be a step toward a civil code covering marital rights, inheritance, divorce and child custody – issues that currently favour males under most religious codes. And such changes could in turn encourage gender equality in other areas of law such as criminal codes relating to honour killings that currently treat male killers leniently.

The activities of trade unions, women's movements, and

amorphous mass movements like that which gathered in Beirut in March 2005, show there is a vibrant, multifaceted, and often optimistic, counter-cultural movement in Lebanese civil society. It informs private discourse and even some aspects of public life. Different ideas are represented within it, but what is common is a belief in a united and secular country in which inclusive liberal nationalism can finally overcome those exclusive ethnicities motivated by the romantic ideologies of blood, honour and vengeance. It is too early to judge whether secular sentiments will ultimately triumph over confessional prejudice; but unless they do, Lebanon will continue to be 'meted out' and 'trodden down' by external forces.

References

Amnesty International, *Annual Reports: Lebanon*, 1997-2006, published on the website www.amnesty.org.

Beydoun, Ahmad, 'Confessionalism: Outline of an Announced Reform' in Nawaf Salam (ed.) *Options for Lebanon*, London and New York: Centre for Lebanese Studies and I B Tauris, 2004

Daily Star (The) Lebanese (English language) newspaper, published in Beirut

Gambill, Gary C, 'Lebanon after Assad', *Middle East Intelligence Bulletin*, 2:6, 2000, published on the website www.meib.org

Gambill, Gary C and Daniel Nassif, 'Walid Jumblatt: Head of the Progressive Socialist Party', *Middle East Intelligence Bulletin*, 3:5, 2001, published on the website www.meib.org

Gaspard, Toufic, 'Towards a Viable Economy' in Nawaf Salam (ed.) *Options for Lebanon*, London and New York: Centre for Lebanese Studies and I B Tauris, 2004.

Gibreel, G and Gambill, Gary C, 'A Return to Religious Extremism? Not Quite', *Middle East Intelligence Bulletin*, 2:9, 2000, published on the website www.meib.org

Hanf, Theodor, *Coexistence in Wartime Lebanon: Decline of a State and Rise of a Nation*, London: Centre for Lebanese Studies and I B Tauris, 1993.

Harris, William W, *Faces of Lebanon: Sects, Wars, and Global Extensions*, Princeton: Markus Weiner, 1997.

Hollis, Rosemary and Nadim Shehadi (eds), *Lebanon on Hold: Implications for Middle East Peace*, London: Royal Institute for International Affairs, 1996.

Johnson, Michael, *All Honourable Men: The Social Origins of War in Lebanon*, London and New York: Centre for Lebanese Studies and I B Tauris, 2001.

Khlat, Myriam, *Les mariages consanguins à Beyrouth: traditions matrimoniales et santé publique*, Évry Cedex: INED/Presses Universitaires de France, 1989.

LCPS, 'Civil Society and Governance in Lebanon: A Mapping of Civil Society and its Connection with Governance', *unpublished paper*, Beirut: Lebanese Center for Policy Studies, 1999.

Leenders, Reinoud, *The Politics of Corruption in Post-War Lebanon*, doctoral thesis, School of Oriental and African Studies, University of London, UK

LibanVote, 2004. Lebanese website: www.libanvote.com

Mattar, Mohammad F, 'On Corruption' in Nawaf Salam (ed.) *Options for Lebanon*, London and New York: Centre for Lebanese Studies and I B Tauris, 2004.

MEED Middle East Economic Digest, business weekly, published in London

MEIB Middle East Intelligence Bulletin, journal of the United States Committee for a Free Lebanon, published on the website www.meib.org

MENA, The Middle East and North Africa 1999, London: Europa Publications, 1998.

MENA, The Middle East and North Africa 2007, London: Routledge, 2006.

Nahar (An-) Lebanese (Arabic language) newspaper, published in Beirut

Perthes, Volker 1997. 'Myths and Money: Four Years of Hariri and Lebanon's Preparation for a New Middle East', *Middle East Report*, 27:2

Sherry, Virginia N, 'Disappearances: Syrian Impunity in Lebanon', *Middle East Report*, 27:2, 1997.

Thomson, William M, *The Land and the Book*, New York: Harper and Brothers, 1858.

Younes, Massoud, *Ces morts qui nous tuent: la vengeance du sang dans la société libanaise contemporaine*, Beyrouth: Editions Almassar, 1999.

Chapter Eight

Education: A Means for the Cohesion of the Lebanese Confessional Society

Maha Shuayb

This chapter explores the impact of educational policies introduced by the government subsequent to the Ta'if Accord in order to foster the cohesion of Lebanon. The research compares the educational philosophies and practices of 15 public and private [religious and secular] schools. The study revealed a significant gap between public and private religious schools. Religious schools seemed to achieve the highest level of student satisfaction. Private schools catered for the diverse needs of students and involved them in various activities in the same religious institution. This resulted in a strong sense of belonging to the institution. In contrast, the majority of students in public schools suffered neglect and consequently developed negative feelings towards officialdom. As a result, most of these students expressed their wishes to join a private religious school because it caters for their diverse needs. These findings revealed that the younger generation trust religious institutions to fulfil their needs rather than the public secular ones. The superiority of religious schools over public ones could lead to a more fractured society comprising different ghettos.

Introduction

Following the end of the civil war in 1989, a grand plan for educational reform was launched. A modernised curriculum with new textbooks was designed and introduced in 1997. The main aim of this educational reform was to abolish sectarianism and build a unified Lebanese identity. In this chapter, I shall examine the reform process and the effectiveness of the new curriculum approach for building a unified society.

Studying this topic can be problematic for one major reason. It is difficult to assess the effectiveness of the new curriculum in fostering the social cohesion of Lebanon; the students' sense of belonging is not only shaped by schooling, but other factors such as family and media which are known to be significant in the socialisation of children. Hence, it is difficult to claim that any observed change in the students' sense of belonging is a direct result of the new curriculum. To tackle this problem, I decided to study the practice of the factors common to citizenship research – which contribute towards national upbringing – in fifteen private and public schools. I also examined the impact of these aspects on students' sense of belonging to their school.

Research into citizenship education has constructed a number of factors that are thought to contribute towards a student's sense of belonging. These factors include active discussion of current local, national and international events; critical thinking and discussion; voluntary and extracurricular activities; and student voice and democratic practices in schools (Macedo 2004). Achieving these practices requires the adoption of a constructivist learning theory. The latter theory places the child at the centre of the learning process and emphasizes deductive rather than inductive teaching. The factors that this study was able to cover were democracy, teaching methods and social and extra-curricular activities.

The political dimension of reforming education in Lebanon

The Ta'if Accord (1989) was the starting point of the educational reform that followed. In section two it states:

the curricula shall be reviewed and developed in a manner that strengthens national belonging, fusion, spiritual and cultural openness, and that unifies textbooks on the subjects of history and national education.

Despite this apparent effort to abolish sectarianism the Ta'if Accord elements reflected in the 1990 constitutional amendments are not fully committed to this cause. There are many contradictory articles, some of which institutionalise sectarianism. This inconsistency made educational reform a much harder process. While educational reformists tried to move towards abolishing sectarianism, the sectarian regulations jeopardized this reform.

As a result, the new Lebanese curriculum looks too idealistic and unrealistic. In its attempt to undermine sectarianism, it failed to reflect authentically the current political system in Lebanon. For example, it laid great emphasis on national upbringing through asserting values like human rights, democracy and tolerance. By contrast, article 95 distributes grade one posts and their equivalents on a sectarian basis. This violates a concept much emphasized in citizenship textbooks – that of equal rights to hold a job with no preference being made except on the basis of merit and competence. This inconsistency between textbooks and the current situation will make students doubtful about the practicality of the values they are taught.

The new curriculum also propagates a democracy of the majority. Contrary to this, the Ta'if Accord generates a consociational democracy which puts several strains on equal opportunities and other aspects of human rights. The new curriculum does not provide a lot of information and opportunities for debate concerning the confessional political system in Lebanon. Whilst it is important to teach students about the alternatives to the current consociational system such as democracy of the majority, educationalists should not attempt to suppress any of the current realities. A sustainable and prolonged peace in Lebanon requires awareness from the younger generation of the political and social issues in the country.

The current approach to national upbringing also lacks critical thinking. It does not encourage political debates among students. Students need to be involved in a critical analysis of the current consociational systems and the limitations it puts on democracy and human rights. They should also debate the possible alternatives to this system.

The Ta'if Accord did little to tackle the authority of religious establishments in reforming education which is known to have contributed to the identity dilemma in Lebanon. Article 19 of the Ta'if Accord establishes a constitutional council whose role is to 'oversee the constitutionality of laws and to adjudicate the conflicts stemming from the presidential and parliamentary elections.' Religious heads of sectarian communities are, except for the three top state leaders and ten unspecified members of parliament, the only parties allowed to petition the council. The religious leaders' appeal to the council is restricted to legal matters related to 'personal status, and freedoms of belief, religious practice, and religious education.'

Hence article 19 preserves exclusive control for confessional leaders over all personal status and religious education. In a state where a significant number of educational institutions are religiously affiliated, this puts them in a unique position to block secularisation of education and thwart attempts to create a secular and unifying national identity. This is exactly what happened when the first attempt to reform education began.

The initial educational reform, known as the Educational Development Plan (Khutat Al-Nuhood Al-Tarbawi), was approved by the Chamber of Ministers by decision number 26, dated 10 November 1993. On 8 May 1994 the Minister of Education and Sports enunciated both the objectives and content of the plan. The Educational Development Plan called for national integration through three main objectives: (i) to standardize history and civics textbooks and make their teaching mandatory in all schools; (ii) to protect private education; (iii) to reinforce the public sector of education. However, many religious educational institutions and educational policymakers opposed the objectives of the plan on the grounds that it was unrealistic and was a replica of the Jordanian curriculum (Abouchedid, 2002). Consequently the Lebanese Parliament rejected the Educational Development Plan in 1994 and on 25 October 1995, the Chamber of Ministers replaced it with the New Framework for Education in Lebanon.

> The New Framework for Education in Lebanon represented a tectonic shifting from the political objectives accented by the Education Development Plan to the recognition of the structure, content and styles of pedagogy of Lebanon's curriculum. As a result, a joint committee comprising university professors, policymakers from private and public schools, and education policymakers from the Center for Educational Research and Development (CERD) developed the New Framework for Education in Lebanon, which was officially endorsed by virtue of Legislative Decree 12227, dated May 1997. (Abouchedid, 2002, p.4)

Not only did the New Framework for Education have to give up the political objectives, it was also incapable of producing a standardised history and religious textbooks accepted by confessional communities in Lebanon. The Ta'if Accord (article 19) opened the door for religious and confessional bodies to decide educational policies regarding religious teaching.

Political confessionalism and government corruption continue to hinder educational reform. An extreme example of this is the appointment of the Deans of 'The Lebanese University', the only public university (cited in Ofeish, 1999). This university has the largest student population. The attempt to appoint new deans for its ten colleges was blocked for months in 1996 because the troika members (the president of the state Elias Hrawi, the Prime Minister Rafiq al-Hariri and the Speaker of Parliament Nabih Berri) could not agree on a sectarian distribution of deans that was satisfactory to all three of them.

The initial distribution of deans was three Maronites, three Sunnis, two Shi'ites, one Orthodox and one Druze. Berri protested the inadequacy of his share compared to those of the other troika members and the appointments were put on hold. Finally, the troika reached a compromise, which undermines the claims of educational reform. A new college was initiated (the College of Tourism and Hotel Management) and a Shi'ite dean was appointed to it in order to satisfy Berri.

To sum up this section, there are several articles in the Ta'if Accord that present serious obstacles to fostering the cohesion of a fractured society through educational reform. In fact, it can be argued that the Ta'if Accord manifests the absence of a real commitment to abolish sectarianism.

Public and Private Educational Institutions in Lebanon

Through the history of education, particularly in Europe, private schools preceded public ones (Cole, 1950). The former schools were launched by churches and other religious institutions. The public sector was established in an attempt to diminish the influence of the church and to emphasise the dominance of the civil state (ibid). Similar to other educational systems around the world, particularly Europe, the private sector in Lebanon preceded the public one. However, the private sector still currently dominates, as private schools receive the majority of Lebanese students. According to the Ministry of Education statistics for the academic year 2001/2002, the number of students in private schools was 548,331, while 351,177 students studied in public schools. Despite many secular schools, the private sector consists mainly of religious schools run by religious institutions. Private schools are not obliged to teach the Lebanese curriculum and hence they can use textbooks of their choosing including for the subjects of history, citizenship and religious education.

This means that private schools can convey and emphasise particular ideologies. While this could be considered as a part of the religious freedom that Lebanon wants to guarantee its citizens, when completely unmonitored, this policy has several negative implications for the social cohesion of Lebanon.

On the eve of the protracted 1975-90 war... The Permanent Congress of Superiors General of the Lebanese Monastic Maronite Orders... stated that Lebanon's educational system should arm the citizen with the possibility of connecting history with world cultures. On the other hand, the working paper of the Supreme Muslim Shi'i Council called for a standardized educational system emphasising the national Arab heritage and culture. A similar position was endorsed by the Sunni Muslim paper, which requested that Arabism in Lebanon be established once and for all. (Abouchedid, 2002, p: 3).

The lack of inspection of private schools is alarming because it allows these schools to teach certain identities and religious ideas while ignoring other identities. This single dimensional education will eventually lead to a generation centred on their sect that does not know much about the other sects and communities. Due to the lack of unified history and religious textbooks the situation is further alarming. A recent study by Abouchedid (ibid) revealed that the majority of students in Lebanon do not have sufficient knowledge about other religions and sects.

There have been several governmental attempts to monitor education in private schools. Following the independence of Lebanon in 1943, the first Lebanese government issued a decree which enabled it to inspect private schools. Section 18 of Decree 1436 dated March 1950 stated that the Ministry of Education should supervise all private schools. However, the decree failed to provide a mechanism for carrying out the inspection and to specify exactly what should be inspected.

Due to the interference of many confessional leaders and the influence of religious institutions and following the 1958 civil war, in 1959 the Lebanese government backed down from its policy of exercising its authority over private schools. It transferred the responsibility of inspecting private schools from the Ministry of Education to the Governors of Lebanon's Governorates (Section 40 of Decree number 2869). Governors are considered grade one posts, which according to article 95, are distributed on a sectarian basis. Hence the objectivity of inspection can be jeopardised.

> Under this arrangement, the government entertained only a nominal administrative authority over private schools. As a result, the role of education entered into a state of political moratorium within the boundaries of the 1946 National Pact which accentuated consociationalism as a 'fair weather model' of political settlement or a sort of 'live and let live' pattern of multi-communal coexistence. (Abouchedid, 2002.)

After the Ta'if Accord much effort was invested in drafting history textbooks. However, until now the various religious and confessional leaders can not agree on a common version of Lebanese history. One of the difficulties in creating unified history textbooks probably rises from the didactic approach to the study of history. The teaching of history in Lebanon has been mainly associated with memorising facts rather than analysis, research and debate.

Research Methodology

The research methodology included quantitative and qualitative techniques. I conducted a content analysis of the goals of the new curriculum. I also designed two questionnaires that examined the views of students and teachers. 1,220 students and 300 teachers from 15 schools were asked to comment on Likert scale statements whose range extends from 'agree' to 'do not agree at all'. These statements explored the school teaching methods, learning theory, facilities, democracy and activities. The quantitative data were coded and analysed using the computer statistics software SPSS 11.

The qualitative techniques included focus group workshops with 150 students, 60 individual interviews with teachers and 15 with principals. These interviews allowed me to gain an understanding of the participants' views and increased the reliability of the quantitative data. The qualitative data were analysed following the grounded analysis method. A pilot study of all the research techniques was conducted and the reliability of the questionnaires was tested (alpha Kronbach =0.9121).

The Research Sample

The sample consisted of fifteen schools selected from two administrative areas in Lebanon (Beirut and South Lebanon) and belonged to the public and private sector. It represented the various major sects within Lebanese society – Maronite, Catholic, Orthodox, Sunni and Shi'ite. Secular schools were also included. 1220 students and 300 teachers were surveyed. The average age of students in the secondary stage ranged between 14 and 18. Fifteen principals were interviewed.

Content analysis of the New Lebanese Curriculum

The main aim of the new curriculum according to The Educational Centre for Research and Development (ECRD) is.

> to construct a citizen who is proud and dedicated to his/her country...participates in the social cohesion of Lebanon... respects his/her cultural and religious heritage... works on developing his/her cultural, scientific and artistic knowledge... and capable of choosing independently his/her future career (ECRD, p. 4).

From this brief summary, one notices the emphasis placed on the civic, social and moral duties and obligations which the student should be trained in.

The new curriculum is based on three principles: cognitive/humanitarian, national and social. The content analysis of these principles revealed that they too revolved mainly around one goal which is 'citizenship'. This impression is further emphasised in the content analysis of the aims and goals of the new curriculum.

Table 1: Aims and goals of the new Lebanese curriculum

The goals	The number of times each term was mentioned in the curriculum goals
Citizenship	12
Social	8
Moral	4
Environmental	2
Education art	2
Personal	1
Physical	1
Vocational	1
Technological	1
Psychological	0

Table 1 revealed that citizenship was the top priority in the new curriculum. This was followed by a considerable emphasis on social and moral education. Little emphasis was given to the child's personal, emotional and psychological needs that are essential for a balanced and rounded education (Noddings, 1992). Furthermore, when examining the curriculum's social goals closely, they were mainly concerned with the child's duties and responsibilities towards the society rather than his/her own needs and expectations. This suggests that the designers of the new curriculum placed the expectations of the society above those of personal needs of the child.

These results reflect a didactic and totalitarian view of education, which contradicts the proclaimed aims of constructivist education, human rights, democracy and participation. Lecturing students about their duties towards their state and teaching them about the election system in Lebanon is not sufficient to enhance their sense of belonging. The best available evidence suggests that teaching students to think critically about current events, the political process, and how to get involved can make them more willing and able to practice active citizenship. Furthermore, participating in simulations of democratic institutions may increase students' political knowledge, skills, and interest. (Macedo, 2004; Osler and Starkey, 2004).

The new curriculum disregarded the importance of the student voice and students' councils. Although it adopted a constructivist learning theory, which demands an active change in the role of the teacher and the principal, the internal regulations describing their roles were not updated. Furthermore, the disciplinary policy – derived from the behaviourist educational theory adopted during the sixties – was not altered to fit the ethos of the new curriculum.

Although the new curriculum emphasises democracy and participation it did not tackle the hierarchical management policy dominant in public schools. The Ministry of Education School Integral Regulations reduced the principal's role merely to a functional and technical one. The principal's role is mainly to ensure that the teachers and students obey the regulations. The designers of the new curriculum did not train principals in school leadership and the empowerment of teachers and students, nor did they conduct workshops prior to the inauguration of the new curriculum.

In conclusion, the goals of the new curriculum are quite ambitious and seem more like slogans. This impression is further enhanced by the failure to design a practical plan that upholds these goals. The major pitfall that could hinder the effectiveness of the new curriculum aiming to build social cohesion lies in the purely functional, technical and academic role of public schools. No plans have been designed to connect public schools with their local communities. This relationship is essential for empowering students and allowing them to develop social and political skills. As a result, under the new curriculum, the younger generation of Lebanon might gain some factual knowledge about their country but they will only acquire limited skills on how to contribute towards building a unified state.

Results of the Empirical Research

In order to study the current educational practices following the inauguration of the new Lebanese curriculum, I investigated the views of principals, teachers and students in 15 schools. The research sample included public and private (religious and secular) schools. Since the designers of the new curriculum claimed to develop a democratic, active, critical thinking, responsible, and tolerant generation, I decided to design the questionnaires and interviews around three main points: democracy; teaching practices; and social and personal education.

Democracy in Lebanese schools

Giving students a voice in the management of the classroom and the school is thought to increase civic skills and attitudes (Macedo, 2004). Great emphasis has been placed on democracy in the new curriculum. In order to assess its current application, I asked 15 principals, 60 teachers and 1,220 students about the current practice of democracy in their schools.

Principals' views on democracy in school

Principals' views and practice of democracy differed considerably among the different types of schools. The majority of principals in public schools did not favour democratic practices in their schools and adopted a centralised and hierarchical management policy. By contrast, those in religious schools took several steps to provide students with opportunities to express their views and play an active role in their school. Principals in the latter schools adopted a less centralised management policy.

Most public schools did not have student councils. Furthermore, most of the principals interviewed in public schools were sceptical of students' ability to participate and play an active role in the school. During my interview with a public school principal, I asked him if he had any plans for developing student councils. His response was negative, saying that there was no need because students would use them for political debates or for trivial matters that are of no importance for their academic achievements. It is worth mentioning that this particular principal was appointed because of a recommendation of a political party leader. Hence, this principal would not have been happy to see students expressing political ideas which may favour other parties. In fact, four out of the five surveyed principals of public schools were affiliated to a political leader.

Principals in public schools did not only prevent students from having a say in the school, teachers too were not encouraged to participate in the school policy. The teachers' role was restricted to teaching and marking students' results. The majority of public schools had two to three meetings for teachers each year at which they discussed mid and end of year exams results.

During the individual interviews, it became apparent that the main concern of the majority of principals in public schools was the results of official exams. Citizenship was not high on their agenda. This could be partly due to the lack of workshops for principals on the aims and goals of the new curriculum. Furthermore, none of the interviewed principals in public schools had received any professional management courses. As a result, the majority of them seemed to struggle in applying citizenship concepts such as empowerment, democracy and decentralised management.

In contrast, principals in the surveyed private religious schools adopted a humanitarian approach to education and were more concerned with empowering students and teachers. They had students' councils and clubs and organised many school and community activities that encouraged students to play an active role in society. Some had university degrees in school management and leadership, while the majority had received and attended management and leadership training.

Teachers' views on democracy

In order to understand the current practice of democracy in schools, I investigated how teachers applied democratic principles with their students and the extent to which the teachers had a say in what went on in the school. Teachers' views on their current practice of democracy with their students will be presented first.

Table 2: Frequencies of teachers' views on their current practice of democracy in school

Answers / Teachers current practice	Agree	Sometimes	Do not agree
Students should be given the freedom to choose to study some topic or another	25%	16.1%	58.9%
Students' opinions should be sought about examinations and the testing of course work	10.6%	30%	59.4%
I teach students the way I want and believe without seeking their opinion	23%	35.2%	41.8%
My students obey my orders without discussion or questions	64.8%	16.8%	18.4%
If students were allowed to plan what they wished to study they'd probably waste a great deal of time trying to decide what to do.	50.4%	37%	12.6%

The above table revealed that the majority of the teachers surveyed had limited democratic practices in the classroom. Sixty-four percent stated that their students obeyed their orders without discussion or question. Only 10 per cent of teachers said that students should be allowed to express their opinions about examinations. The above results largely reflected the fact that teachers played a mainly authoritarian role. They had little trust in the students' ability to organise and have some control over the learning process.

When asked about the opportunities available to participate and express their views within the school, teachers were hesitant to open up and to speak freely about the school. They tended to idealise the situation. However, during the individual interviews where the matter of confidentiality was stressed, intensive discussion of the current situation took place and they talked more openly.

The majority of the teachers interviewed complained of a lack of discussion and opportunity to express their views and opinions. The majority of them said that they were not involved in the school policy. A teacher commented:

> If you lack something, you cannot give it. If you lack democracy you cannot be democratic with others, you will oppress others. We teachers do not have any say in the school, similarly the students do not have a say. Everything is decided from above. In the school, the principal decides everything.

These results showed that the authoritarian and hierarchical practices of the teachers towards the students were also applied on and with the teachers by the principals. It seems that a hierarchical, undemocratic and centralised management culture dominates the Lebanese public sector. This culture continues to haunt the school democratic life, limiting any opportunity for developing an egalitarian society.

Students' views on the practice of democracy in their schools

Students were asked to comment on the following two statements:

Table 3: Students' views on the current practice of democracy in their school

Answers / Statements	Very much	A little	Rarely
There are lots of opportunities for all the students in this school to have a say in the school's activities and rules	17.5%	22.3%	60.2%
Students play a part in making the school a better place to learn	19.6%	25%	55.4%

Looking at the above table, we notice that 60 per cent of students were not satisfied with the opportunities given to them to have a say in what goes on in their school. In the group discussion with students they disclosed that they did not have any chance to express their views. Students claimed that teachers did not even seek students' feedback on their teaching methods.

When asked about what they would like to change in their school, the enhancing of student participation was a major recommendation by students.

> Student: I would like to establish a student council that should be concerned with the students' needs and work on their problems and organise activities with the administration.

Although citizenship textbooks in the new curriculum are full of lessons and topics on democracy and its importance, students in their daily life were not given any chance to experience and live within a democratic environment in school. This contradiction creates a negative image among students about democracy which might lead them to conclude that democracy could be an unworkable idea.

The Ministry of Education Internal Regulations require that student councils and societies should be established in every school. However, the majority of the public schools surveyed lacked students' councils. This was partly due to the principals who were not in favour of allowing students to participate in the school life.

It is important to point out the differences that were found in the practice of democracy between secular public schools and private religious schools. Students in religious schools were more satisfied with the opportunities given to them to express their views. Most of the religious schools surveyed had active student councils. In contrast, most secular public and private schools did not have students' councils. Principals and teachers in these schools were very suspicious of students' opinions.

The impact of democracy on students' sense of belonging to their school is apparent from the strong statistical relationship found between the two factors[1]. This strong relationship implies that when the practice of democracy in the school increases, students' sense of belonging to their schools is likely to increase. Where democracy and participation were available to students in private religious schools it made them feel worthy and empowered. They were able to develop skills such as electing and running for student committees. They also developed organising, management and leadership skills. By comparison, the lack of trust in students' views and ability to manage themselves responsibly in the public schools surveyed made them feel alienated and undervalued. As a result, students in private religious schools had a strong sense of belonging to their schools.

The gap in students' sense of belonging in public and private schools can present a serious problem for abolishing sectarianism in Lebanese society. Students in religious schools who have experienced care by their sect will probably have strong trust in that sect. By contrast, the passive education in public schools will lead to negative feelings towards the secular state. This situation will emphasise sectarianism in Lebanese society and will deter any hope of developing a unified society. A study conducted in 1998 found that students in religious secondary schools considered sectarian affiliation stronger than national ones (LAES, 1998, cited in Frayha, 2006), a fact which emphasises this argument.

Teaching Methods

Active discussion, problem solving, and applying knowledge and linking it to real life are some of the learning methods known to improve students' critical thinking and communication skills. These skills are essential for developing an active and critical thinking citizen. The designers of the new Lebanese curriculum adopted these pedagogies in order to develop active and democratic citizens. In order to assess the current teaching methods applied in schools, I decided to survey the views of the principals, teachers and students in 15 schools.

Principals' views on the teaching methods

A number of principals in public schools were not very up-to-date with the teaching methods required by the new curriculum. For instance, one of the principals interviewed expressed the view that the teacher's role is to transmit the information from the book to the student whose task was to memorise it. This particular principal did not allow teachers to take students on fieldwork trips because he was concerned about being held responsible if anything should go wrong. Whilst the majority of principals in public schools sought practical learning particularly in teaching science, two of the five public schools studied had chemistry and computer laboratories.

What could be concluded from studying the principals' views on teaching in public schools is that the majority were mainly concerned with finishing the textbooks and the results of official exams. Developing active and critical thinking students was not their top priority. Some of these schools were struggling to contract teachers. Hence, outdoor activities, practical learning and school and community activities were not high on the agenda of some of these principals. As a result, the majority of public schools surveyed continued to adopt didactic teaching methods.

In contrast, principals in private schools, particularly religious ones, adopted a constructivist educational philosophy. They were adamant about using active teaching methods. They had enough resources to establish laboratories and to train teachers in active teaching. They organised many outdoor and school/community activities. Developing active students who are capable of playing a full role in the future was an essential target for these principals.

Teachers' views

In order to understand the pedagogies teachers used in their classes I investigated their educational philosophies.

Table 4: Teachers' views of the current teaching methods

Answers Statements	Agree	Sometimes	Do not agree
Students are here to learn what the teacher knows	77.7%	10%	12.3%
The school works at encouraging students to take part in community school activities	67.7%	25.7%	6.6%
I teach students the way I want and believe without listening to their views	74.8%	10%	15.2%
Students acquire valuable skills when they are directly involved in planning their studies and the ways in which they are to be examined	72.6%	23.2%	4.2%
Students are given an opportunity to decide whether to work in groups, pairs or individuals	21.2%	50.3%	28.5%

From the above results, we noticed that 77.7 per cent of teachers perceived themselves as the source of information, thus reflecting the old educational approach which dominated Lebanon for more than 50 years. The significant number of teachers, (74 per cent) who stated that they taught students the way they want, further supported this authoritarian view. Only 21 per cent of teachers gave students the opportunity to decide whether to work in groups or individually. This centralised view of education contradicted the philosophy of citizenship, which stressed democracy, respect, and the empowerment of students.

Students' views

In order to assess the current pedagogies used in teaching citizenship education I asked students to comment on the current teaching methods applied in schools. Their answers were as follows:

Table 5: Students' views on the teaching methods practised in their schools

Answers Teaching Methods	A lot	A little	Rarely
My teachers encourage group work in the class	27%	56.6%	16.4 %
My teachers are interested in students' views of their lesson	24.7%	41.5%	33.8%
The teacher often explains the purpose of the lesson or a series of lessons	50.8%	31.5%	17.7%
My teachers encourage me to set goals for my learning	41.4%	8 %	50.6
My teachers ask me to do a lot of memorising	62.7%	27.9%	9.4%
Teachers help me to relate what I am learning in class to real life outside school	35.3%	36.6%	28.1%
My school organises a lot of outdoor activities	13.8%	24.6%	61.6%

The above results revealed that didactic teaching methods were still dominant in the schools surveyed. Memorising was still seen as the most common method of learning, while group work and practical application of the information learnt were not as common as students would like.

During the interviews, students in public schools revealed that the teaching methods mostly applied in their schools were lecturing, transmitting knowledge without adding anything new and didactic teaching. They complained that few teachers explained the role and the goal of the lesson.

A student: I always want to know why we are learning, but the teachers say you will know later. If we know the aim of the lesson, we understand better.

Outdoor activities were very rare. Active learning was limited. Students were learning without understanding the application and the practical relevance of the information. By contrast, the teaching methods which students recommended included collaborative learning and linking learning to daily life.

Through this study of the current teaching methods in 15 Lebanese schools, we notice that active and critical thinking learning, much emphasised in the new curriculum, is limited particularly in public schools. Newmann et al. (1996) argued that learning can be considered as 'authentic' only if it involved the construction of knowledge, a disciplined inquiry, and a value beyond school. In relation to civics education, 'authentic pedagogy' is appropriate given the consideration of 'value beyond school', where emphasis is placed on the practicality of learning out of a school context. If the designers of the new curriculum strive to develop individuals who can function purposefully as citizens within their society, then such an emphasis on value beyond an academic setting is a necessary consideration for pedagogy and citizenship.

Social Education and Extra Curricula Activities

Social education and extracurricular activities are essential for developing skills needed by students for playing an active social and political role in the community. Extracurricular activities have long been known to contribute to students' tendencies to become and remain civically engaged, even after decades have passed. In order to assess whether these activities were being carried out, I investigated the current practice of social and extracurricular activities in 15 Lebanese schools.

Principals' views

The majority of the principals interviewed stated that the role of the school should not merely be restricted to academic duties.

They argued that its role also involves developing students' social, physical and political skills. However, a small number of principals in public schools stated that the school's role according to the internal regulations set by the Ministry of Education is mainly academic.

> According to the ministry, our role is academic. We have to prepare our students to pass the official exams and to join university (the principal of a public school in the south of Lebanon).

One principal of a public school was completely against any social role of the school as this in his opinion might encourage students to express political ideas. Student councils which enable students to develop important social, political and democratic skills were not encouraged and in fact were absent from all the five public schools I surveyed. Community and outdoor activities were very rare in the majority of public schools.

By contrast, principals in private schools, mainly religious and secular schools, considered the development of a student's social, personal and political skills at the heart of their school mission. Empowering students and preparing them to play an active role in their community and other religious institutions was essential. Hence, these schools had active student councils, social clubs, extracurricular and community activities. The majority of private schools had a schedule for extra-curricular and community activities.

Teachers' views

Teachers' perception and involvement with social education varied considerably between the public and private sector. In four out of the five public schools surveyed, teachers were only responsible for academic teaching. They did not participate in any other activities. In contrast, the duties of teachers in private religious and sectarian schools involved organising social activities and participating in social clubs.

Students' satisfaction with social activities

The following figure presents students' satisfaction with the current emphasis on social activities.

Figure 1: students' satisfaction with the social activities in their school

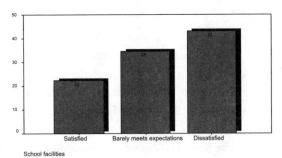

In this figure, we notice that 43 per cent of students were dissatisfied with their school's social and extra-curricular activities. Only 22 per cent were satisfied with their schools' facilities while 35 per cent saw they barely meet their expectations. Students' satisfaction with their schools' facilities differed among the four types of schools. Students in private religious and secular schools were more satisfied with their schools' facilities compared with their colleagues in public schools. Statistical tests revealed that these differences were significant and hence they are unlikely to have occurred by coincidence.

Schools' policies and students' sense of belonging

Students were asked about their sense of belonging to their schools. The results revealed that students in private schools had a greater sense of belonging compared to their colleagues in public schools.

We can see in the table below that 63.8 per cent of pupils in private schools had a strong sense of belonging compared to 53.3

Table 6: Students' sense of belonging in private and public schools

| | | | I feel I really am part of this school | | | | | |
			very much	much	a little	very little	Not at all	Total
Type of schools	private schools	% within public	32.2%	31.6%	23.0%	5.5%	7.7%	100.0%
	public	% within public	21.4%	31.9%	27.8%	10.4%	8.4%	100.0%

per cent in public schools. By contrast, 34 % in private schools and 46.6 per cent in public schools did not have a strong sense of belonging.

Of greater interest were the strong statistical relationships found between students' satisfaction with the social, democratic and active teaching methods on the one hand and their sense of belonging on the other[2]. The strong relationship between these factors implies that in order to foster students' sense of belonging we need to concentrate on the social, democratic and active elements of education. Private schools were successful in engendering students' loyalties by providing a caring and supporting environment. Consequently, students in private schools, mainly religious ones, had a stronger sense of belonging than those in public schools. When asked to name their ideal school the majority of students in public schools named a private religious school because in their view it cared for their needs.

Conclusion

In this chapter, I have explored the Ta'if Accord in the light of its declared aim to reform education in Lebanon in order to develop a Lebanese national identity that is cohesive, unified and tolerant of different sects and ideas. The study concluded that there are political and educational obstacles facing the reformation attempt.

Political obstacles:

There are two political obstacles facing the attempt to reform education in order to foster social cohesion: the Ta'if Accord itself and political affiliation.

The inconsistent policy of the Ta'if Accord towards abolishing sectarianism represents a major obstacle. While it calls for a new curriculum that emphasises national upbringing, it also includes articles which institutionalise sectarianism. As a result, the values of the new curriculum appear to be unrealistic, occasionally idealistic and definitely contradictory. This undermines the authenticity of the principles of the new curriculum.

The Ta'if Accord also failed to tackle the petitioning prerogatives given to private schools and religious leaders. Private schools are still unmonitored by the ministry of education. The interference of religious leaders contributed to the failure to unify history and religious education textbooks. These gaps in the Ta'if Accord reflect a lack of political commitment to abolishing sectarianism.

Another obstacle to educational reform is political affiliation. The appointment of deans at the Lebanese University crisis was an example of political affiliation. Confessional leaders usually distribute the public sector jobs among them. This sustains confessionalism. We have seen in the empirical study that four out of five principals in public school who participated in the study were appointed because of their good relationship with a political leader.

Educational gaps

The new curriculum's educational theory and practice suffers several gaps that present serious obstacles to fostering the social cohesion of the Lebanese society. To foster national upbringing, the designers of the new curriculum emphasised the child's duties more than his/her rights. They did not concentrate on providing a school environment which allows students to develop the skills needed to play an active role in their society and local communities. Lecturing about citizenship, democracy and participation is not sufficient for students to acquire these values and attitudes. What is needed is an education which addresses students' rights while at the same time engaging with the concerns of young people themselves (Osler and Vincent, 2002; Osler and Starkey 2005).

> [Citizenship education] must also be carried out using democratic working methods to prepare pupils for active participation in civic life. Pupils should be given experience of participating in the planning and evaluation of their daily education, and in exercising influence and taking responsibility. (Curriculum for the compulsory and non-compulsory school in Sweden, quoted in Birzea, 2004: 61.)

The aims of the new curriculum to develop an active, democratic and tolerant citizen required shifting the schools', principals' and teachers' role from an academic to a social and community based role. While the designers of the new curriculum concentrated on the teachers' role they failed to describe the kind of school management needed to implement this change. There were no workshops for principals prior to the inauguration of the new curriculum. As a result, a number of the interviewed principals were not even up to date on the goals of the new curriculum. Others did not have the knowledge and experience and thus the confidence to follow a decentralised management style as opposed to a centralised, micro-management approach. The principals were used to a merely functional and micro-management style, which requires them to ensure that teachers and students follow the Ministry of Education's internal regulation. As a result, we noticed through the empirical data that there is a significant gap between private and public schools. The five surveyed public schools did not make positive steps towards providing a democratic and pro-active atmosphere for students to develop the necessary skills to become responsible and active citizens.

The designers of the new curriculum also failed to abolish didactic teaching methods. This was apparent in students' and teachers' views of the current teaching methods.

> Civic education should be cross-disciplinary, participative, interactive, related to life, conducted in a non-authoritarian environment, cognizant of the challenges of societal diversity and co-constructed

with parents and the community (and with non-governmental organisations) as well as the school. (Torney-Purta *et al.*, 2001: 30)

The political obstacles and several gaps in the educational reform resulted in a significant gap between the public and the private sector. Although the public sector managed to improve its results in the official exams, it failed to provide a proper school environment to empower students. As a result, students in public schools expressed negative attitudes toward their officialdom and had a low sense of belonging to their school. In contrast, by caring for students' diverse needs and involving them in an active and participative environment, private schools managed to acquire a strong sense of belonging in their students.

To conclude, national upbringing in Lebanon is mainly restricted to citizenship literacy which is not enough for unifying and overcoming sectarianism. Real life experiences of such an atmosphere are more likely to contribute to developing children's sense of belonging to their country. A cohesive society is built on the loyalty of its citizens. Private sectarian institutions were most successful in engendering loyalty in students by demonstratively caring for their diverse needs. If Lebanon is to build a cohesive future, non sectarian schools must adopt these same policies and care for the child.

References

Abouchedid, K, 'The limitations of inter-group learning in confessional school systems: the case of Lebanon' *Arab Studies Quarterly* (ASQ), 2002.

Acra, A, *Evaluating Civics Curricula*. Report in Arabic submitted to the Lebanese Association for Educational Studies, Beirut, 2003.

Akar, B, *A Critical Analysis of Citizenship Education in Lebanon: concepts, Agendas and Student and Teacher Attitudes,* Unpublished MA Dissertation, London Institute of Education, 2005.

Birzea, C, *Education for Democratic Citizenship Activities 2001-2004: all-European study on EDC policies*. Strasbourg: Council of Europe, 2004.

Cole, L, *A History of Education: Socrates to Montessori*. New York: Rinehart & Company, 1950.

Crick, B, *Essays on Citizenship*. London: Continuum, 2000.

Educational Centre for Developmental Studies (ECRD), *The Aims and Goals of the New Curriculum*, Al Sayad, 1997.

Frayha, M, (unfinished PhD). *Secularism under Siege in Lebanon*, Harvard, University of Harvard (Doctoral Thesis).

Garratt, D, Citizenship in the Curriculum: Some Problems and Possibilities. *Pedagogy, Culture and Society*, 8 (3), 322-346, 2000.

Gilbert, R, Citizenship, Education and Post-modernity. *British Journal of Sociology of Education* 13 (1), 1992.

Heater, D, *Citizenship, The Civic Ideal in World History, Politics and Education*, Harlow: Longman Group UK Limited, 1990.

Hogan, D, Fearnley-Sander, M, and Lamb, S, 'From Civics to Citizenship: Whereas the people ... and Civic Education', In Kennedy, KJ (Ed.), *New Challenges for Civics and Citizenship Education*, Canberra: ACSA, Teaching Resource Number 10, 1996.

Kelly, AV, *The National Curriculum: A Critical Review*, London: Paul Chapman Publishing Ltd, 1990.

Kelly, AV, *Education and Democracy: Principles and Practices*. London: Paul Chapman Publishing Ltd, 1995.

Kennedy, KJ, *Citizenship Education and the Modern State*. London: Falmer Press, 1997.

Kinnear & Gray, SPSS for Windows Made Simple, Release 10. Psychology Press Ltd, 2001.

Macedo, S Spring, *Civic Education: can public schools teach good citizenship?* – Forum, 2004.

Marshal, TH, *Citizenship and Social Class and Other Essays*. Cambridge: Cambridge University Press, 1950.

Muncie, J, *Youth and Crime, a Critical Introduction*, London: Sage, 1999.

Newmann, FM, Marks, HM, and Gamoran, A, 'Authentic Pedagogy and Student Performance', *American Journal of Education*, 104, 278-31, 1950.

Noddings, N, *The challenge to care in schools: an alternative approach to education*. New York – London: Teachers' College Press, 1992.

Ofeish, SA, 'Lebanon's second republic: secular talk, sectarian application', *Arab Studies Quarterly (ASQ) winter issue*, 1997.

Osler, A and Starkey, H, *Teacher Education and Human Rights*. London: Fulton, 1996.

Osler, A, and Starkey, H, 2002. 'Education for citizenship: mainstreaming the fight against racism?', *European Journal of Education, 37 (2):* 43-159

Osler, A. and Starkey, H. 2004. *Study on the Advances in Civic Education in Education Systems: good practices in industrialised countries,* Report prepared for the InterAmerican Development Bank, *Submitted to International Bureau of Education UNESCO 3* December 2004.

Osler, A, and Starkey, H, *Changing Citizenship: democracy and inclusion in education*. Maidenhead: Open University Press, 2005.

Shuayb, M, Towards a Theory of Care, A study of students', teachers' and principals' views in 14 schools in Lebanon, Unpublished Doctoral Thesis, University of Cambridge, 2005.

Torney-Purta, J, Lehmann, R, Oswald, H, and Schulz, W, *Citizenship and Education in Twenty-eight Countries: civic knowledge and engagement at age Fourteen. Executive summary.* Amsterdam, the Netherlands: International Association for the Evaluation of Educational Achievement (IEA), 2001.

UNESCO, *Message from the 47th session of the UNESCO International Conference on Education and proposed priorities for action to improve the quality of education for all young people.* Geneva: International Bureau of Education, 2004.

UNESCO-LEAS, *Evaluation of Subject Curricula. In The Evaluation of the New Lebanese Curricula.* A Report of the Lebanese Association for Educational Studies, 2003.

White, J, *The Aims of Education Restated.* London: Routledge & Kengan Paul, 1982.

Zoreik, A, *Civics Education: How do we deal with it.* Beirut: Arab Scientific Publishers, 2000.

Notes

1 A significant statistical correlation was found between students' satisfaction with the practice of democracy in their school and their sense of belonging to this school. This relationship is explained in the following formula (r (1063) = 0.321, p<0.001), where the value of 'p' indicates the significance of the relationship. For further information, refer to Kinnear & Gray (2001).

2 For more detailed statistical information refer to Shuayb (2005).

Chapter Nine

From Beirut Spring to Regional Winter?

Mark Farha

Is the 'Intifada of Independence' and its Promise of Arab Liberalism in Peril?

I would like to broach a familiar topic from – hopefully – novel vantage points. I will try to offer as unvarnished a view as possible. I truly hope that any critical analysis will not be taken amiss as a threatening attack but as the voice of constructive concern. Lebanon is a country I love deeply, albeit from afar.

This chapter provides a broadly conceived, kaleidoscopic overview of the recent cataclysmic events which have shifted the political tectonics of Lebanon and indeed the region, while bringing to the fore latent forces of (secular) liberalism and (religious) radicalism concurrently[1]. It gauges the exuberant optimism which followed the 14 March demonstration, and assesses to what degree a word of caution is in order. The current political polarisation in Lebanon is compared (and contrasted) to that prevailing prior to the last Civil War of 1975, with a focus on three commonly cited causes for inter-communal hostilities: Lebanon's unresolved identity, skewed economic development and the country's continued exposure to the Israeli-Arab conflict and its ramifications. Finally, I propose possible measures to countervail the growing political bifurcation in Lebanon. In short, I suggest that liberal and secular forces in Lebanon must not be drawn into the vortex of the quasi-tribal clash of religious nationalisms which is engulfing the region. Instead, the unprecedented political constellation and momentum should be used to mount a peaceful 'cultural revolution' aimed at full national integration, the only alternative to a further confessionalisation of politics in Lebanon.

I. Lebanon: Cradle and Grave of Secularism in the Middle East

Lebanese of all religions, identities and political persuasions have gone through a series of turbulent emotional vacillations since the assassination of the late Premier Rafiq al-Hariri on 15 February 2005. No sooner had the grey smoke settled from the mighty explosion which shook the entire capital than profiteers, both domestic and foreign, descended on the political scene, seeking to trade in the political party surmised in the debris. While the cataclysmic event did trigger a huge national outpouring of grief and the expulsion of the Syrian security apparatus, a revision, let alone revolutionary transformation of Lebanon's political structure was not in the offing.

Today, many Lebanese are left with vexing questions:

Why did the 14 March 'Intifada of Independence', celebrated as the 'Cedar Revolution' in US government circles[2] and media, and hailed as heralding a dawn of democracy, not usher in the aspired national integration and rid Lebanon of its last sectarian vestiges?

Was the denouement, the sobering consternation after the euphoria inevitable?

Why have the ghosts of *ta'ifiyya* or sectarianism not been exorcised once and for all?

Was Lebanon, the historic lighthouse of the Arab world, not the ideal candidate for a spring of secular liberalism?

After all, from long before George Bush's 'crusade for infinite freedom' until today, Lebanon has managed to retain its historic vanguard position amongst all Middle Eastern countries in terms of levels of education[3], democracy, press freedom[4] and gross number of publications[5].Lebanon was also one of the first Arab countries to introduce political parties, a parliament and suffrage for women.

We may even state that despite Lebanon's long history of resurgent waves of confessional strife[6], a form of ecumenical tolerance and proto-secularism – defined as a posture of non-discrimination of the state vis-à-vis a multi-confessional citizenry – first made inroads in Lebanon long before it was codified in Europe in the nineteenth century. The Emir Fakhr ed-Din Ma'an II (1585-1635) freely shed the sectarian straightjacket, choosing instead to focus on securing vital trade networks running through Mount Lebanon and Palestine, and building a formidable army composed – for the first time – of Maronite, Druze, Sunni and Shi'ite soldiers. Fakhr ed-Din's grandfather had already displayed acumen in wresting limited sovereignty from Istanbul and Damascus, but it was under Fakhr ed-Din II that a pre-existent, quasi-secular policy of religious non-discrimination and equality between Muslim and Christian was reinforced[7].

Well-placed as Lebanon was to become the first modern secular state in the Middle East, the birth of a fully-fledged secular democracy was periodically interrupted by civil, and regional, wars (1840, 1860, 1914, 1958, 1975), while today sectarianism is once again rearing its ugly head. Arab liberalism likewise seems in a state of regression. This holds true on the regional plane as well, as secularism in the Arab world has progressively been losing its shine. Lebanon – which arguably passed through its own 'Clash of Civilisations' from 1975-90 – has not been able to escape this environment and, while there is an ongoing debate as to what degree 'primordial' religious communalisms and atavisms can be held responsible for the repeated eruptions of violence in Lebanese history, few would contest that their substitution with a supra-sectarian solidarity would serve to lessen the potential for future conflict. In short, then, the rest of this chapter shall examine the diverse stumbling blocks to comprehensive de-confessionalisation in Lebanon.

I would like to begin by arguing that the crisis of 14 March and with it the malaise of Arab secularism and liberalism can be related to larger, older and deeper predicaments which may be categorized under three rubrics:

1 A crisis of *religious discourse* and theological-ideological malaise expressed by a totalising 'anti-Westernism', i.e. a posture of undifferentiated Occidentalism[8] and culture of conspiracy and xenophobic suspicion. The facile equation of atheism with the West and secularism was and remains prevalent, even in many an ostensibly liberal or reformist discourse. In the case of Lebanon, the continued persistence of the 'secular' complex is evident in the allergic sensitivity of religious communities in Lebanon and the Middle East to allow for even mild forms of religious criticism. The near sacrosanct status of the religious representatives is also affirmed by the Lebanese constitution and criminal law which grant special prerogatives to religions and their official representatives beyond those given to ordinary citizens or secular ideologies. The likes of the Orthodox Bishop George Khodr, the late Palestinian scholar Hisham Sharabi and the Syrian poet Adonis have argued that the Arab world has not developed – or made space for – critical reasoning vis-à-vis the sacred[9]. In Adonis's words, just as it is anathema to critique all things religious, so too has the image of the particular *za'im* or paternalistic leader become a sacrosanct, untouchable icon. Just as prophets enjoy a stature beyond critical inquiry, so too are the authority and actions of the king, bishop and sheikh in our modern age not to be questioned[10]. Whatever liberalism exists, it is a mere rhetorical mirage hiding these fundamental, hierarchical structures and complexes.

2 A more organic gestation of secularism was also hindered by the *historical legacy* of unresolved conflict and outside political intrusions. Liberal democracy and secularism in the Middle East, since their introduction in the nineteenth century *nahda*, have always suffered from their historic association with Western colonialism and the latter's ulterior motives. Somewhat

ironically, imperialist machinations are also held responsible for having 'invented' sectarianism in the Levant.

Given its non-Muslim majority, situated on the periphery of a Sunni Empire, the Emirate, and subsequent *Mutasarrifiyya* of Mount Lebanon were perhaps the most conspicuous candidates for anti-Ottoman proto-nationalism and secularism. On the other hand, the close historical ties of Lebanon's Christian community to the West has nourished the bogeyman of Lebanon serving as a beachhead for Western designs, a fear which was not always misplaced, but which was bound to hamper a more candid confrontation with Lebanese responsibility and an objective encounter with modernity. It is not coincidental that Lebanon's nineteenth century secularist intellectuals – many of them Christians – have been associated with Mount Lebanon's historic proximity to the European powers and the missionary schools which served as the seedbed for the *nahda*[11]. Stereotypical and reductionist depictions of an ostensibly 'Western', 'Christian' exceptionalism stem from this era and abound to this very day, particularly as regards the depiction of secularism as an alien import[12].

From the French Mandate onwards, initiatives to secularize personal status laws were thwarted repeatedly by a joint Muslim and Christian opposition. While the mandate has ended, the spectre of (neo-)colonialism has not. Indeed, there is no way to underestimate the intense demographic, military and ideological pressures emerging from an increasingly religiously-defined, ever intensifying struggle for land and resources in Israel-Palestine, the chief fulcrum for all fundamentalist movements in Lebanon and the region as a whole[13]. The blatant century-old hijacking of US foreign policy to impose on the region a neo-colonial ethnocracy – in repeated contravention of international law[14] and under the guise of Western democracy – has further besmirched the reputation of secularism, democracy and liberalism in the twentieth century Middle East. George Bush's rhetoric of 'freedom' may sound similar to Pope Urban II's call for '*libertas*'[15], a pious pretext for conquest.

3 *Social-economic* stratification and attitudinal elitism mediated against a dissemination of secular and liberal ideas. In addition to their avant-garde propositions and their elevated social status, the condescension towards their common compatriots burdened the early generation of 'enlightened' *mutanawwirun* intellectuals with an additional freight their cause could ill afford and one which would bedevil their campaign for a dissemination of secular and liberal ideas until this day. Such elitism, both social and intellectual, remains the principal Achilles' heel of secularism and would reinforce a social caste division which – in the case[16] of Lebanon – has often overlapped with or reinforced denominational divides.

Elite-popular divides could and can also adversely affect intra-sectarian relationships. Popular pressures, for instance, partially help to explain the then Prime Minister Rafiq al-Hariri's refusal to sign the 1997 Civil Marriage Bill supported by a majority of the Council of Ministers. Likewise, lack of control over the 'street' was evident in the (largely Sunni) 'Danish embassy' riots in Ashrafieh[17] in 2006 and Hezbollah's apparent difficulty in reigning in enraged followers protesting a program poking fun at Hassan Nasrallah on Thursday, 1 June 2006. To be sure, these visceral popular uprisings can also be related to the aforementioned ideological insecurities, Occidentalist phobias and intolerance of any criticism or pun of religious or confessional icons, both amongst Christians and Muslims. One thinks of the manifold book-bans in Lebanon over the past two decades from Mustafa Juha, Salman Rushdie, Dan Brown to Sadiq al-Nayhum and the respected German scholar Noeldeke, to mention only the most prominent cases. Recent virulent reactions to a Christian politician's criticisms of a bishop's political role or the riots following a comedy spoof of Hassan Nasrallah indicate that Lebanon still has a long way to go before it reaches a level of political maturity. Without undue condescension, we might state that despite its regionally superior political liberties and trappings of modernity, Lebanon is still subjected to a pre-modern political mindset characterised by a personal status code which views the individual not as a citizen before an egalitarian law, but as a member of a larger confessional community.

The above exposé of the ideological, regional and historical context is necessary to properly understand the multiple difficulties Lebanon encountered as the country embarked on a massive reconstruction in the post-war era. In what follows I will try to briefly examine the ramifications of the post-*Ta'if* era. The question I pose here is whether economic development can indeed act as a catalyst for liberalism, or whether Lebanon is in need of a more comprehensive political vision if it is to escape the clutches of communalism.

II. The Post-War Era: Modernisation and Religion, Jihad and McWorld

Both Lebanon's pre- and post-war experience may test the following rather familiar hypothesis: Does economic liberalism invariably induce political liberalism? Does development decrease the attachment to tradition? Or does our latent assumption of an inherent antithesis between modern, 'rational' capitalism and traditional religion perhaps rest on a faulty premise to begin with?

In a much read article entitled 'Jihad vs. McWorld', the American political scientist Benjamin Barber contends that globalisation has ushered in an ambivalent dual dynamic of simultaneous fragmentation and homogenisation, marked by a (parallel) rise of religious fundamentalisms and a heavily consumerist secular culture:

> Just beyond the horizon of current events lie two possible political futures – both bleak, neither democratic. The first is a retribalisation of large swaths of humankind by war and bloodshed: *a threatened Lebanonisation of national states* in which culture is pitted against culture, people against people, tribe against tribe – a Jihad in the name of a hundred narrowly conceived faiths against every kind of interdependence, every kind of artificial social cooperation and civic mutuality. The second is being borne in on us by the onrush of economic and ecological

forces that demand integration and uniformity and that mesmerize the world with fast music, fast computers and fast food – with MTV, Macintosh, and McDonald's, pressing nations into one commercially homogenous global network: one McWorld tied together by technology, ecology, communications and commerce. The planet is falling precipitately apart *and* coming reluctantly together at the very same moment.[18]

Curiously, Barber does not mention Lebanon itself as one of the illustrations of his thesis, though he does conjure the catchy mantra of 'Lebanonisation'. In fact, the Lebanese Civil war has been viewed as much a result of an uncontrolled plunge into economic and social liberalism as a product of the (ostensible) Pandora's box of religious pluralism and culture clash which was only opened with an additional influx of Palestinian refugees in 1970[19]. The latter exacerbated the social and sectarian fault lines even further.[20] According to another study conducted just before the war, 47 per cent of Orthodox Christians had an income below 6000 L.L. in 1974, compared to 47.6% of the Greek Catholic, 52.4 per cent of the Maronites, 59.1 per cent of the Druze, 60 per cent of the Sunnis and 70.7 per cent of the Shi'ites.[21]

In effect, the Lebanese social and economic trajectory after the Second World War puts into question whether economic liberalism, urbanisation, the spread of education and individualism – globalisation if you will – are in fact automatic guarantors of democratic stability, secular modernity and sustainable socio-economic development. After all, economically, Lebanon had become a 'Tiger' by 1973, but politically, the Lebanese state was beset by a crisis of legitimacy which was only aggravated by its minimalist, ostensibly *laissez faire* policy, a policy which in fact protected the privileges of cartels and oligopolies[22] and allowed non-state actors to fill the void in the absence of robust, uncorrupted federal institutions and social services. The Civil War itself may be seen as an extreme form of a centrifugal devolution of power. It marked the ultimate collapse of state authority and at the hands of the militias and patronage networks.

After the guns fell silent, Rafiq al-Hariri emerged as the chief representative of 'McWorld' in Lebanon. Betting on an imminent resolution to the Israeli-Palestinian conflict, the premier pushed his own, highly personalised version of the *Washington Consensus*, an agenda which faced resistance by Baathist Statism, Hezbollah and militant Sunni Islamism, Christian (economic) conservatism, leftist parties and labour unions. It is not for nothing that one political analyst even went so far as to ascribe the motive of the assassination to an attempt to bring down the regional project of liberalisation[23].

Taken as a euphemism for (rentier) capitalism bearing a distinct Saudi imprint, the repercussions of the post-war era, and its effect on strengthening a secular democratic state must be viewed with a jaundiced eye. Hariri was able to spearhead a gigantic reconstruction effort and expand the sway and clout of the Sunni Premiership to a degree hitherto unknown. His unprecedented political stature and his seemingly boundless financial reserves, however, did not allow him to entirely escape the matrix of the confessional triumvirate. Nor was he, anymore than Hezbollah[24], able to elude the watchful eye – and considerable pecuniary demands – of the Syrian security suzerainty. While Damascus and its allies proved particularly resilient to a downsising of state institutions and a slashing of government wages in the post-*Ta'if* state, Syria too, lacked both wherewithal and will to act as a successful agent of de-confessionalisation. Damascus could realign and recalibrate the balance of power between the different Lebanese players to its own advantage. It could – or would – not, however, reform, let alone uproot the sectarian system itself. When Hafez al-Assad backed President Hrawi's bid to introduce a secular, 'civil marriage' in 1997, the seminal venture ended in an acrimonious 'political divorce'[25] filed for by the *Future* block and the recalcitrant religious establishment, both Christian and Muslim.

In the final analysis, it is clear that neither Mr Hariri's financial prowess nor Syria's military might could break the ice of sectarianism since both still relied – willy-nilly – on the same modus operandi, that is to say the inherited patronage system in which political services and philanthropy was – and is – bartered for loyalty and electoral ballots.

In the end, the web of an (intersectarian) *Gemeinschaft* and civil society was weakened by the Syria-Hariri hegemony; the 'gemeine *Gesellschaft*' of clan, confession and class once again continued to foster in consort with the absence of credible trans-confessional state institutions and an independent judiciary. *Homo economicus* may indeed transcend *homo religious* in many a business transaction or investment joint-venture, and even seal the occasional political pact. National integration in Lebanon, however, was ill-served by an emasculated state and the absence of a comprehensive political reform programme. The irony is that for all the acrimonious political debates in Lebanon, there seems to be an unacknowledged unspoken consensus that a weak state in fact serves the private interests on opposing sides. Both the forces close to *'jihad'* on the one hand and those beholden to 'McWorld' on the other may resist the extension of the state for their own particular strategic and economic reasons. As globalisation has failed to bring the aspired economic welfare and political security, and as the government has left its citizens orphaned, the latter have been thrown back to seek succour locally in grassroots networks. Unfortunately, this social reality cannot be uprooted overnight.

Even the seismic shockwaves sent by the 'earthquake' assassination of the late Premier Rafiq al-Hariri followed by a string of further assassinations of anti-Syrian journalists and politicians, while they did result in an unprecedented Sunni-Maronite-Druze realignment, were unable to dislodge the sectarian islands. Indeed, after the end of the 2005 parliamentary elections, the Shi'ite south remains as distant from Beirut as ever. While democracy, freedom and resistance to outside interference are on everybody's lips, none of the parties is willing to seriously tackle the confessional system. Consequentially, unattended socio-economic duress and political disputes are – as was so often the case in Lebanese history – once again being converted into inter-confessional rivalries.

The perilous polarisation we are seeing today in Lebanon, the increasing meddling of murky intelligence networks, the rampancy of rumours and prevalence of parochial foreign interests augur badly for the future. The web of intrigue reminds one of the First World War environment in which Lebanon became the plaything of foreign powers and secret diplomacy; accusations of treason and dual loyalties were traded then just as they are today – with potentially equally costly consequences.

III: Déjà vu? Civil War Analogies:

'Beirut will be destroyed again' Amir Hassan of Jordan, 26 March 2004.

'By our efforts we have lit a fire as well, a fire in the minds of men. It warms those who feel its power; it burns those who fight its progress.' President Bush, Inaugural Address, 2004

'If anything is burning, it's nihilism!' Dostoyevsky, *The Prisoner*

A number of the chief precipitating causes for the 1975 Civil War seem to be discernible in a slightly modified form today. We might enumerate three key factors:

1 Lack of shared national identity, frailty of inter-communal trust (related to crisis in religious discourse – Muslim and Christian, Lebanese and Arab).
2 Economic: Uneven Development (Compounded by Elitism).
3 Political: Domestic imbalance compounded by external pressures and interference (continuation of historical legacy).

1. Competing Lebanese Identities

'Pity the nation divided into fragments, each fragment deeming itself a nation.'

Khalil Gibran, *Garden of the Prophet*

What are the credentials of a bona fide Lebanese citizen? This unresolved question has remained at the core of the modern Lebanese predicament. The clash over identity has fuelled civil strife and continues to constitute the principal source of contention. Can one be striving for a communist state, a Christian homeland, an Islamic state and still be considered a Lebanese citizen? Citing the example of Lebanese espousing Communist or Syrian nationalist ideologies, Hezbollah's Secretary General, Hassan Nasrallah, for instance, has stated that 'there is no inherent contradiction between seeking an Islamic state in Lebanon and being a Lebanese citizen.'[26]

In light of the resilience of competing religiously-tinged nationalisms, Lebanon's unique status as first and sole state in the Middle East – with the exception of Kemalist Turkey after 1928 – which does not stipulate Islam (or Judaism) as the religion of the state[27], may be viewed as a compromise solution to an intractable problem. With the persistent undercurrent of religious nationalisms, the Lebanese quota system amounts to a balancing act continuously living under the Damocles sword of demographics. We may recall that in the prelude to the Civil War of 1975, Lebanese politics were marked by a barren 'dialogue of the deaf'[28] between Christian leaders who may feign interest in a secular system merely in order to provoke the pre-calculated negative response of the Muslim leaders, particularly in light of the latter's opposition to the laicisation of personal status laws, while conversely Muslim leaders raised the banner of 'political secularisation' in anticipation of Christian *angst* of the spectre of an Islamic state imposed by dint of a [Shi'ite] demographic hegemony[29]. Needless to say, demographics would be irrelevant if a common notion of citizenship were to develop.

14 March, however – and the subsequent, sterile sessions of the 'national dialogue' – did not resolve the conundrum of Lebanese nationalism(s). Rather, the domestic impediments to the bright liberal dream of 14 March appeared momentous from the beginning. After all, it was a wager laden with complications, the loud call for 'democracy' issued by precisely those groups which stood most to lose if a direct numerical democracy were to be instituted in Lebanon. The (anti-Syrian) opposition camp was mainly composed of minority sects who – generally speaking – are less favourably disposed to the abolition of 'political sectarianism' than the pro-Syrian, theocratic-inclined Shi'ite

Hezbollah. Thus, Walid Jumblatt publicly disavowed his father's legacy by stating that 'the slogan' of abolishing the current confessional system would lead to 'nothing less that a Syrian dictatorship.'[30]

One might retort that the largest national demonstration in history witnessed on 14 March 2005 might have disproved – or rendered obsolete – such familiar sectarian arithmetics. There was a hope that 14 March had transcended sectarian parochialisms and forged a new trans-confessional identity. After all, Lebanese flags were hoisted next to crucifixes and Qur'ans during the stunning collective assembly of one third of the nation's entire population. What was scarcely recognised in face of this unprecedented moment of mass mobilisation and the melee of religious and national symbols was that this demonstration came about as a coalition of sects, most of which still fell under the aegis of feudal families. From the outset, the near absence of the Shi'ite community was all too glaring.

Conversely, during the previous 8 March pro-Syrian demonstration – which helped to mobilise not a few 14 March demonstrators – Hezbollah had been equally intent on pledging its allegiance by waving only Lebanese flags. The yellow-green Kalashnikov-adorned Hezbollah's flag has since returned, however, indicating the fragility and transience of this phenomenon.

As of 2006, then, the finality of the Lebanese state of 1920 still remains contested, particularly (though certainly not exclusively as witnessed by the myriad *Salafi* groups in Lebanon and some extremist Christian advocates of federalist separatism) for segments of the religious Shi'ites. Hassan Nasrallah's recent outburst is indicative of this latent, unresolved tension:

> [They want us to] speak about Lebanon the country, Lebanon the people, Lebanon the entity, Lebanon the nation, Lebanon the history, Lebanon the geography, and if this continues, two or three years from now we will arrive at Lebanon the god[31].

Nasrallah would drastically temper his tenor in a subsequent interview[32] in which he squarely professed Hezbollah's 'primary allegiance' and issued a stunning, *mirabule dictu* denial of Hezbollah's long-stated goal of erecting an Islamic Republic in Lebanon:

> From its foundation onwards, the party has not suggested that its political project was aiming at the establishment of an Islamic Republic in Lebanon. There were religious scholars and authorities who tabled the idea of an Islamic Republic in Lebanon, yet these were not in the party. This slogan was espoused by a religious scholar who is not Lebanese. The party has not promulgated it, not in its discourse and not in its literature.[33]

Despite such reassuring measures, and his display of accommodationist inclinations, political flexibility and stated readiness for dialogue[34], the Hezbollah leader has in the past indeed outlined the party's mission in Lebanon as entailing the 'Islamisation of the Muslim individual and community, its values and way of life'[35] and the aspired establishment of an Islamic state.[36] From its 'Open Letter' of 1985 down to the present, Hezbollah has neither substantially modified nor terminally relinquished its ultimate goal of an Islamic state, though from the outset the official party line has rejected any forcible imposition of theocracy[37]. Accusations of harbouring divided loyalties and an ulterior Iranian agenda have irked Nasrallah who has become increasingly emphatic in affirming the patriotic contribution and Lebanese credentials of Hezbollah[38].

To be sure, the Shi'ite discourse is not of one stripe on the thorny issue of Iranian guardianship. While Nasrallah has declared his preference for the Iranian-Syrian axis over the one running from Tel Aviv to Washington, Seyyed Fadlallah, for instance, at one point flatly rejected all tutelage (*wisaya*), whether it be Iranian or American in origin[39]. This internal diversity has not prevented some pundits from casting the Shi'ites *in toto* as 'subaltern' outsiders to the modernising Lebanese state – just as some (pro-Palestinian) Sunni Muslims had been previously ostracised during the Civil War. Even so, we would do well to take note that according to a recent Pew study[40], national identity and support for a secular state remains stronger amongst Muslim Lebanese compared to the regional or even international average.

Moreover, Lebanon remains a unique, vital paradigm not only of inter-religious, but also of *intra*-religious diversity. Criticisms of Hezbollah's theocratic agenda have not entirely emanated from the quarters of the Christian right wing; the liberal Shi'ite cleric Hani Fahs has explicitly described Hezbollah as a 'parallel state' or *'al-dawla al-badil al- muwaziya'*[41]. The frequent official and unofficial visits of Hezbollah general secretary Hassan Nasrallah to Tehran have done little to allay these fears and have cast doubt on the so-called 'Lebanonisation' of the 'Party of God'[42]. Afif al-Nablus, the head of the Association of Ulama of Jabal Amil, has further fuelled these 'fifth column' suspicions by averring that: 'we are not allies of Syria but rather we are an inextricable part of Syria. And we shall never forget the contributions of Syria to Lebanon. He who fails to render homage to Syria today has no religion.'[43]

To be sure, inverse charges of foreign sponsorship can be levelled against some of the anti-Syrian parties, many of which have almost spent as much time in Washington and Paris as in Beirut. Certainly seeking succour for a liberal agenda in Western capitals is not a new phenomenon. The total subordination of the most powerful country on earth to an Israeli-driven neo-con agenda[44], however, has heightened the suspicions of even more secular-inclined Shi'ites and Lebanese of all stripes. This highly controversial dalliance with neo-conservativism was reaffirmed when Saad al-Hariri came to Washington and called on the Palestinian government to 'to move forward and make peace with Israel'[45]and with somewhat flippant confidence promised to the *Washington Post* that 'we will disarm Hezbollah'. It was Walid Jumblatt who, only months after he had stood by the side of Hezbollah, let all the masks fall, affirming flat-out that 'Israel is not the enemy, Syria is'[46]. While Jumblatt instantly became the darling of die-hard Zionist pundits such as Charles Krauthammer and William Kristol, his statements served to further antagonise the political arena in Lebanon where 90 per cent of all Lebanese still view Israel as an enemy state. It is difficult to hypothesize whether Rafiq al-Hariri would ever have phrased his stance in such boldness, even though the late Premier was straddling the fences before his assassination and was working behind the scenes for a Syrian withdrawal[47].

The bewildering changes of direction which have marked the Lebanese political scene are not conducive to instilling greater inter-communal trust, perhaps the *sine qua non* building-block for Lebanon's future stability. The self-same Walid Jumblatt who at the height of the war railed against the Israeli-American conspiracy hatched against Lebanon and expressed his preference for a 'reunification' of Lebanon and Syria over a Western-Israeli control[48], would suddenly express his yearning for the return of the 'French Mandate'. Having been barred from the United States for his engagement in 'terrorist incitement' to kill Paul Wolfowitz (whom the Druze leader called a 'microbe heading the axis of Jews'), the same Walid Jumblatt who had again resorted to crude racism when likening the skin-colour of Rice to 'oil'[49] would, barely two years later, find himself warmly embracing and extolling Rice while denying the presence of neo-conservatism in Washington[50]on the very same day he lunched with one of its high priests, Elliot Abrams, the number two at the NSC.

With one wing of Lebanese politics flocking to the doorsteps of the messianic theocrats in Tehran, and another bestowing honour[51] on the likes of former JINSA[52]member John Bolton, a sound,secular vision seems more imperilled than ever. For the lifeblood of Lebanon's pluralistic existence is its secular principles and its 'liberalism' protection of the weak and besieged. Such principles are patently antithetical to the exclusivist Zionist, Islamist and Christian fundamentalist aspirations.

2. Economic Chasms

Yet identity is not formulated in a vacuum, and it is hardly coincidental that the sect/caste which historically suffered from the greatest alienation from the state and its services, and which was the last to be fully recognised in 1926, should be the latest to recognise its legitimacy[53].

In 1968, a prescient work by Michael Hudson drew attention to the 'uneven development', that is to say the gap between rapid economic growth and lagging political sophistication which accounted for part of the tension leading to the outbreak of the civil war and auguring the collapse of the 'precarious' Republic of Lebanon[54]. Albert Hourani likewise argued that it was the absence of inter-sectarian trust and the fragmented form of the state in the pre-war system which made it ill-suited to absorb subsequent economic developments in trade and commerce in the post-war era. Much the same obtains today.

As during the prelude to the war, a flush of oil rentier capital has fuelled a real-estate boom in some areas while governmental neglect has exacerbated rural marginalisation. The parallels to 1975, however, do not end there. Once again, the tertiary sector of the economy, in particular the banks, are flourishing partly due to the exorbitant interest rates on government bonds and partly due to a 'second' oil boom after 2003 which mirrors that of 1973. With gulf money gushing in, Solidere's stocks are soaring, just as prime real estate was a source of many a fleeting fortune in the prelude to 1975.

Such wealth however – spurred by an influx of oil-investments – is accumulated just as the government contemplates a slashing of social benefits and abolishing a ceiling on gasoline prices – which could raise prices 30 per cent and increase the VAT from 10 to 12 per cent. The aforementioned controversial budget for 2006 did trigger an intersectarian counter-demonstration, but, the unions and communists excepted, the two major parties constituted a confessional alliance.

The debt rose from $1.5 billion[55] in 1992 to a staggering 38 billion dollars at present, amounting to double the GDP[56] and a per-capita ratio which arguably is the highest in the world, comparable perhaps only with that strangling a city like Berlin[57]. Not everybody was hurt by the debt however. Two separate recent studies estimate that approximately half of the mountain of the (then) $33 billion debt can be attributed to graft and astronomic, untaxed interest rates on government treasury bills granted to local banks which have seen their profits soar[58].

From a macro-economic perspective, the Achilles heel of the Lebanese post-war economy consists not so much in the absence of economic growth[59] and development, but in its tendency to accentuate rather than attenuate socio-economic as well as inter-regional, cultural and sectarian chasms. According to Butros Labaki, a former Hariri aide and vice-chairman of the CDR, the rate of low-income families has soared from 20.4 per cent in 1974 to 54 per cent in 1997 to 62 per cent in 1999. Conversely, the percentage of medium income families has fallen from 60 per cent in 1974 to 40 per cent in 1992 to 29 per cent in 1999. The Gini coefficient indicating capital concentration has risen accordingly to this study.[60] Other sources, however, show an improving income Gini coefficient from 0.61 in 1951, to 0.51 in 1966 and 0.41 in 1997[61]. The post-war era thus saw a lopsided development and a greater concentration of wealth in fewer hands than ever before, a development exacerbated by the lowest tax rate in Lebanese history. In 1992, 2.4 per cent of depositors owned 40 per cent of total deposits, by the end of 2002 the share of total bank deposits of the same thin oligarchy had risen to 60 per cent[62].

The overall negative fallout of this social stratification and a continuously shrinking middle class for the prospects of secularism in Lebanon cannot be overestimated. The clear, virtually linear correspondence between levels of income and the support for secular reforms have been documented.

The post-war status quo recalls the potentially incendiary effect of gross socio-economic disparities which prevailed before the Civil War. In the prelude to the 1975 war, the escalating social tensions often took on a sectarian colouring when, for instance, Shi'ite laborers protested against wretched work conditions at the (Sunni-owned) Ghandour factory in the summer of 1972, or during the clashes between a Christian dominated army and Lebanese

Table 1: Support for Secularism According to Income (1997, 2002) and Type of Schooling

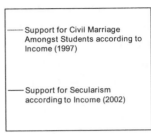

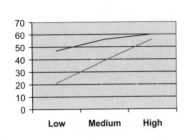

Support for Civil Marriage Amongst Students according to Income (1997)

Support for Secularism according to Income (2002)

Sources: Lebanon in Limbo, *ed. Theodor Hanf and Nawaf Salam, Beirut: Nomos Verlag 2003, p.224; Nahar as-Shabab, 27 January 1998.*

students sympathising with the Palestinian freedom fighters at AUB. A similar mix of external pressures emanating from the Israeli-Palestinian conflict, and internal instability fomented by social disparities – both between and within sects – makes a sequel a portentous possibility. Too apparent are the fragilities and fissures of the Lebanese political system which still has not seen a non-sectarian, socially responsible political vision and national solidarity emerge.

In what is generally seen as one of the emblematic harbingers of the subsequent Civil War of 1975, clashes erupted in Sidon between the army and largely Sunni workers who were protesting the encroachment of businessman and former President Camille Chamoun and his Protein Fish Company. The ensuing conflict between the Christian dominated army and the endangered (mainly Sunni) workers and PLO demonstrated how quickly economic divides could – and can – take on confessional contours[63]. To be sure, today, the Palestinian militias, while armed, have largely been confined to the twelve, largely quiescent camps[64], while the Christian militias have been disarmed, at least as regards the heavy armoury[65].

Another inauspicious omen is the recent edict issued by the Ministry of Education warning teachers not to participate in political affairs, recalling the self-same measure taken to neutralise political discussion by the Ministry three years before the outbreak of hostilities in 1972[66]. Then as now, such measures have not prevented university campuses from once again becoming the scene for violent brawls between partisans of the different sects and parties. Even as wealthy a campus as that of the Lebanese American University was forced to shut down after Druze supporters of Walid Jumblatt, 14 March and (Shi'ite) members of AMAL (8 March) clashed.

3. Domestic Political Imbalances and Foreign Interferences

'According to the Persians best informed in history, the Phoenicians began to quarrel.'

Herodotus, *History*, Vol. I

More discomfiting yet is the regional ratcheting up of the Iranian-US brinksmanship over nuclear weapons. The current standoff with Hezbollah bears an uncanny resemblance to the slow build-up of tension in 'Fatahland' on the southern border in the late 1960s and early 1970s. There are no indications that the Lebanese army has got any stronger, particularly as regards the south while Hezbollah's militia is distinguished by a degree of discipline superior to that of the PLO and Fatah.

After the Hariri assassination and the subsequent withdrawal of Syria, the source of the new *wisaya* (tutelage) moved from the Syrian secret service in Anjar to Aukar, the seat of the American embassy which itself has for decades fallen to the control of zealous Zionists and myopic neo-conservatives. The irony is not lost on many who remember some of the same leaders of the anti-Syrian majority of today having praised and justified the Syrian presence in Lebanon. One example is Jacques Chirac, the chief sponsor of the UN Resolution 1559 who gave an ardently pro-Syrian speech in Lebanon's parliament in 2002, conditioning a withdrawal on a comprehensive regional peace settlement. Several of the political leaders of 14 March were known to have been close to the Syrian secret police in years past. As late as the

2005 elections Jumblatt's PSP, the Lebanese Forces and Hariri's Future movement formed an electoral alliance with Hezbollah to ensure a defeat of Michel Aoun's Free National Movement. The latter has since signed an agreement of understanding with Hezbollah.

It is then the larger confrontation of two religious nationalisms – Zionism with Islamic fundamentalism – that Lebanon, along with its fragile model of Muslim-Christian coexistence, is caught in their throes. Unfortunately, the US – despite its being led astray in Iraq and its entanglement in Palestine – is not bound to come to reason anytime soon and abandon its one-sided, extremely costly blind sponsorship of Zionism for a policy in sync with the most basic requirements of justice, and its own now rather insipid incantation of 'liberty'. At least this is the conclusion reached in a recent Harvard study by Walt and Mersheimer[67].

Conversely, the guerilla party of Hezbollah, while it does enjoy a considerable network of support above and beyond Iran, will likewise not refrain from availing itself of a strategic regional partner, particularly when the contours of the regional chessboard are making the solidification of such an axis almost inescapable. A pessimist might add that the current Syrian regime is in fact coterminous with a secret service apparatus and, perhaps more importantly, mentality as a series of frantic arrests of even moderate opposition members goes to confirm. Yet even though Syria may be enfeebled economically and isolated politically, regionally its (outward) stance of resolute refusal to give in to the Israeli diktat still commands great respect. As for the latter, Tel Aviv has only thinly concealed its glee at the opportunities afforded by the Hariri assassination and the turning of the historically pro-Syrian Sunni majority against Damascus. On 23 February 2005, Israeli Foreign Minister Silvan Shalom laid out the aspired goal to the Knesset (parliament) in no uncertain terms: 'Giving back Lebanon's sovereignty to the Lebanese depends on the dismantling of Hezbollah. Israel is acting towards the realisation of this vital objective in a worldwide political campaign.'[68]

The fear now remains that Hariri's death, momentous as it may seem, may be dwarfed in time by the regional cataclysm to which it merely served as a prelude. Kamal Salibi has likened Lebanon to a fish piloting the whale below the sea. This may be an exaggeration and indeed one might feel prompted to invert the metaphor: Lebanon more often than not has been the – not entirely helpless and not entirely innocent – hostage to outside powers, the staging ground for the 'wars of the others' to quote the somewhat apologetic mantra invoked by Ghassan Tueni.

IV. Weathering the Tempests of Ta'ifiyya: Concrete Steps to be Taken to Stave off Further Tension:

In light of the current deadlock and the impending dangers of a further escalation, it is easy to succumb to pessimism, but it would be irresponsible not to offer possible solutions, cognizant that a talisman-like solution for the conundrum faced by Lebanon does not exist. It would be incumbent on all those interested in safeguarding Lebanon's unique model of diversity to take the initiative in order for Lebanon to withstand the sectarian storms brewing in its immediate neighbourhood; the window of opportunity may be brief.

Above all, an internal strengthening of all non-sectarian structures is in order. Such an endeavour would necessarily have to encompass all aspects of society, from education to the media to the political and legal system.

Concretely speaking, such a revamping could begin with a desegregation and expansion of public schools – if need be, forcibly by governmental decree. The Civil War and emigration have exacerbated segregation and resulted in a de facto cantonisation of the country. Only concerted state action can redress the proliferation of virtual ghettos. Moreover, the historical dominance in Lebanon of confessionally homogenous private schools have mediated against inter-confessional integration[69] as each school still follows its own curriculum after a standardised national secondary school history book was withdrawn in 2001 over a concocted controversy[70]. This book should be re-introduced along with one textbook enabling Lebanese to learn each others' religions, or rather religious histories[71].

In the longer term, by writing a history which highlights peace and violence, failings and achievements objectively, rather than engaging in a selective sectarian hagiography, the Lebanese will not be able to evade a honest confrontation with Lebanon's checkered past. Students must – similarly to their post-war peers in Germany – be taught a history of humility, not hubris, to avert further destructive wars. What is needed is a national historiography aimed at inculcating a secular identity and promoting inter-confessional fraternity by ways of grappling with – rather than sugar-coating or evading – Lebanon's scarlet past of inter-communal strife.

The reluctance to come to terms with its past, however, pervades not only the educational, but also the political realm. Echoing the sentiment of many Lebanese, Seyyed Hani Fahs wants to close the chapter of the past lest the Lebanese continue to be hostage to it[72]. Gibran Tueni likewise cautioned 'not to open the files of the past' in 2002, apprehensive of opening a Pandora's box. As the showdown with Syria intensified, and as the political assassinations multiplied, Tueni found himself increasingly recalling the past martyrs of free thought in Lebanon, before he himself would become the latest victim of such callous bloodlust.

The overall dearth of contrition amongst yesterday's protagonists of the war – who pose as today's peddlers of peace – continues to be perturbing. There are edifying exceptions, to be sure. The truly remarkable profile in courage of former militiaman Assad Shaftari has been well publicised[73]. The 'Beirut Declaration', drafted by Samir Franjijeh and signed by a rainbow coalition spanning the spectrum of political parties, contained the most open admission to date of responsibility for the war crimes[74]. Another example was set by the former head of the Communist Party, George Hawi. Weeks before his assassination he was asked why he chose to take up the burden of searching for peace between the parties; the candour in his reply was startling:

Trust me when I tell you that my conscience is burdened with the names of a number of martyrs. And I believe that I cause suffering to those whose regions I ordered to be bombed. And so I ask myself frequently: Could I have undertaken something to prevent the killing I did? And if there is a lesson to be drawn from the experience of the war, is it not incumbent on us today to exert our utmost efforts to preclude another nihilistic experience for our country? For during the war we all failed. Amin Jemayyel committed a wrong, and I committed a wrong as did the Syrians and Kamal Jumblatt. Starting on this premise I undertook a self-criticism and decided to engage in dialogue with all the enemies of yesterday[75].

To further foster such a public sphere open to (self) criticism, the audio-visual press law of 1994 should be revised. By the same token, Articles 23 and 26 of the Lebanese publication law and Article 219 of the penal code ought to be amended to withdraw the special status enjoyed by heads of state and religion. It is easy to pay lip service to freedom of speech as Lebanese politicians are wont to do; more important is its protection even – or especially – if it affects the symbols/leaders closest to us. Article 9 of the Lebanese constitution solemnly enunciates that 'freedom of belief is absolute'. Consequentially, there should be no sanction for 'blasphemy' since faith has no value if it is rendered a dogma rather than a choice. The late Mahatma Gandhi, who can hardly be charged with a lack of piety, insisted that the state had no business in acting as the watchman of religion[76]. Freedom of belief must not be seen as a threat to religiousness, but as its very guarantee.

In the same vein, the Prime Minister should sign the shelved Civil Marriage Bill and forward it to Parliament for ratification upon raising awareness for the necessity of equality, common citizenship and unity. He can expedite the process by joining forces with numerous like-minded Lebanese NGOs to this end. Over the past decades, numerous NGOs have been set up with suggestive names such as 'The Civil Society Movement' (under the aegis of Gregoire Haddad), 'Towards Citizenship', the 'Peoples Rights Movement' or the 'Alliance for Change and Salvation' led by Najah

Wakim and the Communist Party[77], to name but a few.

Finally, there is an oft-reiterated but rarely acted upon need to follow up on the 1990 Ta'if Accord clause mandating the establishment of a committee of scholars commissioned with studying a roadmap towards an abolition of confessionalism in Lebanon. To remain realistic on this front, it seems clear that electoral reform including the formation of a non-sectarian senate – as stipulated in the Ta'if Accord – will in and of itself not necessarily induce the formation of non-sectarian parties[78].

Given the potential controversy they could stir, the above bold domestic reforms however risk becoming hostages to the regional climate of fear. Reform ideologies – such as secularism – are neither cast in stone nor impervious to the ebb and flow of global events, but subject to the political perimeters which may narrow or widen the scope of inquiry. A recent survey conduced by the Beirut polling office of *Information International* revealed that the percentage of Lebanese citizens who consider their confessional identity paramount to their Lebanese identity surged when posed in a context of conflict[79]. One hastens to add that the current unbalanced ideological environment in the region and the latest escalating confrontation between the US, France and Syria does not promise to redound to the advancement of secular forces in Lebanon.

Thus, it is of paramount importance that the marriage of (in)convenience of self-professing Lebanese liberals with the hijacked US administration should not be concluded without a 'pre-nuptial' agreement refusing a subservience of American (and Lebanese) interests to the ambitions of a discriminatory ethnocracy, even as it is demanded from those seeking succour in Tehran to disavow the project of an Islamic state. Arnold Toynbee's eloquent clarion call on the eve of the civil strife of 1958[80] rings as true then as it does today: Lebanese seeking assistance from the US administration must resolutely refuse any 'extra-marital' affairs which in fact violate the soul of the US, its constitution and bill of rights lest the sweet fruits of democracy promised with great bravado by the neo-conservative US administration continue to be spoiled by the germs of hypocrisy. When it comes to their policies towards the Middle East in general, and Lebanon in particular, successive US administrations have again and again betrayed the 'self-evident' truths of equality they have been charged to uphold by their own Declaration of Independence. The blind, unabashed espousal of neo-conservatism – which, after all, is but a euphemism for zealous Zionism hijacking US foreign policy – plays right into the hands of terrorism by heightening the phobia of a foreign, Western conspiracy. Lebanon must bring its vital message to bear on the US administration rather than let the latter be used and abused by deluded warmongers. Domestically, such a course would endow proponents of liberalism in Lebanon (including 14 March) with greater credibility and contribute to integrate Hezbollah by widening the common ground[81]. By contrast, the current double dealings, friendships based on naked opportunism, trade in principles, and wholesale accusations of a 'Persian peril' will only make the latter all the more acute.

If I may end on a sober note; an unvarnished estimate would tell us that a regional deterioration is all but unavoidable. What Lebanon can do is to insulate as suggested should the winter set in. Is such radical political reform and comprehensive deconfessionalisation – which was proposed repeatedly in twentieth century Lebanese history from Butrous al-Bustani to Antun Saadeh to Gregoire Haddad – a pipedream? As Saffiya Saadeh has bluntly put it, ultimately the advancement of secularism in Lebanon hinges on the formation of a class capable of formulating and implementing it[82], a class willing to tap into the general popular readiness for change. It is precisely, however, this *Bildungsbürgertum,* the mainstay of European liberalism, which has been either silenced, co-opted or eliminated[83] by the guardians of the sectarian status quo.

Surveys reveal that the popular acceptance of reform might be far greater than the will of the political class to dismantle the patronage system they owe their existence to. With cross-sectarian consensus a rarity in today's Lebanon, one precious exception which stands out are the 80 per cent of Lebanese who concur that 'tyrannical egoisms' (*al-ananiyyat al-taghiya*) constitute a greater danger than sectarianism proper[84]. Beyond the string of recent scandals and rampant corruption, the ravages of the savage civil war might be fresh in the memory of some of the respondents. Confessionalism, after all, is but a euphemism for a form of communal egoism. The hope remains – however feeble – that secularism and political liberalism may take root in Lebanon as they did in the West, i.e. as a result of sheer exasperation and nausea with confessional wars of extinction and the bloody experience of theocratic tyranny.

Perhaps then the Lebanese and the region as a whole can move from its stifling preoccupation with 'identity'. For the discourse of identity and authenticity, unlike that of ethics and justice, is backward-looking and bears within it the seeds of exclusionary authoritarianism. It is a discourse which harkens back to the ancestors, the (excessively) revered roots which may become suffocating shackles. By contrast, a focus on political principle, and a commitment to equity towards the country's multiple communities, need not remain oblivious to cultural roots, but rather may embed the latter in the proper turf so they may grow. The vibrancy and beauty which are the hallmarks of Lebanon are not derived from the imposition of a single hegemonic historical, linguistic or religious model but from the country's ability to synthesize a variety of cultures and creeds.

In light of the pervasive suspicions of secularism and the discourse of freedom and democracy in the region, the ultimate goal then should not be to exile religion lock stock and barrel – a challenge which is bound to reveal itself as quixotic at best and counterproductive at worst. Rather, the case must be made for Middle Eastern Muslims, Jews and Christians alike to adopt the basic ethical and political premise of equality they would like to enjoy when living in Western countries. Critics of deconfessionalisation have pointed out that secularism all too easily devolves into a gratifying slogan, a mantra whose mere utterance – thus the delusion – would somehow dispel the spectres of sectarianism once and for all. Yet secularism is no panacea but rather a posture of positive neutrality in both political and personal relations.

If Lebanon fails and fragments anew – in a sequel to the Civil Wars of yore – a critical example of Muslim-Christian co-existence will have disappeared, a loss which is sure to be felt far beyond the shores of this small country. Lebanon bears within it a dual capacity, of clash and comity of civilisations. If barbarism signifies the absence of standards and the final victory of untrammelled, self-centred greed, the mainspring of civilisation could be deemed a creative curiosity and outreaching empathy for the other in all his human needs. Lebanon, as ever, bears within it the seeds for both its own constructive and destructive destinies. It has no weapons to fight the inhuman cynicism of this world save a return to its trans-sectarian, human soul.

Notes

1 I link liberalism here to secularism while defining the latter simply as non-discrimination towards a plurality of confessions: 'Liberalism is the supreme form of generosity; it is the right which the majority concedes to minorities and hence it is the noblest cry that has ever resounded on this planet. It announces the determination to share existence with the enemy.' José Ortega y Gasset, *The Revolt of the Masses*, New York: W Norton & Company, 1994. p.24.

2 The designation of a Cedar Revolution, so ubiquitous in the US Press, was coined by the US State Department Undersecretary Paula Dobriansky. 'In Lebanon, we see growing momentum for a 'cedar revolution' that is uni-fying the citizens of that nation to the cause of true democracy and free-dom from foreign influence. Hopeful signs span the globe, and there should be no doubt that the years ahead will be great ones for the cause of freedom.' Last accessed on 1 February 2006 at: http://www.state.gov/g/rls/rm/2005/42793.htm. The word 'Intifada' is the more commonly heard designation in Lebanon, but due to its associ-ation with the Palestinians it carries unwelcome connotations in the US and thus is but rarely found in the press there.

3 With 9.3 per cent of GDP Lebanon in 1997 spent almost 3 per cent more on education than OECD or MENA countries and with 8.3 students to each teacher Lebanon nominally boasted one of the lowest student-to-teacher ratio in the world in 1996. Numbers refer to 1996. France's ratio is 19, Germany's 17 and Turkey's 28. Tabbarah, Riad. *The Educational System in Lebanon*. Beirut: Center for Development Studies and Projects (MADMA), 2000, p.18. Also see Nemer Frayha. 'Education and Social

Cohesion in Lebanon.' *Prospects* 23, no. 1 (2003), p.87.

4 According to the *Third Annual Worldwide Press Freedom Index* established by *Reporters Without Borders,* as of 2004, Lebanon's ranks at 87, well before Turkey (no.113), Egypt (no.128), Syria (no.155) or Saudi Arabia (no.159) in terms of press freedoms. see www.rsf.org

5 In 1999, 1,358 titles were printed in Lebanon out of a total of 2,714 in the entire Arab world. This means that Lebanon boasts six times more periodicals than Egypt, the largest Arab country, see Franck Mermier in *Monde Arabe,* (2000) 'Beyrouth, Capitale du Livre Arabe', p. 100.

6 There is almost a consensus amongst Lebanese historians that the Western powers concocted confessional identities and cooked up sectarian strife in the nineteenth century. Ussama Makdisi, *The Culture of Sectarianism,* Berkeley: University of California Press, 2000. Khalil Arzuni, *As-Safir,* 18 December 2003, 'Masa'lat al-Ta'ifiyya fi Lubnan'. While it goes without saying that the mechanisms and form of sectarianism have changed over time, a cursory review of Levantine history will reveal the far older legacy of inter-sectarian strife. Lebanese history is brimful with periodic instances of inter- and intra-religious instances of communal strife. Ironically, the efforts to suppress this pre-modern, pre-colonial scarlet past have resulted in a papering over of the instances in which Lebanese rose to oppose sectarian bloodshed, from the Imam Uza'i who protested the collective punishments of Maronite Christians in the eighth century, to the proto-secular Emir Fakhr ed-Din II in the 16th, to the instances of mutual aid in the 1860 massacres. See Phillip Hitti, *Lebanon in History,* London: Macmillan Press, 1957.

7 akhr ed-Din's contemporary, the Mughal Emperor Akbar (1542-1605) embraced a religious syncretism which to a certain degree resembled Fakhr ed-Din's 'open door policy' towards religion. In many ways Akbar had even more leeway in abolishing the *jizya* and declaring himself 'infallible' in all matters, religious and secular, in 1579. Akbar's liberalism, however, was successfully resisted by Shaykh Ahmad al-Sirhindi's (1564-1624) subsequent Islamist polemics which culminated in the harsh rule of Aurangzeb. For Akbar and the even more liberal Dara Shoko, see Eugene Smith, *India as a Secular State,* Princeton: Princeton University Press, 1963. p.435 and TN Madan. *Modern Myths, Locked Minds: Secularism and Fundamentalism in India,* New York: Oxford University Press, 1987.

8 See Sadeq al-'Azm 'Orientalism and Orientalism in Reverse', *Khamsin* 8 (1981). One should add that the defensive and reactive origins of Occidentalism alone do not erase the kindred symptoms it shares with Occidental essentialisms as claimed in Ussama Makdisi, 'Ottoman Occidentalism', *American Historical Review,* 107 (June 2002): 768-797.

Western colonial efforts at domination and subjugation of the 'Orient' have on occasion given rise to a discourse of counter-dominance and a no less essentialist counter-orientalism. Carter Vaughn Findley, 'An Ottoman Occidentalist in Europe: Ahmed Midhat Meets Madame Gülnar, 1889,' *AHR* 103 (February 1998): 15–49. Nor has Occidentalism waned with formal, flag independence and the end of the overt colonial era. Thus, Hassan Hanafi has been one of the most prominent late twentieth century Egyptian intellectuals to embrace openly Occidentalism (*al-istighrab*) as a response to the distortions and damage inflicted by western Orientalism. See Hassan Hanafi, *Muqaddimah 'ilm al-Istighrab*, al-Qahirah: al-Dar al-Fannya, 1991. An even more virulent strain of Occidentalism is found in the works of Anwar al-Jindi who has attached the defamatory epithet to even remotely Western-oriented authors as foreign traitors, from Salama Musa to Taha Hussein to Adonis. The *Shu'ubiyya* refers to an early ethnic-religious resistance movement in the Abbasid Empire which opposed Arab dominance. Anwar al-Jindi. *Al-Shu'ubiyyat*. Tarablous: Dar al-Shamal, 1978.

9 George Khodr, *An-Nahar*, 27 December 2004. Hisham Sharabi, *Neopatriarchy: Theory of Distorted Change in Arab Society* New York/Oxford: Oxford University Press, 1988.

10 Lecture delivered by Adonis as cited by *An-Nahar and As-Safir*, 23 November 2003.

11 Farah Antun (1874-1922) at once offered a critique of imperialism and an acknowledgement of the contributions of the foreign schools which he – like Georgi Zaydan – credits with the Arab renaissance: 'For its age of a modern *nahda* is the age of the entry of the American missionaries and French Jesuits' *Ibn Rushd Wa Falsafatuhu*. Beirut: Dar al-Tali'ah, 1983. p. 273.

12 Such anti-Westernism extends into the present day. The late Muhammad Mahdi Shamseddin has depicted secularism as 'an exclusively European phenomenon'. Shamseddin, Muhammad Mahdi, *al-'Almaniyya: Tahlil wa naqd lil 'Almaniyya Muhtawan wa Tarikhiyyan*, Beirut: al-Manshurat al-Dawla. 1980, p.160. Lebanese Christian postures towards secularism however have not always been more positive though stemming from a fear of a numeric democracy. Kamal al-Haj's anti-secular discourse for instance is designed to justify Lebanon's sectarian system which he equates with (the preservation of) religion; political sectarianism thus is posited to be the sole guarantee against (personal) atheism. See Kamal al-Haj, *Constructive Sectarianism and the Philosophy of the National Pact* [Arabic], Beirut: 1961.

13 Virtually all Islamic fundamentalist groups in Lebanon, both Shi'ite and Sunni, define their foundational struggle in response to the Zionist

colonies and later establishment of the state of Israel. For a good study on how Israel has undermined secular forces in Palestine, see Loren Diller Lybarger, *Between Sacred and Secular: Religion, generations, and collective memory among Muslim and Christian Palestinians in the post-Oslo period*, PhD Dissertation, The University of Chicago, 2002.

14 The 42 US single SC vetoes since 1970 shielding the Jewish state from recriminations have severely undermined trust in international law and thus supported a retreat to parochial identities and a portentous recourse to brute force and terror as the most viable means to settle disputes. For the list of US vetoes in the security council, including those directly pertaining to transgressions in Lebanon, see: http://www.jewishvirtuallibrary.org/jsource/UN/usvetoes.html. For the additional 65 UN resolutions of which Israel stands in direct violation, see: http://www.jerusalemites.org/facts_documents/un/22.htm

15 Baldric of Dol *Historia Jerosolimitana* as cited in *The First Crusade: The Chronicle of Fulcher of Chartres and Other Source* Material, trans. Edward Peters. Philadelphia: University of Pennsylvania Press, 1971.

16 Sophia Saadeh has rendered *ta'ifiyya* as (religious) 'caste', akin to the Indian notion of caste signifying hereditary identities of closed, endogamous groups see Saffiye Saadeh, *The Social Structure of Lebanon*. Beirut, Dar an-Nahar, 1993.

17 The government was quick to identify Syria as the instigator of the riots, only to find itself acknowledging in the aftermath that over 80 per cent of the rioters were Lebanese. Rachid Mezhar, the judge responsible announced that of 137 arrested, 111 were Lebanese, 16 Syrian and 10 Palestinian. *L'Orient de Jour*, 7 March 2006.

Some of the militants were members the notorious *Dinniyeh* Group, Islamists who in January 2000 launched a failed attempt to establish an Islamic 'mini-state' in north Lebanon. The insurgents, many of whom were non-Lebanese Arabs and had trained in al-Qaeda camps in Afghanistan, were evicted from dozens of villages they captured in the Dinniyeh district east of Tripoli after several days of clashes with Lebanese troops and 40 casualties. The leaders of this terror cell were imprisoned until 2005 when Saad al-Hariri paid $48,000 in bail for their release. Hariri described this as 'a humanitarian action', in conjunction with a concurrent amnesty of Samir Geagea, the Lebanese Forces leader sentenced to life imprisonment in connection with political assassinations, most notably the murder of former Prime Minister Rashid Karami in 1987. Geagea was the only prominent warlord to be sent to jail. After the elections, Hariri used his parliamentary majority to secure amnesty for 22 of the Islamists as well as seven militants detained in September 2004 on suspicion of plotting to bomb the Italian and Ukrainian embassies in Beirut,

Crisis Group interview, Beirut, 27 October 2005. See *Al-Mustaqbal*, An-Nahar and *The Daily Star*, 10 June 2005.

18 Benjamin Barber, 'Jihad vs. McWorld' in *The Atlantic Monthly*, Volume 269, March 1992; No. 3; pages 53-65.

19 I believe Farid al-Khazen in his magisterial book on the Civil War overstates his case when he holds that 'beginning in the late 1960s, the major crises that destabilised the country and brought the political process to a standstill were not linked to social-economic factors'. Farid al-Khazin, *The Breakdown of the State in Lebanon (1967-1976)*. Cambridge: HUP, 2001, p.261. Only additional concrete data could vindicate this claim and Khazen cites only one concrete economic indicator of income inequalities before the war of 1975, from 1959 (p. 258). Not only does he fail to present comparable data from the subsequent years leading up to the war, which would have illustrated the considerable overlap of sectarian and class divides, Khazen also ignores considering any possible correlation between confessional and social identity and the economic state of the players. Yusuf Sayigh, *Entrepreneurs of Lebanon*, Cambridge: Harvard University Press, 1964. Theodor Hanf has sought to deny these well-documented findings while citing scant statistical data to refute them. See Theodor Hanf, *Koexistenz im Krieg*, Baden-Baden, Nomos Verlag, 1990. Hanf however does acknowledge Butrus Labaki's findings that two thirds of the industrial and trade firms of Lebanon are controlled by Christians.

20 Chamie concludes that 'whatever reasonable criteria one chooses to utilise, the [socio-economic hierarchy] is unmistakably clear: non-Catholic Christians and Christians at the top, Druze around the middle, Sunnis near the bottom, and Shi's at the very bottom'. Chamie, who currently serves as the head demographer at the United Nations, further observes that fertility rates are inverse to levels of income. Joseph Chamie, 'The Lebanese Civil War: An Investigation into the Causes', *World Affairs*, January 1977, Vol. 139 Issue 3, p171. The same findings were confirmed by a study by Salim Nasr.

21 See Y Shmeil, *La Sociologie du Systeme Politique Libanais*, Unpublished Thesis, Université de Grenoble, 1975.

22 The degree to which Lebanon may be said to meet the requirements of a *laissez faire* economy is very much in the eye of the beholder. The movement of labour and capital has been relatively unrestricted in Lebanon since the 1948 official decree authorising a free foreign exchange market. Gates however points out that the Beirut elite's slogans of *laissez faire* in Lebanon did not allow for true domestic competition and smacked of hypocrisy: 'While powerful merchants and bankers hailed the Smithian invisible hand, they were also engaging in price-fixing and manipulation made possible by their market power' Carole Gates, *The Merchant*

Republic. London: Centre for Lebanese Studies in association with I B Tauris. New York 1998, p.96.

23 Eli Khayr cit. in *An-Nahar,* 20 September 2005. In responding to these rumors, Saad al-Hariri has vowed to fight critics of his father's economic program with 'more economic development projects'.

24 Robert Fisk has related the brutality with which Ghazi Kanaan cracked down on Hezbollah in 1987, killing two dozen cadres in cold blood and subsequently parading the bodies in the suburbs. Robert Fisk, 'The Ghazi Kanaan I knew was not the sort of man who would commit suicide,' *The Independent,* 13 October 2005.

25 The final vote in the Council of Ministers ended 21 to 6 in favour of the new civil law, but Prime Minister Hariri refused to sign and forward the bill to parliament. The opposing bloc formed around Prime Minister Hariri, Fouad Seniora, Bassem al-Saba', 'Umar Misqawi, Bajij Tabbara and Bishara Merhej. The later two ministers both concluded civil marriages themselves in spite of their opposition to this bill. cit. in Elias Hrawi. *Elias Hrawi: Return of the Republic [Arabic].* Edited by Camille Munassa. Beirut: Dar an-Nahar. p.573. The blocs of Nabih Berri and Walid Jumblatt both supported the bill.

26 *As-Safir,* 27 April 2006.

27 The first modern Arab state to pronounce Islam as the official religion of the state was Egypt in its constitution of 1923, a result of a deal struck between the British and the Khedive Ismail to quell the latter's caliphal ambitions. The Syrian Arab Kingdom of 1920 under Faisal spelled out a 'civil government' but likewise insisted on Islam as the religion of the Kingdom. In Egypt, Law no. 40 of 1977 prohibits the establishment of any party whose tenets challenge any principle of *shari'a* legislation, while Article 2 of the 1980 constitution reaffirmed the *shari'a* as the principle source of legislation, a clause which was also added to the Syrian constitution after it had been removed in 1956. In the constitution of 1938, and under Hafez al-Assad in 1973, a clause was added stipulating that the president must be Muslim. The premature neo-con euphoria of celebrating the dawn of secularism in Iraq – see for instance Kanan Makiyya, 'Secularism and Democracy are the Pillars of a New Iraq' WSJ, February 9, 2005 – has already sadly been replaced by reality. *Kitabat Joseph Mughayzil, vol II,* Beirut: Mua'ssasat J. Mughayzil wa Dar an-Nah?r. 1997. p. 249.

28 '*Hiwar al-atrash'(dialogue of the deaf)* is the often-cited Lebanese designation for this stalemate.

29 The cumulative Christian presence has dwindled from 80 per cent of the residents the *Mutasarrifiyye* until the First World War, to c. 60 per cent after the establishment of the *Grand Liban* and the appendage of the Biqa', Beirut and Tripoli in 1920 to about 30-40 per cent today. Philip Hitti,

Lebanon in History. p.439 and 'Abdallah al-Mallah, *Mutasarrifiyyat Jabal Lubnân fi'ahd Muzaffar Bâsha, 1902–1907.* Beirut 1985, p.105, 256. The number of Shi'ites today in Lebanon varies between a maximum of 40 per cent as published in Klaus-Peter. *Untersuchungen Zur Sozialgeographie Christlicher Minderheiten Im Vorderen Orient.* Vol. 43. Wiesbaden: Beihilfe zum Tubinger Atlas des Vorderen Orients, 1980 and a minimum of 26.2 per cent as published by Interior Ministry in *An-Nahar,* 11 February 2005.

30 *As-Safir, 9* February 2005.

31 Hassan Nasrallah, 30 March 2006, *al-Manar Television.*

32 Interview with Seyyed Hassan Nasrallah in *as-Safir 27* April 2006.

33 Ibid.

34 In the National Dialogue sessions Nasrallah managed to sidestep the thorny issue of Hezbollah's disarmament: 'I am ready to discuss the existence of God or his non-existence for ten hours'. Ibid.

35 Eqbal Ahmed, 'Encounter with a Fighter', *al-Ahram Weekly,* 30 July – 5 August 1998, Issue No.388.

36 'We prefer to await the day on which we succeed in convincing our countrymen – by ways of dialogue – that the only alternative is the founding of an Islamic State.' Hassan Nasrallah cited in *al-'Ahd,* 10 April 1994.

37 'We confirm our convictions in Islam as a tenet and a system, both intellectual and legislative, calling on all to learn of it and abide by its code. And we summon the people to adopt it and commit to its instructions, at the individual, political and social levels. Hence we call for the implementation of the Islamic system based on a direct and free choice of the people, and not through forceful imposition as may be assumed by some.' 'Open Letter to the Oppressed' as cited in Naim Qassem. *Hezbollah: The Story from Within.* London: Saqi Books, 2005. p.31 and published on 17 February 1985 in *As-Safir.* Chibli Mallat has trenchantly summarized the reasons for the deliberate ambiguity of the Shi'ite discourse. See *Chibli Mallat, Aspects of Shi'ite Thought from the South of Lebanon,* Papers on Lebanon, 7, Centre for Lebanese Studies, Oxford. See: http://users.ox.ac.uk/~shehadi/papr_CLS.htm (last accessed April 2005).

38 'My prime allegiance is to Lebanon. So much is clear... Pray show me even a single action of ours which was ultimately designed to benefit Iran... if some say that Hezbollah is serving the Iranian interest, then these people should tell me when Hezbollah has undertaken something to the benefit for Iran. Are we from Sri Lanka?' *As-Safir,* 27 April 2006.

39 *As-Safir,* 18 May 2006. Fadlallah draws attention to the period in which Syria cooperated with the United States: 'the Muslims did not bring Syria to Lebanon, but rather the Americans did so.'

40 *Pew Global Attitudes Project,* 2004. *p.25.* One should add however that a

majority of Lebanese (both Muslim and Christian) supported a greater role for religion in school curricula in contrast to other Arab states such as Jordan. A subsequent survey conducted by the Pew Research Center revealed that a whopping 81 per cent of British, 69 per cent of Spanish, 66 per cent of German and 46 per cent of French Muslims consider themselves as Muslim first (rather than a citizen of their country). In Lebanon, this percentage stood at a record low of only 30 per cent. 42 per cent of US Christians and only 14 of French and Spanish Christians think of themselves as Christians (rather than citizens) first. See Pew study as cited in David Rampe, *International Herald Tribune*, 'Muslims and Europe', 7 July 2006, p.4.

41 See Hani Fahs, *al-Shi'ite wa-al-dawlah fi Lubnan: Malami fi al-Ru'ya wa-al-Dhakira*, Beirut, 1996. p.137.

42 Hezbollah has at once stood in the way of the government sending troops to the south while disavowing responsibility for attacks launched by unknown factions. On the one hand, Hezbollah has asserted that 'it is not an alternative to the government', on the other hand, the party refuses to join its militia to the army as this would allegedly diminish its effectiveness.

43 *An-Nahar*, 20 June 2006.

44 'Israel can shape its strategic environment, in cooperation with Turkey and Jordan, by weakening, containing, and even rolling back Syria. This effort can focus on removing Saddam Hussein from power in Iraq – an important Israeli strategic objective in its own right – as a means of foiling Syria's regional ambitions.... Diverting Syria's attention by using Lebanese opposition elements to destabilise Syrian control of Lebanon... Israel will not only contain its foes; it will transcend them.' 'A Clean Break: A New Strategy for Securing the Realm' last accessed 5 April 2006 at: http://www.iasps.org/strat1.htm

45 *Jerusalem Post*, 'Arab World Divided on Hamas', January 27, 2006.

46 *Daily Star*, 27 January 2005.

47 See the account of the last informal conversation of journalists with Rafiq al-Hariri in *As-Safir*, 15 February 2005. Nasrallah, with whom Hariri met on a weekly basis, himself flatly stated that 'it is true that Hariri became a part of the opposition (to Syria)'. *As-Safir*, February 16, 2004.

48 Cit. in *Lebanon in Limbo*, ed. Theodor Hanf and Nawaf Salam, Beirut: Nomos Verlag 2003, p.709.

49 MEMRI, 7 February 2003, no.466. Middle East Online, November 19, 2003.

50 *An-Nahar*, Saturday, January 6, 2006. Jumblatt has recently espoused aggressive, anti-Iranian and anti-Syrian rhetoric. However, it was Jumblatt who facilitated the conduit of Pasdaran fighters through the port of

Khaldeh in exchange for a handsome compensation at a time when Syria was trying to limit the power of Hezbollah. See Houchang Chehabi, 'The Islamic Republic and Hezbollah', in *Iran and Lebanon in the Revolutionary Decade*, 2006, p.227.

51 Bolton, who had previously expressed his disdain for international law and the UN, was honored on 12 March 2006 by the Lebanese American Delegation in a ceremony attended by some of the leaders of the Cedar Revolution.

52 The Jewish Institute for National Security Affairs is perhaps the most militant lobby for the Jewish state in Washington. Besides Bolton, Douglas Feith and Richard Perle, Michael Leeden, Dick Cheney and Paul Wolfowitz served as members and as architects of the wars on Iraq and the campaigns against Syria, Iran and Hezbollah. Jason Vest, 'The Men From JINSA and CSP' *The Nation*, 2 September 2002.

53 Tamara Chalabi, *Community and Nation-State: The Shi'is of Jabal 'Amil and the new Lebanon, 1918-1943*. PhD thesis, Harvard University, 2003. and Roschanack Shaery-Eisenlohr, *Constructing Shi'ite Nationalism*, PhD dissertation, University of Chicago, 2004, p.52.

54 Michael Hudson. *The Precarious Republic*. New York: Random House, 1968.

55 In Hariri's election booklet *Government and Responsibility*, the pre-1992 debt is put at 3 billion US$. However, this computation neglects the pound stabilised at around 1.500 LP to 1 US$ only after Hariri assumed power late in 1992. Before that, the going rate was at 3.000 LP to 1 US$ which would indicate a cumulative debt of ca. 1.5 billion US$ before the arrival of Hariri. A similar 'numbers game' was played when it came to assessing the costs of Horizon 2000 which were originally put at $11.672 billion but when counted in current prices actually amounted to $18.4 billion. See Tom Najem, *The Collapse and Reconstruction of Lebanon*, 1998, pp.29, 39.

56 See *The Economist Intelligence Unit Report on Lebanon*, July 2003; Neil Ford, 'Lebanon Weighed Down by Debt', *Middle East*, June 2003, p.52. While the official figure as of the end of 2003 hovers around 32 billion USD, Premier Hoss has argued that this number is deflated and that the actual cumulative of money owned by Lebanon's national bank amounts to 42 Billion USD (see An-Nahar, 30 December 2003). According to Hoss, the official government figure for the national debt does not include government expenses for the national social service fond (SSNF), electricity or ongoing projects such as the real-estate development project Elisaar.

57 Berlin's size ($3.4 million) almost equals Lebanon's, yet its deficit has reached 46 billion euros (see *Time*, 'Lost in the Dark', 30 June 2003).

58 At least half of the 18 per cent on Lebanese lira Treasury Bills (i.e. $8.5 bil-

lion) was paid in excess of 'what the cost would have been in a normally operating market'. see Toufic Gaspard. *A Political Economy of Lebanon.* Leiden: Brill, 2004 and Samir Makdisi. *The Lessons of Lebanon.* London: I B Tauris. 2004. 204ff. The inordinately high domestic interest rates made it lucrative for banks to borrow in the foreign market to buy up government bonds (rather than invest domestically), a sign of the times observable in other debt-ridden Middle Eastern countries such as Turkey for instance where the absence of a currency peg and the depreciation of the lira augmented windfall profits to an even greater degree. See Caglar Keyder, 'The Turkish Belly Jar' *New Left Review* July/August, no. 28 (2004) p.76.

59 The rapid (expected) post-war GDP expansion petered out by 1995 and turned negative by 2000.

60 See *An-Nahar*, August 24, 2003, Labaki: 'Al-Faqr wa al batala wa al-Tanmiyya fi Lubnan'. One study of 1998 calculates a pre-tax Gini-coefficient of 0.71 and an after-tax coefficient of 0.69. Abdullah Dah, Ghassan Dibeh, Wassim Shahin 'The Distributional Impact of Taxes in Lebanon'. Beirut: LCPS. 1998. Other sources show an improving income Gini coefficient from 0.61 in 1951, to 0.51 in 1966 and 0.41 in 1997. Gaspard, *A Political Economy of Lebanon*, p.74, Leiden: Brill, 2004.

61 Gaspard, p.74. Disparities of income may be slightly inflated in view of the informal economy and remittances, the highest per capita in the world.

62 Samir Makdisi. *The Lessons of Lebanon.* Beirut: I B Tauris, 2004. p.150.

63 Michael Johnson, *All Honourable Men: The Social Origins of the War in Lebanon,* London: I B Tauris, 2001. p.197. The assassination of Nasserite leader Maarouf Saad on 6 March 1975 during an anti-Chamoun demonstration is often seen as the date marking the beginning of subsequent civil war in Lebanon.

64 Contrary to occasional claims of the press, and in contrast to the pre-1975 situation, the majority of the Lebanese camps have not seen violent flare-ups. The notable exception seems to be the camp of 'Ain al-Hilweh.

65 'Light' weaponry and guns unfortunately still are readily available in many private households in Lebanon.

66 Memorandum no. 35/72, 17 March 1972.

67 Stephen Walt and John Mersheimer, The Israeli Lobby and US Foreign Policy, *London Review of Books,* vol.28, no.6, March 23, 2006.

68 *Asia Times,* February 2005.

69 In Beirut, 74.4 per cent of students attended private schools. In the poor, largely Shi'ite suburbs of Beirut only 13.5 per cent of students attended governmental schools, so that confessional schools exerted a full domination.

70 See Nimr Frayha. 'Education and Social Cohesion in Lebanon.' *Prospects*

23, no. 1, 2003, and Maha Shuayb, *Towards a Theory of Care, A study of Students, Teachers and Principals Views in 14 Schools in Lebanon*, Unpublished Doctoral Thesis, University of Cambridge, 2005.

71 Adib Saab has suggested a possible pedagogical approach in this regard. Adib Saab, *al-Din wa al-Mujtama'*. Beirut: Dar al-Nahar, 1983; *Muqaddima fi falsafat al-Din*. Beirut: Dar al-Nahar, 1995; *Wahdatun fi' al-Tana'u'*. Beirut: Dar al-Nahar, 2003.

72 As-Seyyed Hani Fahs, 'Al-Mawarina fi Lubnan' [The Maronites in Lebanon], *al-Hayat*, Thursday, 4 March, 2005

73 *An-Nahar*, February, 10, 2000. Also see the excellent work by Sune Haugbølle, *Looking the Beast in the Eye: Collective Memory of the Civil War in Lebanon* Thesis for the Master of Studies St Antony's College, Oxford, June 2002.

74 See www.beirutletter.com

75 George Hawi interview with Paul Marodis, *Al-Afkar*, Beirut, no.1062, 14 October 2005, p.22.

76 'If I were a dictator, religion and state would be separate. I swear by my religion, I will die for it. But it is my personal affair. The state has nothing to do with it. The state should look after your secular welfare, health, communications, foreign relations, currency and so on, but not your or my religion. That is everybody's personal concern', cited in TN Madan, p.237.

77 See the website of the Mouvement Sociale at www.aalmana.org, *Nahwa al-Muwatina* at: www.na-am.org also see *as-Safir*, 13 March 2006.

78 This was the fear voiced by Ghassan Tueni in *An-Nahar*, 5 June 2006, p.12.

79 The poll revealed that 34 per cent stated that they belonged to Lebanon first while 37.3 per cent affirmed their confession as their primary identity. This latter number surged to 48.8 per cent in a hypothetical context of conflict, underscoring the precarious fragility of national identity in Lebanon. Cit. in Jawad Adra, 'Crisis of Identity and the Role of the Zu'ama', *II Monthly*, no.47, May 2006. p.19.

80 During his keynote address at the *Cénacle Libanais* in May 1957, Toynbee warned that Lebanon could not survive as a garrison outpost of Western interests and was forced by dint of its geography and history to find a *modus vivendi* with its environment.

81 In dealing with Hezbollah in particular, and militant Islamist movements in general, comprehensiveness and consistency are key. The exclusive preoccupation with the anti-Syrian UN resolution 1559 – without consideration of the plethora of prior anti-Israeli UN resolutions (including the over 70 vetoed by the United States) – cannot conceivably lead to an equitable resolution.

82 Saffiya Saadeh, *The Social Structure of Lebanon*. Beirut: Dar an-Nahar,

1993. p.123.

83 SSNP leader Antun Saadeh was abducted and summarily executed after the collusion of the icons of Lebanese independence, Bishara al-Khoury and Riyyad al-Solh with the regime of Hosni Za'im. It is mentioned but rarely that the Syrian Premier at the time, Muhsin al-Barazi, was the brother-in-law of Riad al-Solh, the Lebanese Premier. Together they coordinated the arrest and execution of Saadeh with the head of the Lebanese security forces. Adel Beshara, *Lebanon: Politics of Frustration - the Failed Coup of 1961*, London: Routledge, 2005. p.181. Kamal Jumblatt subsequently took the mantle of secularism in Lebanon but reneged somewhat from full secularisation prior to his assassination in 1977, in all likelihood at the behest of Damascus. The list of liberal journalists assassinated in Lebanon – from Samir Lawzi to Riad Taha in the 1950s and 60s to Samir Kassir and Gibran Tueni in 2005 – is too long to list here. The sheer number of such brutal murders however testify to their strength.

84 As-Safir, Ghassan Yaqub, 28 January 2005.

Chapter Ten

The Philosophy of Lebanese Power-Sharing

Michael Kerr

Dedicated to the memory of Professor Malcolm Kerr

During my last visit to Beirut, I thought long and hard about the likelihood of a future Lebanese state being governed by the sort of democratic power-sharing system it experienced before the country collapsed in 1975.[1] The people who lived through that period are getting older and older whilst the new generation has little or no memory of anything but war or a form of government, far removed from the 1943 National Pact.[2] So what does this mean for the future of power-sharing and democracy in Lebanon? Does the democratic deficit the country has experienced since 1975 make it less likely that power-sharing will successfully manage Lebanese politics in the future, through the full implementation of the Ta'if Accord or a new inter-communal pact? The conclusion I came to was probably not. This view is, naturally, influenced by my formative experiences in Northern Ireland, a divided society situated in an environment more predisposed to democratisation than Lebanon, yet one with no history of successful power-sharing government or pluralist democracy as we understand it in Beirut.

So whilst the civil war does not necessarily make a return to some form of democratic power-sharing any less likely, to my mind, whether this proves possible in the future will be determined by external intervention, regional stability and state sovereignty.

On 18 April 2002, I heard Professor Joseph Maila deliver a very interesting lecture at St Joseph's University, Beirut.[3] He spoke of how Lebanon's three largest communities had all contributed to the formation of the state: the Maronites in 1920 pressing the French to create greater Lebanon; the Sunnis in 1943 seising independence under the National Pact; and the Shi'a in 2000 triggering the Israeli withdrawal. This is a compelling argument and one that adds weight to the view that Lebanon has a long tradition of tolerance and coexistence. It is important to note, here, that many Lebanese leaders have viewed such inter-communal engagement as fundamental to their interests, regardless of their conflicts over what form the state should take. Yet it was precisely this division, over 'which Lebanon', that saw its communities invite negative external intervention: Hezbollah through its attacks on Israel on 12 July 2006; the Maronites through their support for the 17 May Agreement in 1983; and the Sunnis through their support for the Palestinians in the early 1970s. During periods of instability Lebanon's communities have felt compelled to take shelter under the umbrella of foreign sponsors who offer protection. Consequently, their actions have broken the National Pact on the basis of this patronage. Whilst each major Lebanese community has contributed to the consolidation of the state with the assistance of external powers, they have all contributed to its disintegration, at different junctures, by supporting foreign actors, which have pursued their own strategic interests in Lebanon at the expense of the Lebanese.

Unsurprisingly, war and conflict are the issues that many academics focus on when detailing the modern history of Lebanon. Speaking of the wave of democratisation that followed the Second World War, political scientists forget to mention Lebanon. When Western journalists comment on the prospects of Iraq becoming the Arab world's first democracy, it is not due to their understanding of the thorny question of whether Lebanon is an Arab state or not. The decades of power-sharing democracy in Lebanon seem to have been forgotten by the outside world, such was the ferocity of its civil war. Many states have also found it convenient to overlook Lebanese democracy, alongside their complicity in bringing about its collapse. Ironically, a civil war with many similar internal and external features has broken out in Iraq, following the US led invasion in 2003. This military action was conducted with the aim of imposing democracy and in the hope that Iraq's three main communities, the Kurds, Shi'a and Sunnis, would engage in a successful confederal state-building venture. Policy makers attempting to engineer a 'nation state' in Iraq should heed the lessons of Lebanon's halcyon days. The chances of successfully building a state in Iraq will increase if the West focuses on creating institutions that reflect the country's religious or ethnic heterogeneity, rather than the ideal of moulding a new Iraqi nation.[4]

The serious difficulties the US led coalition encountered following its invasion, raises questions over the ability of democratic Western powers to establish pluralist forms of government in nationally, ethnically and religiously divided societies. Given the interventionist foreign policy decisions the US has taken since the invasion of Iraq – more often than not within the rubric of its special relationship with the UK and in ignorance of the historical lessons that can be drawn from Britain's colonial experience in the Middle East – much can be learnt regarding the use of consociation as a tool for ethnic conflict regulation and its prospects for successfully managing nationally-fractured societies.[5] Should America succeed in establishing a stable multi-communal government in Iraq, the new Iraqi elite will be highly dependent on Washington for political survival. The new Iraqi state, in its present form at least, is dependent on the US government's ability to bring stability to the region. The Bush administration, despite its great power, has, however, proved susceptible to domestic and international pressures that have limited its capacity to guarantee such stability in the absence of regional and internal support for its intervention. The flagrant disregard the US government showed for Lebanon's power-sharing arrangements in 2006 is unlikely to instil consociationalists in Baghdad with any confidence. One might be tempted to view this policy as the actions of an imperial power that has become frustrated by its apparent inability to get its own way. In the post 9/11 world, the US has appeared increasingly constrained by the checks and balances of an international state system that is to some extent formed in its own image.

There are, therefore, limitations on how successful a democratic power can be when it acts to pursue its strategic and economic interests outside the rubric of international diplomacy. As a result, the failure of intervening powers to impose democracy or power-sharing in divided societies has had negative consequences. Putting the clock back in a state that has begun to disintegrate, rather than democratise, may prove impossible for an external power regardless of its military and economic prowess. So when the term 'exit strategy' is used in relation to Iraq, we can infer two different meanings. In Western political speak, it indicates a managed admission of failure and an attempt to check falling domestic poll ratings. In a practical sense, in the Arab world, however, it may mean protracted civil war and ethno-national conflict.

Brendan O'Leary has questioned whether this means that viable power-sharing systems, which seek to regulate ethnic conflicts or civil wars between ethno-national or religious communities, have to be the *de facto* or *de jure* protectorates of external powers.[6] Some realists might view this as an ideal, given the proliferation of ethnic conflict since the end of the Cold War. Whilst the suggestion may be abhorrent to some, such an idea is not so different to the French influence in Lebanon under the Règlement during the nineteenth century.[7] Consociation – the sharing of executive political power through proportionality with communal veto rights and the maximisation of autonomy – has often been a source of colonial or extra-colonial control, enhanced when a regional state system or empire weakens. Iraq is the modern day example of this and, as such, might be described as a consociational guinea pig, building on the Lebanese model.

After the first Gulf War, America left the implementation of

Lebanon's Ta'if Accord and the resuscitation of its power-sharing institutions to a country lacking any democratic attributes, but with *de facto* regional agreement or at least acceptance of this settlement.[8] In 2002, I asked a senior American diplomat in Lebanon why the US government had not pressured the Syrian government to implement the Ta'if Accord to the letter and spirit of that agreement. The answer I was given came as a reality check. The frank response was that the Lebanese government had never asked them to. This was the realism of post-Ta'if power-sharing in Lebanon. In contrast, the US has sought to impose democracy itself in Iraq in the absence of regional or international agreement, acceptance or support for such intervention. The immediate beneficiary of this intervention was Iran, who not only lost an aggressive rival in Saddam Hussein's Iraq, but became vital to the US led coalition in its struggle to provide a stable decentralised democracy in its place. In 1989 Lebanon traded state sovereignty in return for having its civil war brought to a close and its constitutional vacuum filled. In contrast, Iraq has had civil war thrust upon it and with many of the negative external variables familiar to the Lebanese. The choice presented to Iraqis was power-sharing or chaos. But what does this mean for Lebanon and the future of power-sharing in this country? To answer this question, we must assess Lebanon's position within the regional state system.

In May 2006, I had the pleasure of seeing his Excellency Prime Minister Fouad Siniora speaking on Lebanon's economic outlook at my institution, the London School of Economics and Political Science, in the UK. He argued that the world had a 'duty' to help Lebanon recover from its long years of civil war and economic repression.[9] When the subject turned to international relations he focused on the urgent need for the Sheba Farms issue to be resolved diplomatically. He reminded listeners that international and regional dilemmas remain as central to the Lebanese equilibrium today as they have done in the past.

Old Lebanese pacts hinged on the realism of external relations with either patron states or international powers. This is the philosophy of power-sharing in Lebanon. The National Pact papered over inter-communal differences to enable Lebanon to gain state sovereignty from the Free French authorities. Lebanon's founding fathers believed that the contradictory elements that made up the state could coexist, provided the country remained neutral in its foreign policy orientation, both regionally and internationally. Such a philosophy was based on the regional status quo of 1943.

By 1989, the political impact of civil war and the regional conflicts it brought to Lebanon, meant that a new national pact was forged, this time premised on forgoing sovereignty in order to reconstitute the state. This was the opposite of the 1943 formula, when a Christian-Muslim alliance set aside conflicting Lebanese and pan-Arab nationalist aspirations to gain state sovereignty. To some, the Ta'if formula was a violation of the National Pact, a justifiable view, particularly if it was to be considered the real constitution, or the constitution under the constitution, of the country. The problem confronting the old Lebanese elite in 1989 was that they were attempting to strengthen the political fabric of the state from a position of abject weakness at the end of a civil war. While this was a very risky position for those seeking a return to the National Pact, it was also reason to be optimistic about the possibility that the regional situation might change and allow a more proportionate Lebanese equilibrium to re-emerge. This would mean a pact underpinned by Lebanese interests above, or at least equal to, the interests of the external powers that brokered an agreement and acted as stanchions overarching the communities. In the short to medium-term, at least, this dilemma leaves the culture of constitutional dependency at the heart of Lebanese politics. This would appear to be a symptom of consociational government in divided societies. Lebanon remains reliant on the 'politics of anticipation' – the hope that positive external forces will help reconstitute a National Pact, as opposed to manipulating its power-sharing arrangements to serve their own interests. It is safe to conclude then that external events remain central to Lebanese power-sharing and the prevention of future civil war. As Farid el-Khazen has argued, 'Lebanon has been interdependent on the negative aspects of the regional system of security and not on the positive aspects.'[10] The impact Syria's 2005 troop withdrawal had on Lebanese society reinforces this view. We should not, however, dismiss the impact that positive variables might have on Lebanon's power-sharing institutions should they materialise or outweigh the negative variables. After Syria's withdrawal, it was not long before Lebanon required robust external support to enable a new Lebanese government to fill the power vacuum and stabilise its power-sharing institutions. The fact that this was not forthcoming does not mean that the potential for positive intervention was not there.

Strong centralised states can often resist what would be destabilising exogenous pressures for weak plural societies, from both regional and international sources. Clearly, societies divided by ethno-national conflict cannot easily resist the gravity of regional turmoil, as the Lebanese experience illustrates. Such societies require long-term positive external support if they are to consolidate what remain national pacts into national constitutions. Preferably, if an external power supports or oversees the implementation of a constitutional agreement in a divided society, it would be in the interest of that power to enable the new government to survive, both politically and economically, on its own merits. In an ideal world, external actors would have an interest in ensuring this was the case. For example, America and Britain had a clear interest in reviving German democracy following the Second World War and reconstituting a stable sovereign state. It was fortunate for West Germany that this interest was positive and, because of the regional dynamics of the Cold War, the US went to great lengths to ensure its political survival. It should not be forgotten that Lebanon also gained its sovereignty from positive intervention, when Britain played a role in partially creating an environment where independence could be achieved through a national agreement.[11] The British harassed their Free French allies into fulfilling their pledge to grant Lebanon independence and promoted a Christian-Muslim elite that realised it during the Second World War.

In contrast, the Ta'if Accord bounds Lebanon's reconstruction to policy coordination with Syria in all fields. This was open-ended and those negotiating the US-Saudi sponsored agreement did not know how much sovereignty they were conceding to Damascus. Regional events and international relations determined the nature of that agreement's implementation. The violation of the Ta'if process is well documented by Theodor Hanf in his seminal study of Lebanon's civil war, *Coexistence in Wartime Lebanon: The Decline of a State and the Rise of a Nation.*[12] Fellow political scientist, Joseph Maila, reminds us that Ta'if had a tightly bound consociational formula for the re-establishment of a confessional administration, but one that would only be implemented after the sovereignty of the state had been compromised through the external sections of the agreement.[13] Without such external linkage, however, there would have been no agreement at all. This is the realism of Ta'if. The rehabilitation of consociation was a quid pro quo – the Lebanese were assisted in the re-establishment of their pact of coexistence and, in return, conceded an unknown quantity of state sovereignty to Damascus.

So what lessons can we draw from Lebanon's modern history and political circumstances? Firstly, when it comes to maintaining democratic power-sharing, the problem facing divided societies like Lebanon, Bosnia, Northern Ireland and Iraq is that external forces were paramount in the making and breaking of their political systems. External actors can successfully facilitate accommodation between domestic elites and help establish power-sharing governments. Equally, if it does not suit their interests, or they are too weak to act, external powers can undermine power-sharing governments or simply fail in their attempts to support them. If external forces have a positive interest in consociation, i.e. a strategic or economic interest that is not wholly selfish and, in turn, supports the pro-power-sharing domestic elites in a divided society, then they can provide the motivations and incentives for them to engage in consociation. This has been the experience in Northern Ireland through the British and Irish governments' attempts to implement the Belfast Agreement after 1998.[14] This case illustrates clearly that proximity to a democratic state system and the willingness/ability of internal elites to share power considerably influences the prospects of the long-term stabilisation of ethnic conflict through democratic power-sharing. It also helps enormously if they are unhindered by other regional actors who hold a conflicting interest in the divided society and if the internal elites are prepared to work the consociational arrangements of their own accord but simply lack the power.

Lebanon's experience shows that exogenous pressures do not have to be unselfish to impose power-sharing successfully. The Ta'if Accord was brokered due to the convergence of the selfish interests of external actors. Whilst their interests coincided with those of the traditional Lebanese elites, the intervening powers were not entirely dependent on the Lebanese to reach agreement. Lebanon's politicians had agreed many of Ta'if's political reforms between 1976 and 1989 – they simply lacked the power to implement them. By consenting to the external aspects of the agreement, Ta'if granted the old Lebanese elites a chance to regain power in 1989. Refusal would have led to their exclusion from any post-war consociational settlement or simply a continuation of a conflict that was beyond their control. This was typical of the regional dilemma facing Lebanon. Antoine Messarra illustrates this, suggesting that, as with the Cairo Agreement of 1969, the 1988 presidential election crisis over Mikhail Daher and the 1992 parliamentary election boycott, for the Lebanese, 'in all cases, the alternative was either acceptance or chaos.'[15] Here, again, we see the philosophy of Lebanese power-sharing.

The actual timing of Lebanon's 1943 and 1989 agreements was dictated by the agendas of external powers. Whatever arguments can be raised against this point, the Lebanese did not have the power to implement new power-sharing arrangements in the absence of external support for those settlements. But, as has been argued, powers that intervene in divided societies are susceptible to changes of government and foreign policy agendas. Such changes may have both positive and negative influences on the consociational constructs that regulate ethnic conflicts. Dutch political scientist, Arend Lijphart, has argued that 'elite cooperation is the primary distinguishing feature of consociational democracy,' adding that 'conflict management by cooperation and agreement amongst the different elites rather than by majority and competition is the second feature of consociationalism.'[16] Neither of these two features has proved possible in the long-term in Lebanon, as the variables that might provide elite cooperation or conflict management are highly inter-dependent on the regional environment and have not proved static or consistently positive. The shifting dynamics of the Arab-Israeli conflict was the catalyst for the outbreak of civil war in Lebanon in 1975 – regardless of the National Pact's inherent weaknesses – just as the collapse of the Soviet Union saw a convergence of interests in the Middle East that brought it to a close in 1989. More recently, the international standoff between the US, Iran and their regional allies, Israel and Hezbollah, threatened Lebanon's power-sharing system. In these times of crisis, Lebanon failed to adhere to its defensive doctrine of foreign policy neutrality. A policy, which has had a mixed record in a region where pre-emptive strikes, intervention and proxy wars have been favoured foreign policy options by many of its neighbours.

On this question of neutrality, Machiavelli advised that 'A prince is [also] respected when he is a true friend and a true enemy: that is, when he declares himself to be on the side of one prince against another, without reserve. Such a policy will always be more useful than remaining neutral, for if two powerful neighbours of yours come to blows, they will be of the kind that, when one has emerged victorious, you will either have cause to fear the victor or you will not. In either of these two cases, it will always be more useful for you to declare yourself and to wage open warfare.'[17]

Whilst the logic of Machiavelli's view will resonate with students of Lebanese politics, it is of little use to the regulation of divided societies in unstable environments in the twenty-first century. One lesson from the civil war period is that the Lebanese have too often been the loyal supporters or opponents of others at the expense of themselves as a collective multi-ethnic national unit. Lebanese power-sharing, however, continues to oscillate on the changing dynamics of regional and international diplomacy – such is the nature of consociational government in unstable regions where neutrality is seen as a weakness. Conversely, if Lebanon's neighbours have no interest in the stabilisation of power-sharing government in Lebanon, then it is likely that this will have a negative effect. The phrase, 'good social fences may make good political neighbours' is often heard in this debate.[18] Societies weakened and divided by ethno-national conflict are, however, often incapable of building fences or competing with neighbouring states and fall foul to those who have an interest in the failure of their particular political system. Professor James Anderson has noted that neither 'good fences' nor 'weak fences' alone make 'good neighbours', 'only the neighbours themselves can' do that.[19]

Modern Lebanon exemplifies this dilemma as its first consociational agreement was founded on the premise that it would have a foreign policy based on neutrality. Thus, Lebanon's political dependence on the external status quo illustrates both the potential and limitations of its consociational framework, as external forces not only influenced its system of government, but its different communities as well. Just as some states in the Middle East had an interest in Lebanon remaining divided, weak or war torn, it is apparent from the internal and external aspects of the Iraq conflict that some regional forces have an interest in spreading chaos rather than consensus. Like the Lebanese civil war, it has developed into a conflict that is being fought out on many fronts between internal and external forces and, like the Lebanese after 1975, the Iraqis have little control over its outcome.

Ghassan Tueni once suggested that, 'the reality of sovereignty' in Lebanon 'is itself a function of external coercive forces and their interests.'[20] The same can be said of Iraq after 2003. The outcome of any Iraqi pact will be determined by the balance of power between these external forces and whether a collective interest in creating and maintaining stability can be forged. This raises questions over how sovereign ethnically or religiously-divided societies regulated by consociation can actually be. The answer to this, with regards to Lebanon, depends entirely on whether the internal conflict over the state has been finally resolved. Recent events in

Lebanon would suggest that it has not. Hezbollah's vision of Lebanon, as the front line of the Palestinian-Israeli conflict, clashes dramatically with the *laissez faire* urban capitalism of the old Christian-Muslim elite. The irony of Syria's departure from Lebanon, was that, while the Lebanese regained an element of independence or state sovereignty, its power-sharing system lacked the regional stability required to underwrite its new found freedom or prompt a return to democratic power-sharing. There was no symmetry in the external support received by the rival proponents of these conflicting Lebanese visions. Hezbollah relied on its sponsors in Tehran for military, financial, political and spiritual support. In 2006, this support appeared to be a 'constant' in Lebanese politics, whereas the financial and diplomatic aid their opponents received from the Arab states and their Western sponsors could not be taken for granted. There simply is no 'constant' support for democratic power-sharing in Lebanon at the time of writing. For democratic power-sharing to stabilise and reduce tension between Lebanon's different communities or factional alignments, its existence must be guaranteed by Western governments and international institutions. Without a balance of forces within the Lebanese system – an externally sponsored compromise that protects the position of all the communities in Lebanon and in the Middle East – instability will prevail. Lebanon needs positive external intervention if peaceful coexistence is to be realised, if democratic political reforms are to take root and if democratic power-sharing is to be consolidated. These, of course, are big 'ifs', which would require a dramatic u-turn by the US government in its approach towards democratisation in the region as a whole.

So what would an environment that was positive or conducive to the stabilisation of democratic power-sharing in Lebanon look like? As has been argued, external forces may have a selfish interest in regulating a conflict by consociation when it generally suits their purpose and this may facilitate power-sharing. It is an unstable basis for conflict regulation, however, if the interests of intervening powers are purely selfish, as Syria's 2005 exit clearly illustrates. The Assad regime's interest in Lebanon was primarily strategic and, to a lesser extent, economic. Syria's interest in stabilising Lebanon's power-sharing institutions was, therefore, purely to assist in extending its control over the country. A negative external influence would be one where the regional powers have a direct interest in destabilising the divided society's political institutions and possess the ability and desire to do so. Thus, external influences do not have to be strictly positive, in the sense that they are conducive to producing democratic political consociation, as has been defined by consociational theorist Professor Brendan O'Leary.[21] Non-democratic external powers can regulate ethno-national conflict under a form of weak or virtual consociation, as Lebanon's Ta'if Accord demonstrates. This raises questions over just how long consociational governments that regulate divided societies in regionally unstable environments can last. What is apparent from Lebanon's case is that power-sharing arrangements may stabilise so long as the regional status quo, which initially facilitated the inter-communal agreement's implementation, remains relatively static. This is not to say that a slight change or shift in the power or interests of external powers will necessarily result in governmental collapse, but if there is a major change the plaster of consociation may begin to crack. A consociation in an unstable region may well appear fairly static, yet abrupt political changes to its regional environment can fracture its internal and external balance.

O'Leary reminds us that consociation is fundamentally a bargain and nowhere is this more evident than in societies where it is used to regulate ethno-national conflict.[22] As such, the apparent deep-rooted traditions of democracy and consociation amongst the Lebanese failed to prevent any community from retreating to its confessional bunker, or reopening old ethno-national sores that had been bandaged over by the establishment of the state. Lebanon's small size, and the high degree of familiarity and continuity amongst its elites, did not prevent the revival of inter-ethnic hostilities in 1975 and intra-ethnic conflicts thereafter. Nor did the civil war experience, or the prospect of independence from Syria in 2005, temper Hezbollah in its pursuit of a regional agenda that goes against the grain of Lebanon's National Pact. The summer of

2006 served only to remind us that in times of crisis Lebanon's communities will look for external sponsorship to reinforce their domestic positions. More often than not, taking such a stance has led to their participation in externally driven actions that have proved fundamentally detrimental to the National Pact.

Lijphart also stressed that the 'consociational model requires the leaders to have at least some commitment to the maintenance of the state.'[23] But in Lebanon's case, following the Syrian withdrawal, the question again seemed to be: 'which state?' The deadlock in Lebanon's National Dialogue Committee in 2006 indicates that even after the long years of civil war, the question of what it means to be 'a Lebanese' remains unresolved. The country became polarised between the two conflicting 'visions' of what Lebanon's place in the Middle East should be and what sort of independence it should take. The anti-Syrian camp wanted to build on the progress Hariri had made in reconstructing Lebanon as a modern capitalist country. However, they needed Western diplomatic support as well as Saudi financial investment to succeed in those endeavours. In contrast, the pro-Syrian Hezbollah-led faction wanted Lebanon to take a lead role in supporting the Palestinian resistance against Israel and US policy in the region. It was no wonder many Lebanese had a sense of *déjà vu* when Israeli tanks began rolling across the border in July 2006.

To conclude, the fact that a power-sharing government's integrity and continuity is largely dependent on its relationship with external powers remains one of the fundamental limitations to the use of consociation in ethnically divided societies. The internal elites often have little influence over this political equation, hence the need for coercive or supportive consociational engineering. When internal elites do not favour power-sharing as their first constitutional preference – which is often the case – by accepting or supporting its implicit or explicit imposition by exogenous forces they become largely reliant on the ability of those powers to maintain it. Furthermore, they are totally reliant on the constant willingness and inclination of a colonial power or rival regional powers to preserve the external status quo. In other words, the external elites must at least have an interest in maintaining the internal and external equilibrium that facilitates the sharing of power. For example, even if Lebanon's elites agreed the arrangements for a pact of national coexistence, a power-sharing government on that basis might never be realised if the external elites held no interest in the implementation and maintenance of that system. The role played in Lebanon's civil war by Syria, Israel and the PLO illustrates this point.

The prospect of Lebanon successfully implementing a national pact on the consociational model in the long-term should be judged on the existence of stable exogenous forces – the existence of an environment that facilitates or maintains inter-communal power-sharing equilibriums. One of the most fundamental truths in Lebanese politics, at least since the Règlement, is that the communities coexisting on Mount Lebanon and then in greater Lebanon had a shared interest in living together. The premise of this interest is their diversity and need to share Lebanon. The paradox or problem of societies like Lebanon is that where there are powerful external actors with a selfish interest in the state, it is often relatively easy for them to exacerbate inherent tensions within the system to serve their own purposes. This is not to say that Lebanon's problems are exclusively determined by alien forces, but that it often proves impossible for politicians or elites to act in the interest of the state against the grain of regional and domestic zero-sum politics. This is especially so when external actors side with one religious group against another. Internally, even if three quarters of the elites see and pursue a wider Lebanese agenda, it only takes a minority to destabilise such a coalition. Therefore, if external powers provide incentives and motivations for inclusive inter-communal power-sharing, or at least desist from exacerbating the zero-sum nature of consociational electoral systems, the prospects for returning to a true national pact increase.

By 1989, the dynamics of Lebanon's ethno-national tension had radically changed in some respects. Before 1975, inter-communal divisions between the Lebanese were exacerbated as the consociational system failed to deal with the challenges of modernisation and political reform. After the war, however, there appeared to be more agreement on what it was to be Lebanese, and that a return to the pact was the only way for the country to be governed. Hezbollah's Janus-faced position as the country's strongest military force and its largest governing party, in a coalition that had no control over its activity, provided Lebanon's national pact with a divisive ingredient it could not digest. Logically, it was a dilemma that could only be resolved through some regional settlement, which dealt with the constitutional disputes and power relations of those involved in the struggle for the Middle East.

What then would a true Lebanese national pact look like? This is a difficult question to answer and before making any evaluation one must consider whether political conflict in Lebanon remains ethno-national. By that, I mean a society where the state lacks the support of any significant ethnic community or religions grouping. Maila's illustration of religious groups contributing to state formation and Hezbollah finally joining a Lebanese government may lead one to a rather optimistic conclusion on this matter. Lebanon does not suffer from the type of national division over the nature of the state as it did in 1943. Furthermore, Lebanon is populated overwhelmingly by people who see themselves as Lebanese. But does that mean it is safe to conclude that, following a further escalation of regional conflict, the Christians would not look to separatism for their security, the Shi'a community would not promote pan-Islamic interests above Lebanese and the Sunnis would not become hostage to wider Palestinian, Syrian or pan-Arab concerns?

Given the history of conflict and coexistence in Lebanon and the seemingly permanent feature of regional instability, the answer to these questions must be no. We can also be quite sure that if one community was to act in such a fashion, then others would likely follow suit, such is the zero-sum nature of Lebanese politics. Given its long-term success in regulating Lebanon's ethno-national conflict, one of the most interesting observations regarding the National Pact is that it was never intended to be the bedrock of the Lebanese state. The difference between that loose arrangement and the internal aspects of Ta'if are crucial in assessing Lebanon's dilemma. Ta'if's internal reforms, whilst they remained unimplemented, were meant to be lasting. This change in approach was partly a result of the shared learning experiences of the National Pact period and the civil war itself. This is why Lebanon has such great potential to implement a national agreement in the future, to put Lebanese interests ahead of factional concerns and to resuscitate the democracy and vibrant society that it is no longer famous for.

Whilst the Maronites, the Sunni and the Shi'a have all contributed to state formation, the Lebanese elite as a whole have taken advantage of favourable external circumstances in the past: gaining independence under the British; ending the civil war and agreeing constitutional reforms at Ta'if; and making a fresh political departure after the tragic assassination of Prime Minister Rafiq al-Hariri. They can, of course, do so again when the winds of international diplomacy shift.

Notes

1 On consociation in Lebanon, see B. O'Leary's foreword and Chapters 1 & 8 in M. Kerr, *Imposing Power-Sharing: Conflict and Coexistence in Northern Ireland and Lebanon*, (Dublin: Irish Academic Press, 2005).

2 M. Kerr, *Imposing Power-Sharing*, Chapter 5.

3 Lecture given by Joseph Maila at St Joseph's University, Beirut, 18 April 2002.

4 See B. O'Leary in Brendan O'Leary, John McGarry & Khaled Salih, Eds. *The Future of Kurdistan*, (Pennsylvania, University of Pennsylvania Press: 2005).

5 See A. Lijphart, *Democracy in Plural Societies*, (Yale: Yale University Press, 1977); J McGarry and B O'Leary, *The Northern Ireland Conflict: Consociational Arrangements*, (Oxford: Oxford University Press, 2004) and 'Consociational theory, Northern Ireland's conflict, and its agreement. Part 1: What Consociationalists can learn from Northern Ireland', *Government and Opposition* 2006, 41:1, pp. 43-63.

6 B. O'Leary's foreword in M. Kerr, *Imposing Power-Sharing*, page xxxi.

7 See J Spagnolo, *France and Ottoman Lebanon: 1861-1914* (London: Ithaca Press 1977); 'Constitutional Change in Mount Lebanon: 1861-1864', *Middle Eastern Studies* 7(1), 1971, pp 25-48.

8 See T Hanf, *Coexistence in Wartime Lebanon: The Decline of a State and the*

Rise of a Nation (London: IB Tauris, 1993), pp. 621-35; M. Kerr, *Imposing Power-Sharing*, Chapter 7.

9   *The Daily Star*, 10 May 2006.

10 A. Messarra, 'A Problematic Approach to the State of Lebanon: A Debate,' *Panorama of Events*, 1988, 12 (51).

11 M. Kerr, *Imposing Power-Sharing*, Chapter 5.

12 T. Hanf, *Coexistence in Wartime Lebanon,* pp. 621-35; M. Kerr, *Imposing Power-Sharing*, Chapter 7.

13 Lecture given by Joseph Maila at St-Joseph's University, Beirut, 18 April 2002.

14 M. Kerr, *Imposing Power-Sharing*, Chapter 4.

15 A. Messarra, 'Between Good Luck and Bad', *The Beirut Review*, 1993, 6, p.9.

16 A. Lijphart, *Democracy in Plural Societies* (Yale: Yale University Press, 1977) p.1.

17 N. Machiavelli, *The Prince*, (Oxford: Oxford University Press, 2005), p. 77.

18 A. Lijphart, 'Consociational Democracy,' *World Politics,* 1969, 21, p. 219.

19 J. Anderson, 'Partition, consociation, border-crossing: Some lessons from the national conflict in Ireland/Northern Ireland', Submitted to *Nations and Nationalism*, 2006.

20 A. Messarra, 'Between Good Luck and Bad,' *The Beirut Review*, 1993, 6, p. 14.

21 B. O'Leary, 'Consociation: What we Know or think we Know and What we Need to Know,' Unpublished manuscript, 2003, p 3.

22 B. O'Leary, 'Consociation,' 2003, pp. 5-19.

23 A. Lijphart, *Democracy in Plural Societies*, p. 53.

Chapter Eleven

Intifada 2005:
A Look Backwards and a Look Forward

Halim Shebaya

I was asked to discuss how national unity can be built based on the experience of 2005. Inevitably, one's perception of the current situation is dependent on and determined by where one stands. And since there is a widespread consensus that we are witnessing the peak of sectarianism (*ta'ifiyya*)[1] in the aftermath of last summer's elections, I find it hard to claim impartiality or objectivity. So from the perspective of someone who comes from the Lebanese Christian[2] community, I will offer one reading of the prevailing state of affairs.

An important issue that I would like to draw attention to is the state the Christians found themselves in after the end of the war in 1990 and following the Syrian withdrawal in 2005. It is my conviction that dealing properly with Christian representation and participation in the governance of the country will prove to be a watershed in the long journey towards a Lebanese renaissance and away from any possibility of a rekindling of new wars. Any hopes for the coming about of a secular state in Lebanon and the abolition of the confessional system have to be preceded by a general mood of trust in the state institutions and policy-makers by all the different communities present on Lebanese soil. This matter becomes more poignant in the case of the Christians, to whom Lebanon is the last breathing space in the region, and whose concerns and fears tend to possess a more existential nature.

I will discuss this issue (Christian representation) with particular attention given to the events that have taken place since the extension of President Emile Lahoud's term, the passing of UN resolution 1559, the assassination of former PM Rafiq al-Hariri and the subsequent waves of demonstrations and counter-demonstrations, the parliamentary elections (summer 2005), and the current debate over the presidency. While the historic day of 14 March is held in the highest esteem as a memorable day of unity and protest against the Syrian occupation, I will argue that what Lebanon witnessed was by no means a revolution, and hence the popular usage of the term, the 'Cedar Revolution', is misleading and wrong. This will be shown by an analysis of the 8 March and 14 March demonstrations and the 'revolutionary' (or rather traditional) policies adopted after that, most notably (1) the infamous 2000 electoral law under which the elections were held and (2) the manner in which the 'Reform and Change' victory among the Christians was received by the 'new majority'[3].

In spite of this, there are a number of positive and negative elements that can be extracted from the experience of the so-called 'Spring Revolution.' I mention a couple of those in the conclusion of the essay which, in addition to being suggestions on how to avoid a new civil war, may be helpful in avoiding the mistakes of the last 15-16 years – a question that I believe to be of more crucial relevance and significance for Lebanon in the present times. In other words, a modest pragmatic answer to the question of this session is offered: the chance of the eruption of a civil war will be cut down by dealing with what seems to be an overriding concern among the Christians, (namely fair representation in state-power), and by drawing lessons from the experience of the last fifteen months.

A final note before I start, is apologetic (in the sense of defending my choice of emphasis and argument): while it will become clear that I have a particular position vis-à-vis the contentious issues debated in the country that are polarising public opinion, I embark on this 'mission' because of a strong conviction that discussing these issues in an academic setting is useful: the fact that an issue is and can be a source of hostility and political antagonism does not necessarily imply that it ought to be sidelined from academic discussion; on the contrary, academic debate on Lebanese society ought to reflect what the society is thinking here and now (and only then can one suggest that a certain debated topic is over-rated or under-rated). And as the issues I will discuss here represent the views held by a significant portion of the Lebanese population and a majority of the Christian population, they consequently deserve attentive reflection.

Al-Ihbat Al-Masihi

The catchphrase that encapsulated the mood among the Christians during the post-Ta'if Accord era was 'the despair of the Christians' (*al-ihbat al-masihi*). Despair is inevitable in the aftermath of war, but the reason the word 'Christian' became predicated to 'despair' (and not a more general *Lebanese* despair) can be explicable in terms of an analysis of the outcome of the Syrian entry on its famous 'peace-keeping' mission. According to Farid El-Khazen, 'The Christian communities have been most concerned, not only because they lost power as a result of the war, but more because of developments occurring since the ending of the war in 1990.'[4] Former interim Prime Minister General Michel Aoun[5] was exiled to France after 13 October invasion/occupation of Baabda in 1990. A few years later, Samir Geagea[6] was tried and sentenced to life-long underground solitary confinement furthering the opinion among the Christians that they have come out on the losing side of the battle.[7] Furthermore, the successive governments were unsuccessful in reassuring the Christians, most notably with regards to parliamentary elections.[8]

The rationale offered by politicians and the media alike to justify Syrian hegemony ran as follows: Israel is the arch-enemy of the Arabs; Lebanon is an Arab country whose lands are occupied;

Hezbollah is the national resistance and Lebanon's foreign policy was one of unity (*wihdat*) or harmony/concurrence (*talazum*) of tracks (*masarat*) with Syria. Challenging Syria's presence in Lebanon was tantamount to national and Arab treason. In a sense, this foreign policy brought about a quasi-national unity and Lebanon's society, fragmented after the civil war, was reunited as it was now in a 'state of war' with Israel[9].

On a deeper level, this shows that the country never dealt with the civil war properly (i.e. through national dialogue and reconciliations). 'Something has been missing – what might be called 'communal reconstruction,' or national reconciliation among Lebanon's communities while attending to the grievances and concerns of each group.'[10] Issues were never dealt with squarely, that is, and there emerged a politically-correct/orthodox line of reasoning, usually referred to as *al-khatt al-watani* (the patriotic line). So, for example, according to that *khatt* a group of twenty unarmed students protesting against the Syrian presence in front of the *'Adliyyeh'* (Court of Justice) was deemed a threat to 'national security' (*al-amn al-qawmi*).[11] Very few people were willing to question this state of affairs before the Israeli withdrawal, as the most obvious question to be asked by an observer would have been, 'Is there still a Lebanon?'[12]

Israeli Withdrawal and its Aftermath

Against this backdrop, the Israeli withdrawal in May 2000 from the South of Lebanon was a turning point in internal Lebanese politics, as hitherto calls for Syrian redeployment or withdrawal had been written off as being in bad taste within the primacy of the wider conflict with Israel,[13] i.e. Syrian presence was justified on strategic Arab and national grounds. The famous 'Bishops' call' of September 2000 inaugurated a new age where Christian politicians in particular, under the auspices of Bkerke (the Maronite Patriarchate) in the form of the *Qurnet Shehwan Group* (April 2001), began to profess publicly what the people they were supposed to represent used to say in private (and on the streets in the case of the FPM): 'The two taboo issues raised by the QCG – the phased withdrawal of Syrian troops and national reconciliation on the basis of the Ta'if Agreement – led the government to mobilise all its resources, both legal and illegal, to neutralise the QCG and to divide it from within.'[14]

One instance foreshadowing later developments in terms of the Christian electorate was the Murr-Murr[15] parliamentary battle in 2002 when the Christians turned out for the elections (after a majority boycott since 1990). Some analysts[16] suggested that the FPM's involvement in that campaign (for the first time since the 1990 coup) was a major factor and was a reason behind a larger turnout at the ballot boxes. For those who were sensitive to the sense of the people, Aoun's parliamentary sweep in June 2005 came as no big surprise as it was only natural that the 'silent majority' that had boycotted the elections of 1992, 1996, and 2000 would grant its vote to those who had been boycotted by the ruling regime during the period of 'Christian despair' or *ihbat*. At the time, this was a clear indicator that the majority of the Christians were opposed to the Syrian-backed Michel El-Murr and Emile Lahoud – Christian leaders who claimed to be true representatives of the people according to the *khatt al-watani*. Jebran Tueni congratulated Gabriel el-Murr, the opposition and democracy after the elections. He said: 'there remains in the country – unfortunately because of the dire implementation of the Ta'if since 1990 – a state of confessional seething (*ihtiqan*), rather a denominational (*madhhabi*) one that might evolve, if left unchecked, into a direct danger to Lebanon and its unity.'[17]

More instrumentally, the years following the liberation of the South witnessed an increased interest in Lebanon from the US administration, now embarked on its so-called war on terrorism and for democracy in Kabul and Baghdad in the aftermath of 9/11. By September 2004, the shift in international policy vis-à-vis the region and Lebanon (from complete marginalisation to broad internationalisation[18]) had culminated in the passing of UN resolution 1559[19] and the galvanisation of internal opposition against the Syrian presence at the Bristol Meeting (*Liqa' el-Bristol*).

In response, Syria forced the extension of Lahhoud's term[20] and signalled to the newly-founded opposition that it would not acquiesce to international pressure and that it would strike any dissenting (and especially any apostate) politician, hence MP Marwan Hamadeh's failed assassination attempt; removal of security bars from in front of Walid Jumblatt's house in Clemenceau; the demonstration of the 'one-million' opposed to 1559; and most significantly, the assassination of Hariri in February 2005.[21]

February 2005 Earthquake in Beirut

Between the 'earthquake event' of 14 February 2005 and the 14 March largest demonstration in the country's history[22] a cocktail of different segments of the Lebanese population rallied in Martyr's Square in a unique display of national unity. Two immediate concerns animated this unity: first, a clear outright condemnation of and disgust with the manner in which the towering national figure of Hariri was dealt with, i.e. a unity against murder and a possible outbreak of violence and a rekindling of civil strife. The second uniting thread was a protest against the status quo, or more aptly, against the canonisation of a new status quo of Syrian occupation/presence in Lebanon whereby the state of affairs will be conducted in the fashion of the forced extension of President Lahhoud's term in September 2004. According to Jebran Tueni, 14 March was a 'yes' to both Syrian withdrawal and truth regarding Hariri's murder.[23] He also noted in the same editorial that the opposition[24] was not seeking parliamentary or ministerial seats and political gains. Unfortunately, this was subsequently belied by the behaviour and actions of the opposition members (as we will see later), and soon thereafter, the opposition started to falter such that by 20 May 2005, Nabil Bou Mounsef (political analyst in the *An-Nahar* paper) was writing about the 'last days of the opposition.'[25]

Why this rapid demise of the opposition? A careful reading of the two March demonstrations (8 and 14) helps to bring the reader back to reality, i.e. from myths and legends about national unity, to the divisive and opportunistic acts of the members of the opposition, whose only merits were knowing that the dictates of realpolitik would prevail among the political elite with or without the Syrian military presence.

Three Views on 1990-2005

Three judgments on the 1990-2005 period can be discerned through an observation of the 8 March and 14 March demonstrations and what ensued thereafter during the parliamentary elections. The main bone of contention in my opinion is the manner in which the post-Ta'if era in general was seen by the different Lebanese parties, and more specifically, the manner in which the Syrian presence in Lebanon was accounted for. A big part of the confusion after 14 March is due to the fact that it became common to speak exclusively about two camps: 8 March (pro-Syrian) and 14 March (anti-Syrian), and to try to understand the whole picture in reference to these two camps. I will suggest a more useful categorisation in order to understand the present political scene. There were three judgments on the 1990-2005 period that can be distinguished among the major forces (Hassan Nasrallah, Nabih Berri, Saad Hariri, Walid Jumblatt, and Michel Aoun) in the country today.

The 8 March *shukr wa-wafa' li souriya* (thanks and loyalty to Syria) demonstration represented a significant portion of the population's view that Syria had done no harm in Lebanon, and in the case of Hezbollah, it had provided the arena and patronage for a victory over Israel. In this light, what was being expressed was the sentiment that it was only right to thank her for a fruitful presence in Lebanon since 1990. Also, it was a demonstration against UN resolution 1559. Interestingly, the Future bloc thanked Sayyid Nasrallah for his stress on the need to discover the truth regarding Hariri's murder.[26] (As we will see, the substance of many statements on 14 March did not differ as much from what was said on 8 March as some people would like to believe. I am speaking, of course, at the level of the politicians' discourse and not of the people's orientations.)

A second interpretation of the 1990-2005 era (Line 2) can be discerned in Prime Minister Fouad Siniora's comments in March 2006 where Syria is on the one hand credited for preventing *taqsim* (partition) and liberating the land; but on the other hand, it is blamed for becoming a burden on the economic, social, and political life in Lebanon. An unspoken assumption behind this and other statements by the so-called '14 March forces' (and particularly Hariri and Jumblatt) is that Syria's role was positive until 1998, the year Lahoud was elected as president.[27] The stress on Lahhoud's illegal presence in power today and the priority accorded for his resignation by the self-called '14 March forces' sums up this second *khatt* in Lebanese politics: Lahoud as head of the security apparatus is the country's disease and the cure lies in his resignation. Such an approach acquits the politicians in this group as the majority was in the opposition[28] during Lahhoud's term. (A question that comes up from this stress on Lahoud's guilt is whether many of the Line 2 members would have opposed the Syrian presence in Lebanon had Hariri's assassination not taken place and/or had the balance in power been shifted back by Damascus in favour of Hariri.)

Comments from Jumblatt during the last months are revelatory: he understands his conversion from pro-Syrian to anti-Syrian as being triggered essentially by the forced extension of Lahoud and the attempted assassination of Mr. Hamadeh.[29] He actually corroborated this view by being consistent from the start of the popular outbursts by unequivocally calling for Lahoud's resignation alongside the heads of the security apparatus (the latter being the official demand of the opposition during the first few months after the assassination).[30] A 'moral' problem facing this group, however, was the fact that many MPs in this group had voted, albeit unwillingly and under threats from the Syrian regime, for the renewal of Lahoud's term. Jebran Tueni, in his editorial following the 'Good Friday' (as he called Friday 3 September, the day on which the parliamentary session was held to extend Lahhoud's term for three years), had the following words for the 96

MPs who did not stand up against the forced extension and voted against the constitution: 'they participated in slaughtering the constitution. We will not call them Judases because they were loyal to their masters who placed them in that position to perform precisely this kind of task.'[31] Some people consider the penitential petition signed by some of the MPs claiming to have been placed under extreme pressure as only a further condemnation of the signers themselves, as implicit is the recognition that they voted not only against their will, but against the constitution and yet remained in office thereafter as if nothing had taken place, at a time when defenceless students and opposition members were being arrested and convicted for lesser crimes.

Worth noting from the 14 March demonstration was the statement made by MP Ghazi al-Aridi (representing Jumblatt) that 'we have come to say we are against UN resolution 1559.' Thus, already on 14 March, there were divergences on sensitive political issues between the different figures hurrying up to the podium in the fear that the crowds would not see or hear them. So on the issue of UN resolution 1559, there seemed to be no difference between Jumblatt and 8 March, as early as 14 March. What this signifies is that 14 March was never a political coalition united by a common agenda. It was a popular movement united only, as was mentioned earlier, on the matter of Syrian withdrawal and the demand for the 'truth' with regard to Hariri's murder.

The Free Patriotic Movement (FPM) that represents the third line (Line 3) considers the whole period of the post-Ta'if accord as a Syrian occupation and usurpation of Lebanese freedom, sovereignty and independence and hence Aoun's refusal to single out Lahoud and the joint Lebanese-Syrian *nizam al-amni* (security apparatus) as the *sole* culprits of the 'Second Republic'. According to this reading, the entire political elite (*al-nukhba al-siyasiyya*) was responsible, in varying degrees, for the state Lebanon found itself in 15 years after the end of the war, as the Syrian troops withdrew in April 2005. In this light, it was logical that Aoun would consider the resignation of Lahoud (as early as April/May 2005) as premature, as one would be yielding the fate of the new president to the same MPs who extended Lahoud's term in the first place, to the same MPs who 'slaughtered the constitution' in September 2004, and more so, to the same MPs who acquiesced to the holding of the parliamentary elections in the summer of 2005 under the 2000 law.

As Alberto Fernandez, US foreign officer in relation to the Near East said, 'the guilt is immense, but it is the fault of many. Responsible for it are the Americans, the Syrians, the Israelis, the Arabs, and the International community; and in particular (*khususan*) the Lebanese political elite… therefore the Lebanese people claim an open account (*hisab maftouh*) from all the aforementioned culprits.' This is the reason for the split within the 14 March ranks. A major popular movement, the FPM, claimed self-righteously and perhaps justifiably that they had been right all along. They had opposed the Ta'if Accord and the Syrian presence in Lebanon when this issue was deemed a red line and above the political ceiling (*al-saqf al-siyasi*) in Lebanese politics. Aoun summed up this line of thinking during one of his polemical outbursts saying: 'they are the people of 13 October and we are the people of 14 March.' At another point he accused Hariri and Jumblatt of being only in opposition to the *tamdid* (extension) and not proponents of *tahrir* (liberation).

Whereas Line 2 wanted to go back to 1998 or 2004, Aoun advocated a return to 1990. Interestingly, it was harder for Line 2 and 3 to meet than for Line 1 and 3, as we have witnessed during the last couple of months, a case in point being the Tayyar-Hezbollah paper of agreement on 6 February 2006[32] whose repercussions on the internal scene, in my opinion, will be felt for years to come. An interesting element in this agreement is that Hezbollah still maintains strong ties with Damascus while the FPM persists in issuing strong denunciations of the Syrian era (until April 2005).[33] They have agreed, however, to move forward in spite of that. It is worth noting, however, that the alliances we see today (i.e. Line 1 and 3 versus Line 2) were not a natural outcome of last year's events. A major rapprochement took place (immediately after the demonstrations) between Line 1 (Hezbollah and Amal) and two major figures from Line 2 (Hariri and Jumblatt). This came to be known as *al-tahaluf al-ruba'i* (the quadripartite agreement) or the 'marriage of 8 March and 14 March'. It is worth pausing upon this event before discussing the rapid demise of both the popular 14 March coalition and the aforementioned alliance.

8 March versus 14 March: 'Catholic' Electoral Marriage

The news editorial on LBC TV station on 14 March, 2005 stated that all of Lebanon went down to Freedom Square… except those who went down to Riad el-Solh Square on 8 March. Those able to transcend the general euphoria of the historic day were unable to go home thinking that 'it is finished.' To the general public, 14 March was a victory in numbers: 'they were 750,000; we were one and a half million'. I believe many people wished deep inside that 8 March 'would be thrown into the sea'. Pragmatic politicians, lured by upcoming elections, knew that 8 March 'was there to stay.' The 2000 electoral law (sometimes called the Kanaan-Sayyid law) dictated a forced marriage between the two camps. It was a 'Catholic' marriage however, as the two sides were unable to divorce. One or the other partner could walk out of the house (as we saw in the ministerial 'national theatre' during the last year) but they were doomed to coexist because they were, at the end of the day, Lebanese politicians whose interests still necessitated (under the 2000 law) co-existence, albeit in a forced, hesitant mode. It was truly a marriage of convenience. Today, one can argue that the two sides are separated awaiting the formal divorce when a new electoral law will be passed.

Line 2 or the '14 March forces' narrowed down the list of culprits to members of Omar Karami's government. However, the marriage with 8 March occurred at the same time. This then triggered unorthodox alliances by Aoun with former pro-Syrian politicians. He was accused of being a Syrian agent and his response was in turn to point out to the other side's partner in marriage, i.e. if pro-Syrian is a crime, then is not your partner guilty as well? Accusations and counter-accusations have been the name of the game between Aoun and the '14 March forces' ever since.

What is worth noting is that this marriage was the end of the spontaneous 14 March coalition. If 14 March was an alliance of veterans of anti-Syrian rhetoric (FPM and LF) and new converts (Future bloc and Jumblatt), what should have followed in principle was an electoral alliance bringing the true 14 March forces to parliamentary majority and hence embarking on a revolution in the full sense of the word, i.e. a comprehensive purge of security forces and administration along the lines of the waves of protest that swept the country for one month. That is, a revolution against the status quo should bring about a change of personnel as a minimum. A revolution against an occupying force usually brings about a change in leadership and also a trial of collaborators.

None of this took place and what remained hereafter was the '14 March forces,' a misnomer par excellence, for as 'Adnan Hubballa notes, '[The demonstration] was an unprecedented display of unity that no politician had predicted and that no politician can claim to be the 'father' of... and that no politician has any power over because it did not come out of his pocket.'[34] What Line 2 sought to achieve was an eclectic passing of verdicts of *'amil* (agent) and *watani* (nationalist) in the hope that the use of the political term '14 March' would have the same effect as the popular '14 March.' Whereas 14 March was, to use Aoun's words, the people's 'deadly blow', those claiming to represent it today are having a hard time meeting their deadlines, a case in point being the 14 March, 2006 date set for the change in the presidency.

Can one seriously still talk about 14 March as being a Cedar/national/ spring revolution? I believe the term revolution is only appropriate when it comes to the Christian electorate, as only there did we see a new force coming to Parliament, a force that was not there during the Syrian era and that swept the Christian votes throughout most regions of the country.

Alienation of the Christians

In addition to being the end of the popular 14 March coalition, the quadripartite agreement[35] alienated a majority of the Christian portion of 14 March. For the Christians, 14 March was a total revolution against a corrupt system that had marginalised them for 15 years; led the country to economic bankruptcy; acquiesced to all forms of national humiliation under the Syrians, climaxing in the Lahoud forced extension; and most recently killed the vanguard of reconstruction, former Prime Minister Rafiq el-Hariri. The last event triggered a feeling of national unity among all the Lebanese except the majority of the Shi'ites present on 8 March. As I mentioned at the beginning of this paper, two overriding issues united those present on 14 March: Truth regarding Hariri's murder and Intifada regarding the status quo. Very soon however, it became apparent to the discerning eye that a settlement/marriage was in the making that once again would keep the Christians in their *ihbat*. Suffice it to say that the elections were held under the 2000 election law[36] spreading fears that the whole euphoria of a national revolution was merely a myth and that once again, the Christians would emerge on the losing side of the new leadership.

Nabil Bou Mounsef in a sense predicted the outcome of the elections after what he called the *al-mahzala al-sakhifa* (ridiculous display) of the MPs regarding the election law. 'Baabda and the Parliament Square became a battlefield where each borrowed from the Ta'if what they liked... What we witnessed was a sample that shows a sick regime (*nizam*) with or without Syria... This is a further gift for Aoun but also a responsibility on his shoulders.'[37] Aoun had considered the performance (*masrahiyyat al-lijan*) of the MPs as constituting destruction for the national unity achieved on 14 March. He (and also Patriarch Sfeir) warned against unfortunate consequences. The *An-Nahar* paper was right in its analysis that the episode of the election law would be the test for the opposition's unity. The popular 14 March was dealt a divisive blow and would remain in the memory of the Lebanese as a spontaneous day (and month from Hariri's murder) of national unity and progressive hopes for change. Deception, however, would emerge shortly thereafter. Jebran Tueni had written about the need for a 'political 14 March' to redeem the 'popular 14 March'[38] but what ensued was a political marriage of 8 March and a major part of 14 March confirming the death of 'popular 14 March.' (At that point, the FPM was already at odds with the rest of the '14 March forces.' It was easy to ignore Aoun at the start as there seemed to have arisen a working arrangement between the two partners in the marriage. Soon however, the Shi'ite duo (*thuna'i al-shi'i*) would clash with the '14 March forces' government laying the bricks for the FPM-Hezbollah paper of understanding.)

One of the best analyses of the year following the 14 March demonstration is given by Edmond Saab (*Al-Nahar* Chief Editor) and it deserves to be quoted at length before dealing with the 'Aoun phenomenon':

What was supposed to take place, a year after 14 March, was for the leaders to grasp the morals, and to look to the future, proceeding from the challenge set forth by the Syrian withdrawal from Lebanon on 26 April. It was hoped that the response would be a rational assessment of the Syrian presence (*wisaya*) period and an inspiration from the martyrs' souls in preparation for a unification of ranks and coming out as one people wrought with distress and tyranny, such that all sides would transcend political, sectarian, and denominational disputes – and even class struggle – for the sake of reformulating a regime of whom can be rightly said that it was 'made in Lebanon' free of foreign interference.

But what happened unfortunately… was that some of those who were 'slaves' in the eyes of the Syrian regime remain in that condition even after its withdrawal – albeit with no chains on their legs or on their necks. For it is hard to transform a slave into a freeman overnight. For slavery is essentially in the souls and not in the chains…

And there ensued further fragmentation because those who considered themselves to be a majority, monopolised power, repeating the mistakes of the former regime, and thus replacing a foreign tutelage for an internal one taking command on its own. This has led to the isolation of many central political parties in the country instead of isolating those who were allies of the Syrian regime…[39]

'Reform and Change' Sweep in the Christian Districts

As was mentioned, a large number of the Christians present on 14 March felt isolated, and the vehicle for channelling this deception came on 5 June 2005, the day the 'Reform and Change' bloc swept the Christian votes on Election Day. The aftermath of this victory alienated the Christians even more and they adopted a fundamental defiance vis-à-vis the emerging leadership. An interesting parallel can be drawn with Hamas's victory in Palestine under a similar slogan, 'reform and change' with regards to two matters: (1) both victories came as a protest by the electorate against perceived corruption and abuse of power, and both lists came at the expense of well-established political parties and figures. (2) More interestingly, a parallel can be drawn between the way in which Hamas's victory was received internally and internationally and the way in which Aoun's sweep was received by the losing side. In short, both victories are still not properly acknowledged in two displays of disrespect for democracy and the people's choices.

An instance on the night of the victory is highly revelatory: Jumblatt (and another Christian former MP who lost in Kisrwan) called LBC and warned of an upcoming civil war. Aoun was also accused of being sectarian and tending towards isolation and extremism[40]. Artist Elias Rahbani responded to these accusations angrily and asked, 'are we animals such that our choices are not respected. Enough! The people made their choice and that is the end of the discussion!'

Snubbing the results of the aforementioned elections was a very unfortunate moment in the history of post-liberation Lebanon. Aoun became the main opponent of the new government, in which, once again, Christian representation did not reflect the results of the elections. Aoun had previously spoken on 15 May of three betrayals his party had suffered as a major member of the 14 March coalition: (1) when the Najib Mikati government was formed, he was not consulted; (2) when the Parliament decided to hold the elections on the 2000 law; (3) when the electoral lists were formed.[41] The following day he declared al-muwajaha (confrontation) in the elections and he has remained at odds with the self-called '14 March forces' ever since.

The Question of the Presidency: What is really at Stake?

This is a moment of truth regardless of the person or party chosen by the people. If one wants to abide by the 2000 law results and the later mode of conduct of the new 'regime', i.e. the re-election of Nabih Berri as Speaker and Fouad Siniora as Prime Minister, it is natural that Aoun should be elected to lead the country as President (given the results of the elections and countless opinion polls[42]). One of the strongest arguments supporting Aoun as President runs as follows: if the Shi'ites and Sunnis are represented by their strong men (or their electorate choice), why should not the Christians receive the same treatment? A counter argument is that the President should be a conciliatory figure and Aoun's opponents claim that he can be aggressive and undiplomatic, owing to his personality and military background. Worth noting as well is the fact that Berri's re-election as Speaker of the House also strengthened Lahoud's position as there ensued another sectarian argument: 'why should Lahoud alone pay the price for Syrian hegemony and occupation? Why should a Maronite pay the price while a Shi'ite (avowedly Syria's man) remains in power?'

If, on the other hand, some people claim that Aoun does not truly represent the Christian community and that his sweep can be attributed solely to pre-election circumstances that are no longer relevant today (inane sociological and psychological analyses of the Christians and their need for a leader also abound); and moreover, if the 'parliamentary majority' today is the rightful majority on the popular level, then the holding of parliamentary elections as soon as possible is the natural step to take, whereby a new Parliament coming from a fair electoral law will reassure all parties concerned, and a President elected from such a Parliament will enjoy popular and legitimate support. The '14 March' argument is that there should be a change in the Presidency to start with, followed by parliamentary elections. This will allow them to capitalise on their gains during the 2005 elections. Opponents of this view claim that what is really at stake is an attempt by the '14 March forces' to bring a 'loyal' President who would acquiesce to Saad al-Hariri's leadership of the country. Hariri and his allies argue that Lahoud is the last remnant of the Syrian era and should hence be ousted.

This, to be sure, is revelatory concerning the complexity, uniqueness, and anomalous condition Lebanon seems to perpetually find itself in. Following an occupying armies' withdrawal, a simple 'black and white' solution was not found, i.e. one where former pro-Syrian politicians would be ousted and anti-Syrian parties and figures would run the country. The main obstacle was the fact that the Shi'ite community's main representatives[43] were avowedly pro-Syrian (or 8 March) and hence attempts to canonise a new *khatt watani* according to the '14 March forces' would not see the light, as an entire denomination would feel threatened and targeted. Moreover, attempts by the latter forces to portray themselves as vanguards of the opposition and builders of the new Lebanon forgot that 14 March was also in a large part a popular response to 8 March. And since we have seen that 8 March would not be 'thrown into the sea' the continual allusions to the glories of 14 March was bound to fuel tensions and hostilities such as those we saw in the 'ministerial theatre,' most notably the seven-week abstention by the Shi'ite ministers from attending the meetings.

In other words, working to build a new outlook based on 14 March was tantamount to a 8 March defeat (as the latter thanked Syria while the former did the opposite). And since 8 March became an ally during the elections, one could no longer revert back to an earlier situation where the main bone of contention was the Syrian presence or withdrawal. Contentious issues were now different; Syria had withdrawn, and as much as one wanted 14 March to retain a sort of magical power, 14 March was able to be effective on 14 March, 2005 because it was the appropriate national response for that day. There was no political platform, no political agenda, simply a euphoria created by the frustrations of 15 years of occupation for some, and six years of bitter rivalry with the President for others. As soon as the Syrian element lost its primacy, 14 March was no longer relevant and what was needed, as was advocated by some, was a new '14 March' that would represent a national unity regarding the manner in which Lebanon should move forward.

Going back to the Presidential issue, either way one looks at it, the Christian vote is not respected. There are a lot of statements about coexistence and Lebanon's role/message/mission of communal dialogue and harmony, but the apparent mood seems to point in the opposite direction. Coexistence is called for, that is, but on the terms and conditions of a select number of leaders and not on the basis of what the people actually think. If Lebanon is truly the haven of coexistence and plurality, and is to serve as a prime example of the absence of the clash of civilisations and the ability of different communities and faiths to live in a democratic free society, then dealing properly with Christian representation and equal participation in the governance of the country will be a watershed; one from which its people will be able to discern whether there is hope for the future of a country seemingly doomed to live in fear and instability because it is a free and open society in a region of autocratic and abusive regimes.

What is really at stake in the whole debate (or more properly the 'megaphone war') revolving around Lahhoud's forced extension, the calls for his resignation, the signing of petitions, and the quarrels etc. is the pivotal issue of Christian participation (*musharaka*) and symmetry (*tawazun*) in governance. This view was expounded in several points by Hiam Qusayfi in an article written on the day of the 27 March national dialogue meeting: (1) the need to understand the roots of Lahhoud's forced extension in order to get to the gist of the matter; (2) the extension should not be treated in isolation, but rather as part of a larger policy vis-à-vis the Christians during the last 16 years; (3) many of the effects of the Syrian presence in Lebanon are still felt, most notably the Parliament itself that came from the notorious 2000 law; (4) Christians on both sides (14 March Forces and the FPM) agree that this is a crucial issue and one of the main achievements of the Tayyar-Hezbollah paper was to achieve greater representation for the Christians by engaging in dialogue over crucial national matters; (5) what is needed (from the dialogue) is not the name of a new President, but an agreement over the nature of the coming political period; (6) the new President should have representative support from the Christians in a similar way as the Speaker and the Prime Minister enjoy support from their constituencies; finally, in and conclusion, (7) those responsible for pushing the Christians aside are those content with the status quo. The current quandary will not be resolved by a new President, but rather by a change in policy with regards to dealing with Christians in the first place and the restoration of a balance of powers.[44]

So in short, am I arguing that 'Aoun is the solution'? Absolutely not, if what is meant is that Aoun alone *without the others* is the solution. Rather, electing Aoun by a parliamentary majority can be part of the solution for Lebanon today, in the sense of that majority respecting the Christian choice and dealing with Aoun accordingly. This will be a sign for the Christian community that they will be equal partners in the building of Lebanon at this new stage in the nation's history. In conclusion to this section, I quote the Prime Minister from his speech at Chatham House in London last month:

> Let us try and address these issues, and I will tell you that you will immediately find that the people too are really going to go hand in hand and side by side with those who are in favour of real solutions in the region. Let us seriously consider that, and you will see how we can really get results. But at the same time we always have to think and not have double standards. The problem is that in the Arab world, people always feel that it is in that manner they are being dealt with. Double standards create such a reaction and a lot of resistance.

One hopes that this is practised vis-à-vis the Christian choice in Lebanon today and as the Prime Minister said, 'We will see how we can really get results!'

Looking Forward: Lessons from the Intifada 2005

One of the arguments often used during the Syrian occupation to justify the status quo was that the Lebanese needed the Syrians to prevent a civil war from re-erupting. The Lebanese were fighting until the Syrians 'stabilised' the country, some people claimed, and the Lebanese would resume their war(s) when and if the Syrians withdrew. To be sure, one of the main cards the pro-Syrian government played during the February and March upheavals was the 'fear factor.' The 14 March demonstration, however, proved to be a sharp rebuttal of those claims and threats and many speakers, (including Jebran Tueni) on that day, made a point of saying, 'there will be no civil war in Lebanon.' Despite the eventual demise of the national unity achieved on 14 March, 2005, as illustrated above, a number of lessons can be extracted from the experience of the month proceeding Prime Minister Rafiq al-Hariri's assassination. It is worth commending and capitalising upon the fact that the Lebanese experienced harmony, accord, and unification unexpectedly, rather than dwelling upon its eventual failure.

A positive aspect during the *intifada* was the peoples' espousal of political leaders not necessarily from their own denomination or religion. For example, Walid Jumblatt rightly became (albeit for a short while) the 'star' of the opposition with his witty and fiery comments against the Syrian regime and its puppets in Lebanon. I recall having conversations with some friends where I would suggest that MP Hamadeh as President would not be such a bad idea, given his eloquence and sharp tongue. No politician fired the crowds during the first weekly demonstrations after 14 February as much as Ghazi al-Aridi. That is, there was no problem for the people to cheer a non-confessional member as long as he/she was denouncing the same wrongs as the people and espousing the same ideas (of freedom, independence and sovereignty) that the people espoused. Notwithstanding the fact that in some cases, 'the public opinion is dumb,' and many partisans simply parrot the words of their confessional leader (with no qualms about abrupt changes in opinion over crucial matters[45]), last year's experience is a positive indicator that the people are ready to forgive and follow an outsider when it comes to matters of national interest and when, more importantly, political leaders forfeit the joker in Lebanese politics, namely religion and *ta'ifiyya*.

A negative aspect from last year's experience was precisely this use of *ta'ifiyya* such that those who played this card (although guilty of damaging the newly-found national unity) can be credited with at least one thing: they were smart enough to know that you could never lose when you play this card in Lebanon. The elections (most notably those in the North) witnessed the abuse of religion to a distressing level. This was not a new discovery, however, as most Lebanese thinkers were aware that *ta'ifiyya* is the country's disease. A major way to restore national unity and shatter dogmatic narrow allegiances will be to deal with this issue openly. Hitherto, the way to deal with this problem has been an outright denial of the disease: coexistence was the virtue in the Syrian-created *khatt al-watani* and anything that does not help in acquiring this virtue was a vice – or so they said. However, the truth of the matter is that most Lebanese are lacking this virtue. For example, devoting a week to this issue where papers and talk-shows would discuss different communities' fears and ambitions and where the tough questions would be asked and answered (not necessarily in a clear-cut way), i.e. the Christian will get the chance to ask a Muslim Sheikh whether he is considered a *kafer* or not; whether he is essentially a second-class citizen; whether Muslims want to rule Lebanon and so forth (i.e. all the questions that people ask and all the prejudices held about the 'other') and vice-versa.

A by-product of the recent polarisation of public opinion between (roughly) two camps not mainly along a Muslim-Christian divide is promising for the country. Having the Lebanese Forces alongside the Sunni and Druze majorities (Hariri and Jumblatt) is worth mentioning, as is the recent rapprochement between Aoun and the Shia leaders, especially Hezbollah. In a way, one can argue that two sacred notions that had been a source of unrest and mistrust during the past have been somehow reconciled: the Christians have recognised the importance of the Israeli-Arab/Palestinian conflict to the Muslim population represented by the world-renowned guerrilla fighters of Hezbollah; while the latter have recognised the importance of Lebanon's sovereignty and border demarcation with Syria[46]. Another element one can note from the agreement is that it captures the best from two schools of thought: if there is anything good that has come out of the last 15 years, it would have to be the liberation of the South; and if there is any doubt that Syria had abused the Lebanese nation during its occupation, accepting the presence of Lebanese prisoners in Syrian captivity is a quasi-confession of the latter's occupying presence and not simply sisterly tutelage since 1990.

An aspect directly related to the abuse of religion is the double-standards approach adopted in 'judging' former pro-Syrian politicians. I touched upon this issue when dealing with the question of the presidency and the counter-argument that developed in response to calls for Lahoud's resignation, namely 'why should Lahoud go without Berri?' (A similar question was asked when Karami's government was targeted: 'why should Karami go without Lahoud?') The trouble became that the more double standards there were in the treatment of the different sectarian figures, the more the threat of sectarian division loomed large. If sectarianism is to be removed, there cannot be double standards in the treatment of important figures from different sects because that obviously will entrench sectarianism even further. The level of sectarianism in the country today is in large part the fault of this kind of double-standard approach taken by the 'new majority'. What is needed is a just approach where judgments will be issued according to clearly demarcated nationalist principles (the new *khatt al-watani*) against which no politician would be immune.

Another major determinant of the shape Lebanon's future will take is the use and abuse of the media. The media in Lebanon can be used during election campaigns for private, denominational, and state purposes; it was used during the Syrian occupation to justify the status quo, it is used to canonise political orthodoxy and heresy, to demonise or divinise a political figure at will, etc. A lot has been written on the organisation of the media and for the promulgation of certain ethical commitments that would safeguard national interests. All things considered, the media in Lebanon is the freest in the Arab world, which unfortunately is not saying much. On the one hand, the media's role in guiding public opinion and assisting in last year's upheaval was well-received and applauded. This shows that if political leaders agree on a platform of national unity, the media could assist the process of raising awareness and keeping the issues alive, to a large extent. And if there emerges a national consensus for spreading new forms of civic education and consciousness, public opinion will probably follow suit. Of course the question is whether some politicians' *raison d'être* lies precisely in maintaining a level of chaos and distrust among the people to remain in office.

On the other hand, the media failed drastically – if the goal is fair representation and truthful reporting – during last year's elections. This is the second side of the coin, namely: just as the media can be a powerful conciliatory building-up tool for the country, it can turn overnight into a deadly divisive and destructive weapon that can reach, literally, every eye or ear (and house, as the Lebanese saying goes). How to maintain the delicate balance between freedom and national 'security' will require a good deal of creativity and compromise, and perhaps pre-emptive acknowledgments of defeat in the upcoming elections for some figures, whose campaigns stand or fall with the effectiveness of their stations' polemics and/or apologetics and whose electoral base might change its mind if the 'other' is portrayed as he/she really is.

The rise of sectarianism and the revolving of most of the political debates taking place in Lebanon today around narrow personal or group interests denotes the lack of trust in the 'other' or 'others'. There is absolutely no way of building a strong country if all sides are not willing to take a willing step in *trust* and *hope*. The absence of trust is a recipe for perpetual rivalries while the absence of hope means that the country will witness an even larger wave of immigration, unemployment, and lack of initiatives for change, particularly from the youth. One of the ingenious methods the Syrians used to maintain quiescence in face of its occupation was to promote hopelessness of anything better for the country: calls for Syrian withdrawal were countered by threats of civil wars, and hence Syria was portrayed as being a 'necessary evil' to prevent the 'greater evil' i.e. violence and bloodshed. Today, one discerns similar symptoms, albeit under the new regime of the 'new majority.' It is interesting to note that the 'bishops' call' of April 2005 emphasized social and economic problems in the country, most notably immigration (and the question of the presidency that the politicians are singling out). One can argue that this is indicative of an absence of a real change from the past errors in the way the government is being run.

Regardless of the political headlines, the hard facts of reality are that people have solidified their distrust in the politicians and lack hope in true governmental reforms that would affect their daily lives. Some people have even gone as far as lamenting the 'good old days of the Syrians' where at least there was no threat of bombs exploding in the market places in addition to the economic distress. Crowning all this, from the Christian perspective, with the remaining *ihbat* (frustration) in terms of representation and participation in governance after the Syrian withdrawal, one worries about the future of the country.

How to avoid a new civil war and/or the mistakes of the last 15 years? First, one must restore balance in Christian representation either by electing Aoun in the place of Lahoud or by holding parliamentary elections followed by an election of a new President. Second, we must deal openly with the concerns (*hawajis*) of *all* the different communities in Lebanon. One of the periods in which a true accommodation of different perspectives can be achieved is in the aftermath of a national disaster (similar to the role the holocaust plays in Israel): Hariri's assassination, Geagea's imprisonment in 1994, the Syrian occupation of Baabda in 1990, the Israeli invasion of Beirut or the massacre at Qana in 1996, and so forth. By acknowledging the fact that each of these dates constitutes a national tragedy, not necessarily owing to the universality involved therein but in the mere fact that *one* group of Lebanese considers it to be so, all the communities in Lebanon will feel respected and included in the new *khatt al-watani*. Third, thorough reforms in the education system, in particular the history textbooks and religious education, will raise awareness in the minds of the youths of the following point: precisely because Lebanon is a pluralistic country, differing perspectives on crucial issues will always be the norm and never the exception. Fourth, the threat emanating from the misuse of the media should be handled. A suggestion would be to have a 'public editor' (as in the New York Times) whose job would be to criticize the paper or station in which he/she is employed. (Imagine an article in *An-Nahar* criticising Ghassan Tueni for instance, or a talk-show on Future TV taking issue with a statement or action by Saad el-Hariri.) Such a step will have a far-reaching pedagogical, democratic effect on society at large.

How to avoid the mistakes of the last 15 years is a more relevant question for the country. In other words, a crucial element that will determine the country's future will be the manner in which judgments will be issued from the new government. *Who will be on trial and for what charges?* Following the 1990 Syrian entry, two main figures were convicted and these show-trials were reflective of the new regime's policy and predictive of the Christian *ihbat* (frustration) we witnessed during the last 15 years. Another important question is: *how will we judge the last 15 years?* I spoke of three general views of the 1990-2005 period which should inevitably converge in order for the country to move forward (unless one side will cement its view and run the country in a similar way as the Syrians). Line 1 (Syria has done no harm) will have to acknowledge the fact that Syria has done at least a little harm in Lebanon. This will not be very hard to establish objectively. Line 2 will have to admit that they were responsible for at least some of the factors that led to the country's desolation and bankruptcy. Line 3 will have to avoid the pride that comes from having been in the right concerning the reality of the Syrian presence in Lebanon. Moreover, they will have to admit that Lines 1 and 2 have managed to move the country forward in one way or another, i.e. Lebanon today is better off than it was on 13 October 1990.

Notes

1 See 'Tahqiq' in *An-Nahar*, 3 February 2006, p. 13. For sectarianism and politicisation among high-school students, see *Mulhak an-Nahar*, 6 April 2006.
2 This by no means implies that I am justifying the status quo; on the contrary, I believe last year presented the Lebanese with a golden opportunity to transcend narrow allegiances for the sake of national unity, but the outcome was different, to the detriment of advocates of a secular Lebanon.
3 I first encountered this term in an article by Edmond Saab in *An-Nahar* that is quoted at length below (see footnote 45). The new majority is in reference to the 72 MPs elected in the summer of 2005 who belong to the '14 March forces,' i.e. mainly Hariri, Jumblatt, and the Qurnet Chahwan Group.
4 Farid El-Khazen, 'Lebanon – Independent No More' in *Middle East Quarterly, (Winter 2001)*, 43.
5 Aoun was opposed to the Ta'if, 'particularly because it did not set a timetable for the withdrawal of Syrian troops.' (El-Khazen, Ibid., 45)
6 Geagea, the leader of the Lebanese Forces, was initially pro-Ta'if but his detention was due to 'his lukewarm involvement in the political process, and, more importantly, to his antagonism to Syria during the war years.' (El-Khazen, 'Political Parties in Postwar Lebanon: Parties in Search of Partisans', in *Middle East Journal*, Vol. 57, NO.4, Autumn 2003 - 612.)
7 On a very superficial glance at the make-up of the 'Second Republic' governments, the Christian main leaders (Aoun and Geagea) were either from the start or gradually sidelined.
8 For other sources of discontent among the Christians, see El-Khazen, 'Lebanon – Independent No More,' 45-49.
9 The southern front would witness guerrilla operations concomitant with the Syrian-Israeli negotiations in the 1990s. In 1996, the 'April Agreement' provided an international de facto coverage for the Israeli-Hezbollah war. (El-Khazen, *An- Nahar*, May 15 2005, p. 9.)
10 El-Khazen, 'Lebanon – Independent No More,' 43.
11 Aoun and the FPM were repeatedly accused of being Israeli agents. The evidence was their protests against the Syrian occupation.
12 The title of an article written by Habib C. Malik in 1997 in *The Middle*

East Quarterly, December 1997, Vol. IV, No 4.

13 The Major states were also content with the status quo in the South, as is evident in Chirac's statement in 2002 (in the Francophone summit held in Beirut) that the Syrian withdrawal was interconnected with a wider regional settlement of the Arab-Israeli conflict. (See Khazen, *An-Nahar*, May 15 2005, p. 9.)

14 El-Khazen, 'Political Parties in Postwar Lebanon: Parties in Search of Partisans', in *Middle East Journal*, Vol. 57, NO.4, Autumn 2003, p. 623.

15 Pro-Syrian Michel El-Murr (represented by Mirna El-Murr) was running against his brother Gabriel El-Murr, owner of the MTV station that was shut down by the government.

16 Hiyam al-Kusayfi, *An-Nahar*, 4 June 2004, p. 6.

17 *An-Nahar*, June 6 2002, p.1.

18 El- Khazen, *An-Nahar*, 15 May 2005. Six reasons that led to the shift are: (1) 9/11 and its effect on US foreign policy, (2) failure of the peace process, (3) the Intifada and Sharon's aggressive policies, (4) the Iraq war, (5) deterioration of US-Syrian relations, and (6) deterioration of French-Syrian relations.

19 According to El-Khazen, the Ta'if accord ('Arabized' in 1989) was 'internationalised' in 2004 (UNR 1559) following a decade and a half of its absolute 'Syrianisation.' (Ibid.)

20 UNR 1559 was a pre-emptive response to the parliamentary session on 3 September 2004 (Jebran Tueni called it a 'Good Friday') that led to Lahhoud's extension.

21 It seems reasonable to assume that the Syrians were responsible, in one way or another, for the assassination. However, even if Syria is finally acquitted, the fact remains that the opposition to Syria in Lebanon capitalised on the event. Even Syrian officials themselves admitted that, in hindsight, they were the party most detrimentally affected by the crime.

22 For two very interesting analyses of the demonstration, see *An-Nahar*, 9 April 2006, p.9: Muna Fayyad presented a sociological reading whereas 'Adnan Hubballah offered a psychological interpretation.

23 *An-Nahar*, 18 March 2005, p.1.

24 At that point, the opposition was in reference to Karami's government and included the main Sunni, Druze, and Christian leaders.

25 *An-Nahar*, 20 May 2005, p.3.

26 *An-Nahar*, 9 March 2005, p.5.

27 Even Syrian official Khaddam represented this line of analysis where he blames Lahhoud and the 1998-2005 period for the deterioration in Syrian-Lebanese relations in an interview after his dissension in late 2005.

28 The term 'opposition' is a very convoluted term in Lebanese politics, especially during the Syrian occupation. 'Present-day opposition in Lebanon is

neither similar to opposition in the pre-war period nor to opposition in democratic or non-democratic regimes. Four patterns of opposition have emerged since 1990: (1) Opposition exercised by the three 'presidents'... [who] veto each other's decisions informally and thus cripple the decision-making process; (2) Opposition within cabinet, that is, between cabinet members loyal to the three 'presidents' and/or to Damascus; (3) Opposition outside government by parties and politicians 'loyal' to the system; (4) Opposition outside the system targeting not only government policy but also Syria's control over the political process.' (El-Khazen, *Political parties*, 620.)

29 For an interesting short article on Jumblatt's reassessment of certain key national issues (the civil war included), see Edmond Saab, 'Jumblatt on the Penitential Seat', *An-Nahar*, 21 April 2006, p. 17.

30 Edmond Saab also called for a new President (to head a new regime) as the logical outcome of the popular demonstrations. However, this must take place *after* the Syrian withdrawal. More interestingly, he quotes Jamil al-Sayyid's (Former head of National Security who is now in custody) view on the political elite that had succumbed to Syrian pressures: they had moved from the war fronts to seats in Parliament and Ministry on the condition that they would be loyal to Syria, *An-Nahar*, 18 March 2005, p. 17.

31 *An-Nahar*, 4 September 2004, p.1.

32 Nabil Bou Mounsef called it the 'Ta'if of Mar Mkhayel' in reference to the Church in which the two leaders met, *An-Nahar*, 8 February 2006, p.3.

33 An interesting element in Lteif's (Tayyar spokesman) word on 14 March where he said that 'we will not forget to thank [in reference to the 8 March demo that thanked Syria] the Syrian worker who helped build our towns and fields, but on the other hand we will not thank the Syrian military that caused thousands of casualties...', *An-Nahar*, 15 March 2005, p.6.

34 'A Psychological reading of 14 March,', *An-Nahar*, 9 April 2006, p.9.

35 See *An-Nahar* 28 April 2005: the alliance was mentioned in conjunction with the talk about the election law and its effect on the unity of the opposition thereafter.

36 Some people justify the passing of the 2000 law as being a forced necessary evil as there were hints about postponing the parliamentary elections, a prospect feared by the new opposition and the Patriarch in particular. According to one observer, 'The most salient issue of dispute was the electoral law, a marvel of political engineering designed by Syrian military intelligence to regulate the parliamentary division of spoils. Most majority Christian administrative districts were bundled with larger majority Muslim districts, making it impossible to win most of the 64 Christian seats in parliament without the endorsement of Syrian-backed Sunni, Druze, and Shi'ite power barons. Although Syrian troops were gone, the

same barons quickly agreed amongst themselves that there would be no amendment of the electoral law.' Gary Gambill, 'The Counter-Revolution of the Cedars,' in *Mideast Monitor,* Vol. 1, No. 2.

37 *An-Nahar,* 9 May 2005, p.3.

38 *An-Nahar,* 12 May 2005, p.1

39 *An-Nahar,* 10 March 2006, p.19.

40 *An-Nahar's* headline the following day was: After the surprise victory of Aoun, Lebanon is confronted with two choices: Coexistence or Extremism. *An-Nahar,* June 6 2005, p.1.

41 *An-Nahar,* 15 May 2005, p.3.

42 *An-Nahar,* 3 April 2006, p.7.

43 Many articles were written arguing that the Shi'ite community can never and should never be represented solely by the two parties in power today. Regardless of the truth involved therein, the fact remains on the ground that Hezbollah and Amal are the representatives of the Shi'ite people.

44 *An-Nahar,* 27 March 2006, p.3. For another article dealing with the same issue, see Toufic El-Hindi, 'The Theory of a weak president and a Strong PM.', *An-Nahar,* 29 March 2006, p.17.

45 See footnote 1 for articles dealing with increased sectarianism in Lebanon.

46 Three articles were published in *As-Safir.*

Chapter Twelve

Democratic Reform in Lebanon:
An Electoral Approach

Rudy Jaafar

Lebanon is a segmented polity with intrinsic structural weaknesses in its governing system. Although these political flaws contributed to the outbreak of both civil wars, the same structure was maintained, with minor adjustments, after the 1989 Ta'if Accord. This chapter argues that Lebanon needs to adopt a new electoral formula, the Single Transferable Vote (STV), in order to enhance political development and eliminate the drawbacks of the present system. It also proposes recommendations on how to effectively implement the STV in Lebanon.

A fragmented country since its origin as a state, Lebanon has struggled to find a successful political system to maintain and promote peace within the various communities, also known as sects or confessions. Historically, a power-sharing agreement between several prominent sectarian groups managed, for the most part, to maintain peaceful coexistence. However, this political arrangement, known as consociationalism, failed to address the cleavages at the basis of Lebanese society; rather, it has reinforced them. Moreover, it has prevented the formation of an efficient government that could respond to rapid social changes within the polity.

A historical arrangement has therefore created a state structure with systemic weaknesses, some of which resulted in the civil wars of the latter half of the twentieth century. The conflicts that plagued Lebanon are not monocausal; external intervention from regional and international actors, as well as the presence of foreign armed groups in the country, contributed significantly to the outbreak of violence. Nevertheless, internal flaws were also responsible for the breakdown of order. The Ta'if peace agreement that ended the 1975-90 war merely re-established the same political organisation, albeit with minor adjustments. The Ta'if modifications have therefore not addressed the historical inconsistencies of Lebanese democracy. Similarly, the latest proposal by the National Electoral Commission, despite its many improvements on the existing electoral formula, fails to tackle the country's political predicament.

This chapter argues that the Lebanese state needs to adjust its governing system in order to preclude a recurrence of its past experience. The focus will therefore be dedicated to the domestic dimensions of the crisis. Although some effort should be exerted to limit foreign interference in Lebanese affairs, more powerful external actors remain beyond the reach of the weak Lebanese state. The thrust of reform should rather be directed towards the domestic dimensions of the crisis, especially since structural improvements could lessen the effects of regional and international whirlwinds on the Lebanese arena. Given the power struggle, deadlock and insecurity that Lebanon has witnessed in the wake of former Prime Minister Hariri's assassination in February 2005, the need to reform the country's governance system, allowing it to absorb society's heterogeneous forces and translate them into a legitimate and functional body politic, is as urgently needed as ever. The recent removal of the three-decade old Syrian hegemony might just prove to be a propitious time in Lebanese history to undertake such restructuring.

In this study, I first explore the origins of the Lebanese system of government, its inherent weaknesses, as well as its demise and rebirth in post-war agreements. Then, I analyse the need for reform and explain why electoral engineering, in contrast to other institutional reforms, could represent a solution to the country's political predicament. Finally, I examine the present electoral mechanism and propose a new formula, the Single Transferable Vote, as a promising solution to the Lebanese democracy deficit.

Origins of the state

The present frontiers of the Republic of Lebanon were drawn by the French mandate authorities in 1920 mainly to accommodate the Christian Maronites, with whom they had strong historic ties. This newly-created, independent Lebanese state comprised within its borders several religious communities. Demographically, none of these religious sects, including the Maronites, constituted an absolute majority by itself. With the end of French control, it would therefore prove difficult to find a governing system for Lebanon since majority rule was not feasible. No single community could control the entire system.

Moreover, citizens' loyalties were parochial, extending from the family to the clan and the sect. There was no feeling of national belonging amongst the majority of individuals regardless of background. In his seminal study of Lebanese politics, *The Precarious Republic*, Michael Hudson describes the situation as follows: 'As a political culture, Lebanon is a collection of traditional communities bound by the mutual understanding that other communities cannot be trusted.' (Hudson 1968, 34). The task of creating a national governing system was daunting.

Consociational agreement

Following independence in 1943, the leaders of the two most prominent sects, the Christian Maronites and the Muslim Sunnis, agreed upon a workable governing solution. Bishara el-Khouri and Riad al-Solh fashioned a power-sharing mechanism and called it *al-mithaq al-watani*, or the National Pact. Lijphart states that consociational democracy is 'government by elite cartel designed to turn a democracy with a fragmented political culture into a stable democracy.' (1969, 216). This unwritten accord was to form the basis of Lebanese consociationalism; offices and seats in government were reserved for each community depending upon its demographic weight.

Roughly based on the 1932 census, the last to date, the Pact dictated that representation of a group would be proportional to its percentage of the total population. The Christians, according to the census, exceeded the Muslims by a ratio of approximately six to five, and were therefore allocated that many more government jobs (Hanf 1993, 90). The subgroups within the Christian and Muslim communities were also represented proportionately. The composition of the parliament reflected proportionate ratios as well; although, unlike other government quotas based upon unwritten agreements, parliamentary quotas were inscribed in the constitution.

To avoid one of the standard dangers of consociational systems, whereby each party can ignore others at the grass-roots level, the government created new electoral districts with significant minorities, therefore encouraging inter-confessional coalitions. Indeed, these electoral provisions promoted sectarian moderation by forcing candidates to reach for support beyond their traditional sects in order to secure elections. Moreover, since parliamentary seats were allocated for every community, electoral competition occurred between the members of each sect; individual candidates competed for positions reserved for their group instead of seeking to increase their faction's influence. As such, the National Pact institutionalised traditional pluralism and channelled sectarian competitive energy inwardly, transforming the inter-group contest into an intra-group rivalry (Smock and Smock 1975, 111). Naturally, this type of competition was less divisive to a Lebanese state dependent upon a delicate communal equilibrium.

Structural weaknesses in the balance-of-power system

Although it succeeded in moderating sectarian tensions, Lebanese consociationalism contained several structural weaknesses. First, it reinforced confessional cleavages by crystallising sectarian identity. It now became impossible for citizens to have a political existence beyond their religious group. Regardless of their ideological or political outlook, citizens were confined to their communal origin (Salamé 1994, 98-99). Hudson argues 'institutionalised sectarianism is Lebanon's substitute for positive consensus . . .' (1968, 116). Ironically, this system therefore sought to transcend communal identity by reinforcing it.

Lebanese consociationalism also had important repercussions on the nature of the state. The state apparatus was intentionally not developed nor expanded in order to prevent it from seizing power from, or disturbing the balance of, the traditional elites. It was feared that a strong government apparatus could be co-opted by people who did not belong to the traditional agreement and used to alter or destroy this arrangement. Moreover, institutionalised parochialism further eroded the already limited power of the central government (Salamé 1994, 98-99).

The subsequently weak Lebanese state resulted in the different groups enjoying significant autonomy. This non-interference on the part of the state in the intra-communal affairs of its citizens was concurrent with the original policies of the Lebanese consociational arrangement. However, a weak government simultaneously undermined the system. Although group autonomy provided a sense of security, weak central rule created insecurity, forcing factions to establish their own independent power structures and to look for support beyond Lebanon's borders (Hudson 1968, 34). In the absence of a strong central government, communal groups relied upon themselves and their allies to ensure their protection, further reducing the power of the state. This destructive, positive feedback loop culminated with the latter appearance of several armed militia, many of which had ties to foreign groups or neighboring states.

The combination of multiple centres of power and the absence of control over the use of force created a classical balance-of-power scenario. 'In Lebanon, as in the international system, there is no ultimate arbiter of conflict and no monopoly of the instruments of force.' (Hudson 1968, 6.) In reality, 'the sub-national communities are compelled by the situation to act as if they were states in an international environment' (Hudson 1968, 9). An examination of the history of European balance-of-power arrangements highlights the static and rigid nature of these systems (Craig and George 1983, 28-48). Adjustments were very difficult and costly, for any alteration would come at the expense of one of the actors and would threaten to disrupt the whole structure.

In Lebanon, the balance-of-power was built to maintain civil peace between the groups. Its purpose was not to emancipate the citizens by encouraging economic, political, and social development. Notwithstanding minor corrections, the Lebanese consociational system was created to uphold the status quo. The executive simply adjudicated between the various parties according to established but non-codified rules. The government's limited-leadership functions were not to organise progress or make difficult public decisions; they were to act as a trustee (Kerr 1966, 188-190). As Edward Shils argues, 'Lebanon is a country which must be kept completely still politically in order to prevent communal self-centeredness and mutual distrust from turning into active and angry contention.' (1966, 4). The politics of Lebanon were the politics of immobilism, and the balance-of-power system served that purpose. With the appearance of new forces, however, the ossified Lebanese political structure was subjected to severe internal pressure.

Static systems and change

Beginning in the 1950s, new social and economic forces assailed the solidified Lebanese political fortress. Population increase, coupled with uneven economic development and the impact of communication technology, resulted in powerful social mobilisations that disrupted the delicate Lebanese balance (Jabbra and Jabbra 2001, 78-79). The new social forces required political avenues to express themselves; yet, the traditional Lebanese system was inaccessible to them. Due to the communal nature of the system, ideologically based political parties were hard to create and sustain, for sectarianism militated against inter-confessional ventures (Binder 1966, 321).

Furthermore, for success under this system, a party interested in change had to include the same communal leaders it sought to displace. Citizens seeking solutions to policy problems could only depend upon the liberal benevolence of sectarian leaders (Hudson 1968, 214). The fathers of the republic were careful to include in their consociational scheme as much of the traditional pluralism as possible. However, they did not, and could not, secure the representation of ideological politics, a necessary element for governing a modern state.

Moreover, dynamic social changes were demographically unevenly distributed. The unequal birth rates among the various sects soon challenged the balance established at the dawn of the republic. The Lebanese state is based on distributing power according to each community's share of total population. If these proportions were now debated, it was the legitimacy of the state itself that was questioned (Hudson 1968, 23).

As mentioned earlier, the Lebanese state was first established with the premise that the Maronite community was the largest of all. This fact was reflected within the power-sharing consociational agreement as well. With new social dynamics, the basis for Maronite predominance eroded. Seeking to maintain their privileges with decreasing numbers, the Maronites entrenched and expanded their position within the system (Salamé 1994, 89). In response, alienated groups also struggled to further their place in the polity. Although wars are rarely monocausal – and in this case there were numerous external strains on the Lebanese system, such as the presence of armed Palestinian groups in Lebanon, the larger Arab-Israeli conflict, and the Cold War (Jabbra and Jabbra 2001, 80-83) – sectarian friction was at the heart of the short conflict of 1958 and the devastating one of 1975 (Hanf 1993 and Salamé 1994). The static Lebanese political structure could not adapt to dynamic changes in its environment. In a rigid system based on sectarian identity and mutual distrust, the threat or use of force and violence became an effective means to alter the governing structure.

The death and rebirth of Lebanese consociationalism

For fifteen years, the Lebanese, Palestinians, Syrians, Israelis and to a certain extent Iranians and Americans, fought a devastating war on the land of Lebanon. The war ended in 1990 with an agreement brokered by the Syrians and the Saudis at the city of Ta'if in Saudi Arabia. The Ta'if Accord, as it has come to be known, provides the basis for the new Lebanese political system. Coexistence between the Lebanese sects remains the *raison d'être* of the state (Hanf 1993, 585), and consociationalism the means by which to achieve that objective.

The change at Ta'if consisted of a redistribution of power. According to a new formula, the Muslims were now on par with the Christians (compared to the earlier five-to-six ratio), and the Shi'ites were recognised as new major political players, together with the Maronites and the Sunnis (The Ta'if Accord 2005). Government posts previously reserved for community leaders were maintained, but their powers were adjusted to reflect the new sectarian demographic distribution. Apart from the new distributive formula and the fact that Ta'if was a more inclusive agreement than one between the Maronites and the Sunnis, the new power sharing arrangement was identical to that of the National Pact (Hanf 1993, 587). The old and the new sectarian consociational systems are structurally one and the same.

Sadly, the devolution of power to a new Triumvirate – a Troika of Maronite President, Sunni Prime Minister, and Shi'ite Parliament Speaker – has increased the paralysis of the state (Hanf 1993). Whatever executive efficiency the old regime contained has now dissipated with the elimination of a strong presidential office. This new diffuse power structure has created a government even more stagnant than its pre-war predecessor. To further complicate matters, the Syrian regime, which withdrew in April 2005 after almost three decades in Lebanon, established a stranglehold on Lebanese decision-making. This transfer of power to an unaccountable foreign government particularly hindered Lebanese political development in the years after the Ta'if Accord.

The present dilemma

Although it can succeed in containing conflict, consociationalism can also engender negative outcomes in the long-term. Pippa Norris states that 'Consociationalism can be regarded as, at minimum, the realistic perspective, representing the necessary conditions to secure peace agreements and negotiated settlements among all parties. Whether it also serves the long-term interests of democratic consolidation and durable conflict management, however, remains less clear.' (Norris 2005, 19.) Nevertheless, Lebanon's experience with consociationalism has not ended. The fundamental weaknesses of the system were not addressed when it was recast following the 1975-90 civil war. The flaws that led to the collapse of the original arrangement were maintained after Ta'if. These include: the reinforcement of sectarian identity, weakening of the state, proliferation of alternate power centres, prevalence of the inert nature of government and its failure to absorb new social forces, and, most importantly, the incapacity of this rigid political organisation to adapt to a dynamic demographic environment.

The present Lebanese state is consequently still unable to contend with the forces that shattered its predecessor. Social mobilisation continues and certain sectors of Lebanese society have started questioning the one-to-one ratio between Christians and Muslims, claiming that it severely underestimates the Muslim population. Many indeed argue that the Shi'ites today form a majority within the country. The subject of Hezbollah's weapons also carries much significance. Although the Party of God's arsenal has, in the past, almost exclusively been directed against non-Lebanese enemies, there is no doubt, as Amal Saad-Ghorayeb argues, that they too serve the function of internal power equaliser, compensating for the Shi'ite community's limited share of parliamentary seats (2005) – 21 per cent compared to an estimated 35 per cent of the population. However, the debate over new majorities is taboo, for the mere mention of the topic drains the whole governance structure of legitimacy, threatening to open Pandora's box. For this reason, and given Lebanon's turbulent history, the country has refused to undertake a new census, the last one dating back to 1932.

That said, it is important to recognise that Lebanese politics do not evolve in a vacuum, but reflect regional and international forces. As a small and weak state in the midst of a very turbulent region, Lebanon is at the mercy of its powerful neighbors. Consequently, many attribute its failures to external pressures. Hanf, referring to the 1975-90 war and expounding a view that is not uncommon, wrote: 'I am convinced the Lebanese would have been able to solve their problems without resorting to arms. . . . . No, in the absence of the Palestinians, this war would never have started.' (1993, 374). Surely, the presence of an armed foreign militia, which allied itself with certain factions of the Lebanese population, strained the delicate confessional equilibrium beyond the limitations of the balance-of-power system and had a major role in precipitating its descent into violence (Fisk 2001). Additionally, the latter interventions of neighbouring armies only exacerbated the hostilities.

Perhaps events would have taken a different path in the absence of foreign intervention; perhaps not. It is undeniable, however, that the Lebanese regime contains inherent structural defects which have contributed to its past adversity, as Hanf also acknowledges (1993, 374). If the Lebanese consociational system is not altered to absorb and channel the domestic forces that disrupted it in the two previous civil wars, those forces could clash again. Worse yet, if the system fails to develop a way of adapting to shifting demographics, it could possibly unravel and produce an authoritarian government the likes of which abound in Lebanon's vicinity.

Requirements for a solution

In the Lebanese parliamentary system, the Legislative Chamber elects the President of the Republic, who in turn appoints a Prime Minister in consultation with Parliament. The Prime Minister then becomes responsible for forming the executive Council of

Ministers, also in concordance with Parliament (The Lebanese Constitution 1990). This paper seeks to devise a political mechanism to generate a democratic Lebanese government that ensures peaceful coexistence between the various groups and excludes the drawbacks of the present consociational arrangement, namely its immobilism, failure to absorb new social forces, and incapacity to adapt to a demographically dynamic environment.

A holistic analysis of viable political arrangements for divided societies should, among other things, weigh the benefits of a presidential versus parliamentary system, or the advantages of unicameral versus bicameral legislatures (Norris 2004, 39). However, the present institutional configuration does not, in itself, obstruct coexistence among the various communities. Parliamentary regimes have proven successful for many stable polities. Rather, the problems arise from the nature of elections, which produce sectarian politics and their aforementioned repercussions. Consequently, this effort will focus on the electoral *formula* that generates the legislative body. As mentioned earlier, the Lebanese Parliament is the centre of gravity of the unicameral state and the source for legislative and executive powers (The Lebanese Constitution 1990). Reforms to the Parliament should therefore echo throughout the governing structure.

First, the reformed electoral law should ensure sufficient representation within Parliament of all minorities if it is to be seen as legitimate. Additionally, the formula should permit the expression of various ideologies and open Parliament to ideological parties, allowing leaders to assume positions of authority based on their political ideas, not their confessional identity. A better management and development of the Lebanese state requires competent leadership to be substituted for confessional politics. Finally, any new system must permit Parliament to reflect demographic and social change; it should therefore avoid the rigidity of sectarian quotas.

As mentioned previously, the latest Troika scheme, established at Ta'if after the war, in order to redistribute power between the three highest offices of the state, has been a source of political stagnation for the country. A rearrangement in the loci of political authority could therefore be contemplated. However, such institutional adjustments are ancillary to the project of electoral development, for they would not resolve the current dilemma. Indeed, the issue of presidential and ministerial powers does not address the crystallisation of sectarian identity or related problems. On the other hand, a new electoral formula could transform politics and open parliament to modern and competent parties. As such, electoral engineering should constitute the core of the reform plan; institutional reorganisation could subsequently be considered if necessary.

The Lebanese electoral system

Electoral formulas generally fall into three categories, majority or proportional representation (PR) systems – in their numerous variations – or mixed formulas that combine both systems. Majoritarian systems accentuate a winning party's gains with more parliamentary seats in order to provide for a strong governing majority. Indeed, such formulas create a 'manufactured' majority at the expense of the representation of minority parties. PR systems, on the other hand, work to increase the representation of all groups in society, who could then bargain and form a coalition government if need be. With their emphasis on representation, PR systems are commonly recognised as superior alternatives for countries characterized by social cleavages. Here, Norris warns about the use of majoritarian systems in divided societies (Norris 2005, 5):

> Majoritarian rules of the game raise the stakes: some will win more, others will lose more. The risks are therefore higher; if one faction temporarily gains all the reins of government power, few or no effective safeguards may prevent them from manipulating the rules to exclude rivals from power on a permanent basis. Established democracies have developed deep reservoirs of social trust and tolerance which facilitate the give-and-take bargaining, compromise, and conciliation characteristic of normal party politics. Yet trust is one of the first casualties of societal wars.

Lebanon currently uses an electoral system known as the Block Vote, a majority scheme based on multi-member districts (The Law of Parliamentary Elections 2003). Under this formula, electors have as many votes as there are seats to be filled in the district. They may not, however, vote more than once for any one candidate (Reilly and Reynolds 2003). In the end, the candidates with the greatest tallied votes are elected. The Lebanese Block Vote guarantees adequate representation by using explicit quotas without which fair representation for minorities does not occur. For example, with a Block Vote devoid of quotas, a community with an overall majority in any district can secure all the electoral seats of that district by fielding as many candidates as there are seats and voting exclusively for them.

Elections in Lebanon, as in other segmented societies, would be perceived as illegitimate if they do not provide adequate representation to all the major communal groups. The Block Vote guarantees such representation by using explicit quotas that are also at the heart of the governance dilemma and should be discarded. However, if the present Block Vote is stripped of these confessional measures, voting would produce non-inclusive results. As such, the majoritarian Block Vote must be replaced with another PR electoral formula if it is to eliminate the rigidity of sectarian quotas and resolve the Lebanese democratic dilemma.

The Single Transferable Vote

The voting formula known as the Single Transferable Vote (STV), a proportional representation (PR) procedure, may offer a promising solution to the Lebanese predicament. STV is used today for diverse types of elections and in several countries, most notably, Australia, Ireland, the United States, and Malta. It has also been used, intermittently, in the United Kingdom, Canada, and New Zealand (Lakeman 1974, 278-280). Although its use for national parliamentary elections has been limited, it is widely acknowledged by experts to be among the most appealing and refined of electoral systems (Reilly and Reynolds 2001). In a multivariate analysis of

164 countries with various electoral systems, nations using STV scored highest in indicators such as political stability, accountability, government effectiveness, and political rights and civil liberties (Norris 2005, 28).

STV was originally devised in the middle of the nineteenth century, and has, since then, experienced several improvements (Lakeman 1974, 113). It is applied in multi-member districts, and does not pose an upper limit upon the number of seats for the constituency (Lakeman 1974, 127). The foundational principle of STV is to render every citizen's vote as effective as possible in the election of representatives. In contrast to majoritarian systems, the number of wasted votes – votes with no impact upon election results, such as defeated candidates' votes – is reduced to a minimum.

The mechanism is as follows. Voters are asked, although not required, to rank candidates according to their preference. They can exclude any candidate for whom they have no affinity, or rank every candidate on the list. Whether independents or party members, candidates are presented as individuals on the electoral list. They therefore compete with their fellow party members in case their party has presented more than one candidate for the district.

On the first count, all first-preference votes are calculated and a 'quota' of votes (no relation here to the fixed sectarian quotas of the present Lebanese system) is established, above which a candidate is declared a winner. Though there are several quota formulas, most theorists prefer the Droop quota, which translates more voter preferences into election results than other formulas and eliminates the possibility that party manoeuvre might ensure a winning seat (Lakeman 1974, 146-149). Moreover, by providing a lower threshold for the number of winning votes, the Droop quota facilitates the election of minority candidates.

However, if no one attains the quota, or if the seats of the district are not filled on the first count, the candidate with the fewest first-preference votes is eliminated, and in a second count his second-preference votes are redistributed to the others (Reilly and Reynolds 2001). This process is repeated, with as many counts as necessary to fill all the seats of the constituency. In accordance with the principle of increasing the effectiveness of all votes, a winner's excess votes (those votes over the quota) are also redistributed according to the voter's next preference. Electors, therefore, impart only one vote each; if their vote is not used for their first preference candidate, it will be used for their second, or third, and so on down the list. Rather than be discarded, every ballot, if it is ranked, will be used to elect a representative.

Single Transferable Vote in Lebanon

The STV process produces a flexible electoral system that translates, to a very large extent, voter preferences for individual candidates and their party affiliations, into electoral results. In a comprehensive analysis of STV, Enid Lakeman states in *How Democracies Vote*, '[STV] allows the voter full freedom to express his preferences for individual candidates, either with or without regard to those candidates' party affiliations. . . . The elected body reflects, within the limits of a few per cent, the strength of the political parties or other groups of opinion among the voters' (Lakeman 1974, 149-150).

In this regard, STV offers the best of both worlds. It makes possible the election of individuals based upon their political ideas, or party affiliations, while ensuring the representation of confessional minorities, if this conforms to the wish of a noteworthy part of the electorate. It therefore permits the representation of both sect and ideology. As Lakeman argues, under STV, 'any party or other group having a majority of votes will have a majority of seats [and] . . . any substantial and cohesive minority is automatically assured of its representation without any special provisions... [or] a stated number of representatives' (Lakeman 1974, 150, 135 and 133). Designed to achieve proportional representation, STV enables the removal of confessional quotas while securing the representation of any faction whose voters choose it.

Furthermore, voters need not subscribe to an exclusive loyalty but can act on an affiliation both to their sect and to an ideological party. With STV, voters can select both, ranking them depending upon their personal inclinations. Similar to the accommodative electoral arrangements proposed by Donald Horowitz (Horowitz 1985), this ranking provides incentives for every party, group, or individual candidate to appeal for second preference votes by promoting centripetal policies bridging the sectarian divide. It also encourages parties to present diverse candidates reflecting the religious composition of the district, thus allowing a voter to combine both confessional and ideological affiliations by voting for a particular ideological stance within their community. Consequently, STV also allows the parallel representation of sect and ideology.

In essence, STV provides the electorate with a variety of choices to suit their ideological and/or religious preferences. It also ensures the representation of minorities by rendering every ballot effective to the greatest extent possible. On a larger scale, STV also facilitates the dissolution of communal identities, which the present system has crystallised. The political incentives provided by STV promote accommodative behaviour, encouraging parochial voters to venture beyond their traditional groups. Minority voters can slowly move towards ideological parties if they are satisfied with the parties' performances. '[Under STV, the] gradual evolution of political attitudes is facilitated' (Lakeman, 1974, 136). STV therefore provides a momentum towards political development.

Implementing the formula

Interestingly, the Ta'if Accord, which dictated the readjustment of Lebanese sectarianism, also calls for its eventual abolition. Leaving the decision to a parliamentary vote and without stipulating a date, the accord, in Article 95, contemplates the elimination of religious identity from Lebanese politics (The Ta'if Accord 2005). Many Lebanese leaders are therefore conscious of the drawbacks of the present system, although they have yet to change it. To strengthen Lebanese democracy and fulfill the provisions of Ta'if, the state should implement the Single Transferable Vote as the national parliamentary election mechanism.

Not only is STV uniquely suited to address the requirements of Lebanese democracy; it can also be straightforwardly adopted by the Lebanese state. First, the presence in Lebanese society of cross-cutting cleavages, in the form of inter-sectarian businesses, political cooperation, or mixed marriages for example, is constructive for the success of STV (Reynolds 2004). Second, most heterogeneous multi-member constituencies currently in use for the Block Vote could fulfill – with minor adjustments for population size – the district requirements for STV. Indeed, as there is no theoretical upper limit on the number of seats in a STV district, either the present *muhafaza* (governorate) or sub-*muhafaza* districts would work. This policy would save the government resources by avoiding the economic costs of redistricting the nation.

STV has sometimes been criticized for its complexity and the formula has not been recommended for illiterate populations (Reynolds 1999). Lebanon's citizens are highly literate, however, and should have little difficulty embracing the new rules. Nonetheless, the Lebanese state should establish an independent elections monitoring body – as suggested by the recent National Electoral Commission – in order to ensure election integrity and preserve the legitimacy of the vote. Indeed, with the need for intricate computations to determine results, vote counting under STV will have to occur not at polling stations but at specified centres that must be under the oversight of an autonomous and impartial institution.

On 1 June 2006, the National Electoral Commission delivered the much-awaited proposal to reform the electoral system to the Lebanese Prime Minister. The Commission's mandate had been extended many months beyond its original deadline because of the need to satisfy the competing interests of Lebanon's political class. While the document's total or partial approval by Parliament remains uncertain, the Commission did suggest significant improvements to the current electoral law. Modifications such as lowering the voting age from 21 to 18, providing for equal access to the media to all contestants, auditing candidates' funding and spending, giving emigrants the right to vote, and establishing an independent body to oversee the elections process are essential revisions (*An-Nahar* 2006). However, by maintaining sectarian quotas – even, as put forward, with the adoption of a mixed Block Vote-List PR formula – the proposal fails to address the problems of consociationalism and the ensuing policy stalemate.

While the ratification of Parliament is required for the adoption of the new electoral formula, it is very likely, as was the case with the National Electoral Commission, that some entrenched Lebanese politicians, fearing the new formula would erode their positions, could resist the implementation of STV. The choice of an electoral formula is, after all, a fundamentally political process. The endeavour to implement STV should therefore be expanded to include the organs of civil society. Non-governmental organisations, the media, and other citizen associations, already a vibrant group in Lebanon, should pressure parliamentary representatives to endorse the new law. In this campaign, activists should make use of the Ta'if Accord by reminding government officials that the accord stipulates the elimination of sectarian politics. Furthermore, today, with what many perceive to be a worrying spike in internal tension and sectarianism, the effort to reform Lebanese governance is a matter of much urgency.

Conclusion

Even though the Lebanese Republic has, for part of its life, promoted some coexistence between the groups, it has yet to solve its sectarian predicament; so far, it has succeeded only in barely containing it. Since independence, whenever communal pressures exceeded a certain threshold, contributing to the outbreak of violence, the political organisation was forced to adjust at tremendous cost. These 'adjustment spasms' have been especially pernicious. More ominously, there appears to be no end in sight to their recurrence. Consociationalism has, at best, proven to be a short-to-medium term solution. Yet, the Lebanese so far have failed to devise a mechanism to absorb the evolutionary dynamic. The Ta'if

Accord merely adjusted the system to a new reality in 1989; Lebanon's society, however, is continuously changing. Ongoing social and demographic mobilisations could therefore confront the rigid Lebanese state with similar pressures in the future.

Electoral engineering is a promising remedy to the Lebanese democratic predicament. The new electoral system is here presented as a mechanism to constitute the governing body of the state, as well as a tool for conflict management. The STV, uniquely suited to the sociological realities of the country, can create a Parliament representative of all major confessional groups without impeding the necessary expression of modern political ideas. The Parliament would, in turn, produce a competent and effective government to run the state.

Although Lebanon's stability is continuously affected by larger regional actors, a strengthening of its governing institutions would improve the country's resilience. Of crucial importance to good governance is the promotion of 'underlying conditions conducive for the development of human capital and economic growth, for example by investing in schools, basic health care, fair trade [...]' (Norris 2005, 20). However, successful investments in human capital require functioning state institutions. As such, a new adaptable and flexible Lebanese democratic system should diminish the potential for future civil conflict and assist in the advancement of the polity.

References

An-Nahar, 2 June 2006. *The complete text of the electoral law project in its mixed majoritarian and proportional formula.*

Binder, Leonard, Political Change in Lebanon, *Politics in Lebanon*, ed. Leonard Binder. New York: John Wiley, 1966.

Craig, Gordon A and George, Alexander L, *Force and Statecraft: Diplomatic Problems of Our Time*. Oxford University Press, 1983.

Economist Intelligence Unit, The (EIU), *Country Profile 2003: Lebanon*. London: The Economist Intelligence Unit, 2003.

Fisk, Robert, *Pity the Nation: Lebanon at War*. Oxford: Oxford University Press, 2001.

Hanf, Theodore, *Coexistence in Wartime Lebanon: Decline of a State and Rise*

of a Nation. London: The Center for Lebanese Studies in association with
I B Tauris, 1993.

Horowitz, Donald, *Ethnic Groups in Conflict*, Berkeley: University of
California Press, 1985.

Hudson, Michael, *The Precarious Republic: Political Modernisation in
Lebanon*. New York: Random House, 1968.

Jabbra, Joseph G and Jabbra, Nancy, 'Consociational Democracy in
Lebanon: A Flawed System of Governance', *Perspectives on Global
Development and Technology*. Volume 17, Issue 2, 2001.

Kerr, Malcolm H, 'Political Decision Making in a Confessional Democracy',
In *Politics in Lebanon*. Ed. Leonard Binder, New York: John Wiley, 1966.

Lakeman, Enid, *How Democracies Vote: A Study of Electoral Systems*. London:
Faber and Faber, 1974.

Lebanese Constitution, The, *International Constitutional Law*.
http://www.oefre.unibe.ch/law/icl/le00000_.html (accessed April 26, 2004).

Law of Parliamentary Elections, The Lebanese Parliament.
http://www.lp.gov.lb/kanoun_intikhab/table1.htm (accessed April 26,
2004).

Lijphart Arend. January 1969, 'Consociational Democracy', *World Politics*.
Vol. 21, No. 2.

Norris, Pippa, *Electoral Engineering: Voting Rules and Political Behavior*.
Cambridge: Cambridge University Press, 2004.

_____, 'Stable democracy and good governance in divided societies: Do
power-sharing institutions work?', *Faculty Research Working Paper Series*.
John F. Kennedy School of Government, 2005. (cited with permission
from author)

Reilly, Ben and Reynolds, Andrew, *Electoral Systems and Conflict in Divided
societies*. Washington, DC: National Academy Press, 1999.

_____, *Single Transferable Vote. Administration and Cost of Elections
Project*. http://www.aceproject.org/main/english/es/esf04.htm (accessed
April 26, 2004), 2001.

_____, Block Vote. *Administration and Cost of Elections Project*.
http://www.aceproject.org/main/english/es/esd02.htm (accessed April 26,
2004), 2003.

Reynolds, Andrew. 1999. *Electoral Systems and Democratisation in Southern
Africa*. Oxford: Oxford University Press.

_____. 2004, July 25. Boston. Phone conversation with author.

Saad-Ghorayeb, Amal. May 2005, 'Lebanon: Shi'ites Express Political
Identity', *Arab Reform Bulletin*. Vol. 3, No. 4. Carnegie Endowment for
International Peace.

Salamé, Ghassan, 'Small is Pluralistic: Democracy as an Instrument of Civil
Peace', in *Democracy without Democrats: The Renewal of Politics in the*

Muslim World, ed. Ghassan Salamé. London: I B Tauris, 1994.

Shils, Edward, 'The Prospect for Lebanese Civility', in *Politics in Lebanon*, Ed. Leonard Binder. New York: John Wiley, 1966.

Smock, David R, and Smock, Audrey C, *The Politics of Pluralism: A Comparative Study of Lebanon and Ghana*. New York: Elsevier, 1975.

Taef Agreement, The, *The Lebanese Constitution*. Beirut: Dar al-'Ilm lil-Malayeen, 2005.

Chapter Thirteen

Ta'if's Dysfunctions and the Need for Constitutional Reform

Nawaf Salam

The purpose of this essay is to identify and propose solutions to Lebanon's enduring constitutional dysfunctions since the Ta'if Accord reforms were translated into 31 constitutional amendments in 1990. We shall therefore discuss both persisting and newly created dysfunctions. The former are the pre-1990 ones which have not been adequately dealt with – or even addressed – by the accord, while the latter refer to those which proceed from it.

Many important reforms provided for in Ta'if have not entered into force yet. Most prominent among them are the formation of the 'National Committee' entrusted under article 95 of the constitution with the task to 'study and propose the means to ensure the abolition of confessionalism'[1], administrative decentralisation, the strengthening of the independence of the judiciary, and the enactment of a new electoral law intended to ensure the representation of the 'different categories of the population' and to guarantee communal 'co-existence'. This eclectic implementation of Ta'if has certainly undermined its character as a 'package deal' accord. Moreover, many other of the Ta'if reforms have been distorted in practice, as illustrated by the emergence at one point in time of an unconstitutional 'troika', consisting of the President of the Republic, the Prime Minister and the Speaker of Parliament, and acting as a 'supreme' decision-making body.

Consequently, it is often argued that any call to consider amending Ta'if shall remain unwarranted as long as this agreement has not been 'fully' and 'properly' implemented. Such an argument fails to account for both Ta'if's intrinsic dysfunctions which have already been revealed through its own problematical experiment that started in 1990, and Ta'if's incapacity to overcome its systemic crises. However, while offering remedies to these dysfunctions we will be keeping in mind that the structures of the main state institutions in Lebanon and the powers enjoyed by their respective officeholders are less an expression of general constitutional principles than a reflection of the distribution of power among the various sects[2]. In other words, the solutions we shall offer are not designed to alter, at this stage of Lebanon's history, the communal nature of its political system. Pending the emergence of a domestic balance of power that would put Lebanon on the track of genuine deconfessionalisation, the objective of such remedies will be to avoid the risks of constitutional deadlocks that are inherent to the post Ta'if constitution, to redress its imbalances, and to bridge its loopholes.

This has become more urgent than ever before for two reasons. First, when Lebanon might have seemed capable of overcoming the dysfunctions of its post Ta'if constitution, this was not due to any 'invisible hand' (à la Adam Smith's) capable of ensuring the smooth functioning of its political institutions. Rather, this was due to the 'heavy hand' of Syria and to the 'arbitration' role it played in Lebanese politics until the withdrawal of its troops in April 2005. Second, Lebanon needs to prevent the development of detrimental new constitutional customs, for as Thomas A. Baylis observes in his comparative analysis of executive power in the emerging democracies of eastern Europe, 'new rules and institutions ... do not instantly produce firm realities but rather create a loose structure that political actors seek to shape in the interest of their own power and policy objectives'[3]. This is why Lebanon is now bound to introduce balancing and arbitration mechanisms within its post-Ta'if constitution, and to remove from its texts any ambiguity which could be the cause of stand-offs and sectarian quarrels. Otherwise, Lebanon will have to concede anew to the interests of foreign actors acting as arbiters in order to avoid the dangers and costs of political stalemates and/or civil strife.

To that effect ten constitutional cases shall be examined here. They deal, in the following sequence, with issues relative to the executive power, to the legislative power, to their relationship, and to the status of the judiciary. In conclusion, this paper shall also identify the articles of the constitution whose provisions need to be clarified in priority.

First: The election of the President of the Republic is governed by Article 73 of the Constitution which provides that 'one month at least and two months at most before the expiration of the term of the President of the Republic, the Chamber shall be convened by its President to elect the new President of the Republic. However, should it not be convened for this purpose, the Chamber shall meet automatically on the tenth day preceding the expiration of the President's term of office'[4].

It is noteworthy to point out that this article does not require the candidates for the post of the Presidency to declare their candidacy. However, in order to enhance the openness of this process and to increase its transparency an act of candidacy should be made mandatory. A practicable option would be to require from candidates for the Presidency to file their candidacy with the office of the Speaker of Parliament one month at least and three at most before the beginning of the period during which Parliament is to convene to elect a new President. This will undoubtedly strengthen the democratic legitimacy of this election and add to the standing of the Presidency. Moreover, such a change will oblige candidates to break away from the prevailing 'culture' of adopting a 'wait-and-see' policy and of shunning 'political exposure' in the hope that they may thus become acceptable compromise – and optimally 'consensual' – candidates.

Second: Article 53, paragraph 2 of the Constitution, reads that 'the President of the Republic shall designate the Prime Minister in consultation with the President of the Chamber of Deputies based on binding parliamentary consultations, the content of which he shall formally disclose to the latter'[5].

This article does not provide for any time frame for initiating such consultations or for designating a new Prime Minister as of the occurrence of one of the events requiring that, such as the resignation of the Prime Minister or any other of the 'circumstances' under which 'the government shall be considered resigned'[6]. To fill that loophole, the constitution should be amended to state that the process for nominating a new Prime Minister must be completed within a period of time not to exceed ten days. Should a Prime Minister not be designated during that time frame, Parliament will be granted the power to 'meet automatically' on the third day after the expiration of this period and directly proceed to elect a Prime Minister.

The issue here is not merely theoretical as Lebanon has already witnessed the dangers associated with the possibility of undue delays in the process of designating a new Prime Minister as in the political crisis of 2005 which followed the assassination of former Prime Minister Rafiq al-Hariri.

Third: Same Article 53, paragraph 4 reads that '[The President of the Republic] shall issue in agreement with the Prime Minister the decree appointing the cabinet and the decrees accepting the resignation of the ministers or their dismissal'[7].

The rationale behind this provision seems to have been based on the assumption that in the event of a disagreement between the President of the Republic and the designated Prime Minister regarding the choice of ministers and/or the respective ministerial portfolios to entrust them with, both will have to compromise to make possible the formation of the government. But, what if they fail to reach a mutually accepted composition of the cabinet and their disagreement persists? What happens? There is no solution in Ta'if to such an eventuality; hence, the need to amend this article of the constitution to provide for a remedial mechanism. In this case as well, the most logical option would be to resort to the arbitration of Parliament. More specifically, to overcome such a potential impasse, it is suggested here that if the designated Prime Minister does not agree with the President of the Republic on the formation of the cabinet, he would have to present, on the thirty-first day after his nomination, his own proposed cabinet before Parliament for confirmation. If he does not present such a cabinet or fails to confirm that it is accepted by the majority of Parliament, he will be deemed to have resigned.

The merit of such a solution is that it addresses not only the deadlock which could result from possible disagreements over the formation of the cabinet between the President of the Republic and the designated Prime Minister, but it also puts a time limit to the latter and thus protects the constitutional process from the risks of political procrastination; a significant illustration of such dangers is how the situation had started to drift with designated Prime Minister Omar Karami in March 2005. Moreover, the principle of introducing time frames for related acts to be accomplished is not alien to the Ta'if constitution which provides, for example, under Article 64 paragraph 2, that the government 'must present its general statement of policy to the Chamber to gain its confidence within thirty days'[8] of its formation.

Fourth: Article 56 of the constitution reads: '[The President of the Republic] shall issue decrees and demand their publication; he has the right to ask the Council of Ministers to reconsider any decision taken by the Council within 15 days as of its registration with the presidency. If the Council of Ministers insists on the adopted decision, or if the time limit expires without the decree being issued or returned, the decision or the decree will be considered automatically operative and must be published'[9].

In other words, if a decision is taken in the Council of Ministers, but the President of the Republic refuses to sign the decree turning it into an operative measure, the constitution states that after fifteen days such a decision would automatically enter into force. But what if it is the Prime Minister, and not the President of the Republic, who refuses to sign a decree to give effect to a decision taken in the Council of Ministers? There is no solution to such a problem in the constitution. Admittedly, the occurrence of a situation of that kind is difficult to envisage because Prime Ministers and the cabinets they preside over – or at least the majority within such cabinets – are not supposed to be in conflict.

However, since cabinets are often formed of heterogeneous coalitions in Lebanon, such a case has presented itself more than once since Ta'if. In 1998, for example, former Prime Minister Rafiq al-Hariri was capable of 'constitutionally' blocking – by not giving it the form of a decree – a decision taken in the Council of Ministers in favour of a draft law intended to authorize 'civil marriage' on an 'optional' basis[10]. Conversely, former Prime Minister Salim al-Hoss writes that he signed the decree approving of the draft law on legislative elections in 2000, even though he had himself a different opinion on the matter, only because that was the position of the majority of his Cabinet[11]. Both positions are hard to defend on either constitutional or political grounds. Their importance, however, is that they attest to the gravity of the problem and to the need to provide for a solution to it.

The argument that no such problem exists since the constitution provides for holding the Prime Ministers accountable for their acts and/or omissions through the legislature's vote of confidence mechanism simply misses the point. The issue here pertains to the proper functioning of the executive; it is not a matter of checks and balances between the executive and the legislative powers. A possible solution to this matter would be to grant the Prime Minister the right – by analogy to that granted to the President of the Republic – to ask the Council of Ministers to reconsider any decision, in its next meeting. If, on the one hand, the Council upholds its decision and, on the other, the Prime Minister does not sign the decree giving it effect within one week, he should then be deemed as having submitted the resignation of his government.

Fifth: A second problem regarding the functioning of the executive is the possibility of a concerned minister not signing a decree to give effect to a decision taken in the Council of Ministers or even unwarrantedly postponing that. Such a situation may arise if the Council decides to appoint a civil servant not proposed by the concerned minister; for example, if the Council of Ministers decides to appoint a Director General to the Ministry of Finance contrary to the initial recommendations of the Minister of Finance to that post. Ta'if is silent on this matter. In order to avoid a constitutional deadlock if such a situation arises, the decision of the Council of Ministers should be deemed operative after fifteen days – by analogy to the period granted to the President of the Republic – even if the concerned minister continues to withhold his signature. The relative decree will then be issued bearing only the signatures of the Prime Minister and of the President of the Republic, and the concerned Minister will be deemed to have resigned. This solution is based on the principle that under Ta'if, the Council of Ministers should operate as a *collegium*.

Sixth: Experience has also shown that the requirements – and/or the process – for issuing 'ordinary decrees' have also been the source of problems with no constitutional solution. In that respect, it should be recalled that 'ordinary decrees' only require the accord – and consequently the signature – of the concerned Minister, the Prime Minister and the President of the Republic, while issues of greater importance would usually necessitate 'decrees taken in the Council of Ministers', meaning a decision by this Council, although they would still bear the same signatures.

It has already been mentioned that pursuant to article 56 of the constitution a decree taken in the Council of Ministers will become 'operative' after fifteen days, even if it remains unsigned by the President of the Republic. And the introduction of new constitutional mechanisms has been suggested here to prevent both the Prime Minister and the Ministers from obstructing such decrees. However, contrary to the logic of the French adage 'he who can do more can do less', the constitution does not address the problems that 'ordinary decrees' might face. As a matter of fact, an 'ordinary decree' cannot see light if it is signed by both the concerned Minister and the Prime Minister but not by the President of the Republic. It may not even reach the latter –

irrespective of his position on whether to sign it or not – if at an earlier stage in the process it has not been endorsed by the Prime Minister. An example of such a situation is the ill-fated 'ordinary decree' relative to judicial nominations and permutations which, after months of its signature in 2006 by both the Minister of Justice and the Prime Minister, could not become 'operative' as it did not win the approval of President Emile Lahoud.

To forestall such possible blockage of 'ordinary decrees', both the President of the Republic and the Prime Minister should be granted the right to bring the matter before the Council of Ministers, if such a decree remained unsigned seven days after its reception by one of them. It would then become subject to the provisions applicable to 'decrees taken in the Council of Ministers'. Likewise, whenever the President of the Republic or the Prime Minister considers that the concerned Minister has failed to initiate the 'ordinary decree' process to address a situation requiring such action, they should also be granted the right to bring the matter before the Council of Ministers to decide on it.

Seventh: As to the legislature, the term of the Speaker of the Chamber of Deputies, which under the original constitution was of one renewable year, has been changed pursuant to Ta'if, to correspond to the 'length of the Chamber's term'[12] – which is usually fixed at four years by the electoral law. Clearly, the objective was to strengthen the position of the Speaker by enhancing the stability of his term in office[13].

However, this amendment suffers from an unambiguous anomaly. For though the Speaker can now be elected for this extended term by 'a relative majority' – albeit 'at the third ballot'[14] – the Chamber 'may, once only, two years after the election of the President [i.e. Speaker] and the Vice President, and in the first session it holds, withdraw its confidence from the President or the Vice President by a decision of two thirds of the Chamber, based on a petition signed by at least ten deputies'[15]. In other words, though he may be elected by 'a relative majority', the Speaker could not be removed from office even if that came to be the will of an 'absolute majority' – if short of two thirds – of the Chamber.

314

Moreover, the 'two thirds' majority is allowed the possibility of acting to that effect only 'once' and at a certain point in time, i.e. in 'the first session' the Chamber holds 'two years after the election of the President and the Vice-President'. Putting such excessive limitations on the 'powers' of the Chamber regarding its Speaker threatens to undermine a basic principle of parliamentary systems, namely that 'parliaments are sovereign'. In addition, the crisis which was triggered in November 2006 by the resignation of all Shi'a ministers from the government has shown – inter alia[16] – how the 'political stability' of the Speaker's position – as enhanced under Taif – also bears the risks of attempts at hegemony. As a matter of fact, during the following 2007 winter/spring parliamentary session, the Speaker, thanks to his exclusive prerogatives to call Parliament to a meeting was able to turn a deaf ear to the majority's repeated demands to convey Parliament to deliberate on the ratification of the treaty signed between the goverment of Lebanon and the United Nations regarding the establishment of a 'tribunal of an international character' in teh Hariri assassination case. To address such aberrations, a new balance between the requirements of accountability, on the one hand, and of stability of the Speaker's office on the other, ought to be struck. For example, while the four-year term of the Speaker and his deputy will be maintained, the 'absolute majority' of the Chamber of Deputies could be recognised to have the power to withdraw its confidence from any of the former at the beginning – and only at the beginning – of each session it holds. Notwithstanding its obvious merits, such a proposition, given the prevailing sectarian culture in Lebanon, may be perceived as an attempt to divest the Shi'a community of its principal gain under Ta'if. Hence, a more realistic alternative at the present time would be not to require such a revision of the constitution but only to amend the bylaws of Parliament so that it becomes mandatory for the Speaker to call Parliament for a meeting if so requested by the absolute majority of deputies. Likewise, due consideration ought to be given to making it mandatory on the President of the Council of Ministers as well to call the government for a meeting if so requested by the majority of ministers, although this will necessitate an amendment of article 64 (par. 6) of the constitution. Manifestly, in both cases, the proposed amendments seek to reinforce the *Raison des institutions* principle. Hence, a more realistic alternative at the present time would be not to require such a revision of the constitution but only to amend the bylaws of Parliament so that it becomes mandatory for the Speaker to call Parliament for a meeting if so requested by the absolute majority of deputies. Likewise, due consideration ought to be given to making it mandatory on the President of the Council of Ministers as well to call the government for a meeting if so requested by the majority of ministers, although this will necessitate an amendment of article 64 (par. 6) of the constitution. Manifestly, in both cases, the proposed amendments seek to reinforce the *Raison des institutions* principle.

Eighth: Let us turn now to the dysfunctions in the relationship between the executive and the legislative powers. The legislative role of the Chamber of Deputies has been strengthened under Ta'if by amending Article 58 of the constitution, whereby bills that the Council of Ministers deems 'urgent' can no longer be put into effect by means of a decree forty days after being sent to the Chamber if the latter does not act upon them, unless – and here is the critical change – they are placed on 'the agenda of a general meeting [of the Chamber] and read therein'[17]. Before its amendment by the Constitutional Law of September 1991, the text of Article 58 read:

> By means of a decree issued with the approval of the Council of Minister, the President of the Republic may put into effect any bill which has previously been declared urgent by the Government in the decree of transmission issued with the approval of the Council of Ministers, and on which the Chamber has not given a decision within forty days following its communication to the Chamber[18].

The amendment of Article 58 was rightfully meant to pre-empt the government from the temptation of inundating the Chamber with bills declared 'urgent'. However, as it did not provide for any time frame for putting such bills, after their transmission to the Chamber, 'on the agenda' of a 'general meeting' and for 'reading' them, the executive is now at risk of becoming hostage to the sole legislature's decision on the matter. It may not be enough here to revise the text of Article 58 to specify that such bills should be put on the agenda of – and read in – the first 'general meeting' held by the Chamber of Deputies after their transmission to it; a ceiling should also be put on the number of bills labelled 'urgent' that the government could send to the Chamber during each of its sessions.

Ninth: A second dysfunction in the relationship between the executive and the legislative powers under Ta'if lies in that the possibility of dissolving the Chamber by the executive has been explicitly restricted to the occurrence of four highly unlikely instances. Under article 65, paragraph 4, the Council of Ministers shall have the authority to 'dissolve the Chamber of Deputies upon the request of the President of the Republic if the Chamber of Deputies, for no compelling reasons, fails to meet during one of its regular sessions and fails to meet throughout two successive extraordinary sessions, each longer than one month, or if the Chamber returns the entire budget plan with the aim of paralyzing the Government. This right cannot be exercised a second time if it is for the same reasons which led to the dissolution of the chamber the first time'[19]. As to Article 77, it states that if the government does not approve of the proposal of two-thirds of the Chamber of Deputies to amend the constitution and its request to the government to prepare a bill to that effect, it shall return the matter to the Chamber 'for reconsideration'[20]. In that case, 'if the Chamber insists upon the proposal by a three-quarters majority of the total members lawfully composing the Chamber, the President of the Republic has then either to comply with the Chamber's wish or to ask the Council of Ministers to dissolve the Chamber and to hold new elections within three months'[21].

In view of these 'conditions', it could safely be affirmed that, pursuant to the 1991 constitutional amendments, the executive has practically lost the possibility of dissolving the Chamber of Deputies. Admittedly, there is always a danger that incumbent politicians could abuse the 'dissolution option' by manipulating the timing of elections for partisan reasons[22]. But the dissolution power remains a key feature of parliamentary democracies. It represents a necessary counterbalance to the power of the 'simple majority' of the legislature to dismiss the government at will.

Moreover, the very existence of such an 'institutional weapon' might well help avert political deadlocks and foster greater cooperation between the government and the legislature in order to avoid early elections[23].

A remedy to this structural dysfunction created by Ta'if would be to remove the enumeration of 'subject matter' conditions on the power to dissolve the Chamber of Deputies while reinforcing the restrictions relative to its circumstances and timing, such as the possibility of prohibiting the dissolution to take place during the first year of the Chamber's term as provided for under article 12 of the French constitution, for example[24].

Tenth: The only article in the constitution devoted to the judiciary is Article 20. It reads: 'The judicial power shall be exercised by courts of various degrees and jurisdictions. It shall function within the limits of an order established by the law and offering accordingly the necessary guarantees to the judges and to litigants. The law shall determine the conditions and limits of the judicial guarantees. The judges shall be independent in the exercise of their functions. The decisions and judgments of all courts shall be rendered and executed in the name of the Lebanese people'[25].

What is in fact guaranteed under this article is the 'independence' of the judges in carrying out their 'functions' and not the judiciary as a 'constitutional power'. Given the unremitting complaints about external – political and sectarian – interferences with the judiciary, it is important that provisions regarding both the structure and organisation of the judiciary, and the selection, appointment, promotion and tenure of judges be introduced in the constitution. Articles 101 to 113 of the Italian constitution would be a good source to go by[26].

In addition to the needed treatment of the main dysfunctions discussed above, ambiguities should be removed from the articles of the constitution that are potentially a source of stalemate, or an object of communal dispute. Articles 49 and 52 of the constitution stand out in that respect.

Paragraph 2 of Article 49 provides that 'the president of the republic shall be elected by secret ballot and by a two-thirds majority of the Chamber of the Deputies. After a first ballot, an absolute majority shall be sufficient'[27]. Here, while the majority requested for each of the ballots is clearly prescribed, the text remains – no less clearly – silent regarding the needed quorum for the meeting of the Chamber. Two opposing interpretations are possible: to infer from the requirement of a two-thirds majority for the first ballot that a fortiori the same applies to the needed quorum; or, to hold that had a two-thirds majority been required for the quorum, it would have been specified in the text, a fortiori because when such a qualified majority was required for the first ballot, it was specified in the text. The battle of legal experts over the 'meaning" of this text has already been fought[28]. No 'clear" winner could emerge from it. Obviously, the only solution to the problem posed by this text is to have its ambiguity removed by the competent constitutional authority empowered to 'interpret" the constitution, i.e. the Chamber of Deputies.

In the same vein, the ambiguities of Article 52 must be removed. It reads: 'The President of the Republic shall negotiate and ratify international treaties in agreement with the Prime Minister. These treaties are not considered ratified except after approval by the Council of Ministers. They shall be made known to the Chamber of Deputies whenever the national interest and security of the state permit. However, treaties involving the finances of the state, commercial treaties and in general treaties that cannot be renounced every year shall not be considered ratified until they have been approved by parliament'[29]. Manifestly, the term 'ratification' (*ibram,* in the original Arabic text), is used here in a confusing manner for it refers on the one hand to the act of consent for signature which concludes the negotiation stage, and on the other to the formal declaration of approval by the State. In addition to the need to have the legal terms set right here, the problem that this article poses is that it does not address the possibility of disagreement between the President of the Republic and the Prime Minister during the negotiation process, whether regarding the strategies to adopt or objectives to attain. In such a case, would the solution reside in submitting the matter to the 'arbitration' of the Council of Ministers? The matter ought to be clarified through a revision of the text of Article 42.

Here, it should also be noted that the Constitutional Council as originally envisaged under the Ta'if agreement was to be entrusted with the power to interpret the constitution . But this competence was dropped from the aforementioned constitutional amendments of 1990 which were meant to give effect to the Ta'if reforms. Reinstating the power to interpret the Constitution to the Constitutional Council will undoubtedly enhance the legitimacy and add to the credibility of such action in view of the neutrality and judicial nature of this Council. Conversely, keeping the power to interpret the Constitution with the Chamber of Deputies may carry the risk of having any such interpretation subjected to criticism on the basis of serving the 'political interests' of the parliamentary majority.

Finally, it should be stressed that all the proposed amendments here aim not at a redistribution of power among the various sects but at strengthening the role of constitutional institutions, as such, at the expense of the prerogatives enjoyed by their respective officeholders – as individuals. Thus, what has been suggested is to redress the imbalances between the executive and the legislative ,and the executive and the judiciary, and to grant Cabinet and Parliament the powers and means to arbitrate any conflict between the President of the Republic and the Prime Minister, a minister and the Prime Minister and/or the President of the Republic, the Prime Minister and Cabinet, and the Speaker and Parliament. No less important is it to recall here as well that one of the main reasons why Ta'if was adopted while other reform plans failed to win enough support is because it was presented as a 'package deal'.

Given that confessional considerations are still prevailing in Lebanon's political culture, if reforming Ta'if is to stand any real chance of success, it will have to take into account the requirements of balance and reciprocity. Hence, the solutions proposed to the ten dysfunctions discussed in this essay should better be read as a 'one package deal'.

It remains that the need to reform Ta'if should not be at the expense of implementing the original reforms it provides for and which have not entered into force yet, more particularly those designed to allow for the 'gradual' deconfessionalisation of the Lebanese political system. Here, along with the formation of the 'National Committee' entrusted with the task to 'study and propose the means to ensure the abolition of confessionalism'[30], concrete and bold steps should be seriously considered such as putting into effect the provision of Article 22 of the Constitution that calls for establishing a Senate to which sectarian representation would be restricted, and have the Chamber of Deputies elected 'on a national, non-confessional basis'[31].

Notes

1   Cf. Article 95 of the Lebanese Constitution, as amended in 1990. (All references are to an English translation of the constitution, with all amendments since 1926, published by the Lebanese Ministry of Justice in 1995).

2   Cf. Nawaf Salam, 'Ta'if revisited' in Theodor Hanf and Nawaf Salam (eds.), *Lebanon in Limbo. Postwar Society and State in an Uncertain Regional Environment*, (Baden-Baden, 2003).

3   Thomas A. Baylis, 'Presidents Versus Prime Ministers: Shaping Executive Authority in Eastern Europe' in *World Politics*, 48.3 (1996) 297-323, p.302.

4   Cf. Lebanese Constitution, op. cit.

5   Idem.

6   Cf. Article 69 of Lebanese Constitution, op. cit.

7   Cf. Lebanese Constitution, op. cit.

8   Cf. Lebanese Constitution, op. cit.

9   Idem.

10 On the debates then over the issue of 'optional civil marriage', see

Ahmad Beydoun, *Tis'at 'asharat furqa najiya, al-lubnaniyyun fi ma'rakat al-zawaj al-madani*, (Beirut, 1999)

11 Cf. Salim al-Hoss, *Lil-haqiqa wal tarikh, tajarub al-hukm ma bayna 1998-2000* (Beirut, 2001), p.61

12 Cf. Article 44 of Lebanese Constitution, op. cit.

13 For a comparative perspective on how a similar amendment to the tenure of the Speaker of the French *Assemblée Nationale* strengthened this position, see the commentaries on article 32 of the French constitution by Edgar Faure and Louis Mermaz in Francois Luchaire and Gerard Conac (sous la direction de), *La Constitution de la république francaise. Analyses et commentaires* (Paris, 1987) pp. 731-741.

14 Cf. Article 44 of Lebanese Constitution, op. cit.

15 Idem.

16 This crisis, including the consequences of the resignation of all ministers of the same sect, is more of a political than constitutional nature. It will therefore not be discussed in this essay. Nevertheless, it remains noteworthy that while article 95 of the constitution provides that 'the sectarian groups shall be represented in a just and equitable manner in the formation of the Cabinet', it is only when the latter 'loses more than one third of its members' that it shall be considered resigned, pursuant to article 69 (b). In this case, the resignation of all the Shi'a ministers from Fouad Siniora's Cabinet did not represent 'more than one third of its members'. However, it has also been argued that the 'surviving' cabinet is to be considered in breach of paragraph (J) of the preamble of the Constitution which reads that: 'There shall be no constitutional legitimacy for any authority which contradicts the pact of mutual existence'.

17 Cf. Article 58 of Lebanese Constitution, op. cit.

18 For an in-depth analysis of the problems raised by the provisions of this article, cf. Edmond Rabbath, *La constitution libanaise. Origines, textes et commentaires*, (Beirut, 1982) pp. 396-412.

19 Cf. Lebanese Constitution, op. cit.

20 Idem.

21 Idem.

22 Cf. Kaare Strom and Stephen M Swindle, 'Strategic Parliamentary Dissolution' in *American Political Science Review*, Vol. 96, No. 3 (September 2002).

23 On the question of 'parliamentary dissolution', see Martin Cabanis, *La dissolution parlementaire a la française* (Paris, 2001); Philippe Lauvaux, *La dissolution des assemblées parlementaires* (Paris, 1983); and BS Markenisis, *The Theory and Practice of Dissolution of Parliament* (Cambridge, 1972).

24 An English version of the French constitution can be found at:

http://www.assemblee-nationale.fr/english/8ab.asp

25 Cf. Lebanese Constitution, op. cit.

26 An English version of the Italian constitution can be found at:
http://www.cortecostituzionale.it/eng/testinormativi/costituzionedellare-
pubblica/costituzione.asp

27 Cf. Lebanese Constitution, op. cit.

28 Cf. Rabbath, op. cit. pp.298-306

29 Cf. Lebanese Constitution, op. cit.

30 Cf. note 1 supra.

31 Cf. Lebanese Constitution, op. cit.